"The passion and commitment of these two esteemed professors is evident in each of these twenty short chapters on key conciliar texts. Combining expert knowledge with strong pedagogical skills, their presentation provides broader access to the legacy of that most memorable event in the history of Christianity since the Reformation—the Second Vatican Council."

—Gilles Routhier
Department of Theology and Religious Studies
Laval University

"With Vatican II for so many an event in the distant past, this book is brilliantly conceived. Selecting twenty significant passages or conciliar 'keys,' unpacking them in their historical contexts, and providing brief theological expositions, it recovers the council's vision and brings it to bear on a host of contemporary issues. With short, non-technical chapters and sidebar definitions, it could serve as an excellent teaching text."

—Thomas P. Rausch, SJ
T. Marie Chilton Professor of Catholic Theology
Loyola Marymount University

"I recommend *Keys to the Council* to anyone interested in Vatican II and its impact on the Catholic Church today, fifty years after the opening of the council. This brilliant introduction to the key documents of the council is absolutely indispensable to understanding which of these keys of Vatican II have been received into the life and culture of Catholicism. Clifford and Gaillardetz have produced a masterful synthesis on Vatican II, the most important event in the history of Catholic theology in the last 500 years."

—Massimo Faggioli
Assistant Professor of Theology,
University of St. Thomas
Author of *Reforming the Liturgy,
Reforming the Church at Vatican II*

Keys to the Council

Unlocking the Teaching of Vatican II

Richard R. Gaillardetz
Catherine E. Clifford

LITURGICAL PRESS
Collegeville, Minnesota

www.litpress.org

Cover design by Stefan Killen Design. Cover photo © 2012 iStockPhoto.

Excerpts from documents of the Second Vatican Council are from *Vatican Council II: The Basic Sixteen Documents*, by Austin Flannery, OP © 1996 (Costello Publishing Company, Inc.). Used with permission.

The diagram on page xx © 2002, Maryvale Institute, was first published in *The Sower* 23/1 (January 2002) and is reproduced by permission.

Scripture texts in this work are taken from the *New Revised Standard Version Bible* © 1989, Division of Christian Education of the National Council of the Churches of Christ in the United States of America. Used by permission. All rights reserved.

2   3   4   5   6   7   8   9

Library of Congress Cataloging-in-Publication Data

Gaillardetz, Richard R., 1958–
    Keys to the Council : unlocking the teaching of Vatican II / Richard R. Gaillardetz, Catherine E. Clifford.
        p. cm.
    ISBN 978-0-8146-3368-7 — ISBN 978-0-8146-3424-0 (e-book)
    1. Vatican Council (2nd : 1962–1965)   2. Catholic Church—Doctrines.
I. Clifford, Catherine E., 1958–   II. Title.

    BX8301962 .G28   2012
    262'.52—dc23   2011045872

For Francis A. Sullivan, SJ,
who has inspired us with his careful scholarship
and commitment to the teaching of the council

Contents

Abbreviations

AA	*Apostolicam Actuositatem*
AG	*Ad Gentes Divinitus*
CCC	Catechism of the Catholic Church
CD	*Christus Dominus*
CIC	Code of Canon Law
CCEC	Code of Canons of the Eastern Churches
CT	*Catechesi Tradendae*
DH	*Dignitatis Humanae*
DS	Denzinger-Schönmetzer, *Enchiridion symbolorum definitionum et declarationum de rebus fidei et morum*
DV	*Dei Verbum*
GS	*Gaudium et Spes*
LG	*Lumen Gentium*
NA	*Nostra Aetate*
OE	*Orientalium Ecclesiarum*
PA	*Pastor Aeternus*
PC	*Perfectae Caritatis*
PO	*Presbyterorum Ordinis*
SC	*Sacrosanctum Concilium*
UR	*Unitatis Redintegratio*

Introduction

January 25, 1959. Few days in the last four centuries would equal its impact on the Roman Catholic Church. Yet that day passed largely without notice for the Catholic Church's nearly one billion members. To appreciate its significance we have to go back three months earlier.

On October 28, 1958, Angelo Roncalli was elected pope. He was a rotund, lifelong church diplomat, an elderly prelate known more for his self-deprecating humor than for his erudition. He succeeded the saintly but severe Pius XII who wielded an unprecedented spiritual authority in the church. Indeed, so far-reaching was his authority that some theologians and ecclesiastical figures speculated that ecumenical councils, formal gatherings of all the bishops of the universal church, had become obsolete. There was nothing a council could do, many felt, that a pope could not accomplish more effectively.

In some respects Roncalli's election was unsurprising. A custom had developed of electing a "caretaker pope" to succeed a papacy of extended length and influence. The theory, not without merit, was that after an extended papacy, the church needed a chance to stop and catch its breath before determining what new direction it must take. Pius's momentous papacy of almost two decades certainly qualified, leading to the election of Roncalli (who took the name John XXIII) as the ideal caretaker.

It is not difficult, then, to imagine the surprise of the small group of cardinals who had gathered on January 25 for a meeting with the elderly pontiff at the Basilica of St. Paul-outside-the-Walls. The context of the meeting was the celebration of Vespers for the conclusion of the Week of Prayer for Christian Unity. At that modest gathering, Pope John announced what were to be the three central planks of his pontificate: (1) the convocation of a diocesan synod for the diocese of Rome, (2) the reform of the Code of Canon Law, and (3) the convocation of a new ecumenical council. It was the last announcement that was most surprising. The last ecumenical council, Vatican I, had ended rather unceremoniously in 1870.

The onset of the Franco-Prussian War required the French emperor to remove the garrison of French troops that had been stationed in Rome to protect the pope. This action, in turn, opened the door for the Italian nationalist army, eager to seize the Papal States and unify Italy, to march

Ecumenical councils are formal gatherings of all the bishops of the universal church. The Catholic Church traditionally recognizes twenty-one such councils, though some scholars consider only the first seven as truly ecumenical councils since they were the only councils to have voting representation of the East and the West. In this schema the fourteen subsequent councils are referred to as *general* councils or synods of the Western church. Councils are generally named after the places where they are held.

unchallenged into Rome. The turmoil that followed led to the hasty suspension of the council. It had been almost ninety years since that sad event. No bishop alive in 1959 had any personal recollection of an ecumenical council; councils were simply not part of the consciousness of the church.

The pope's announcement of a new council stirred the imaginations of many. For some bishops and theologians it represented a remarkable opportunity for church reform and renewal. Still others saw it as a chance for the church to demonstrate the relevance of the Christian message to a world in the midst of unprecedented social upheaval. Many parts of the so-called developing world were breaking free of the influence of European colonialism. The world had just witnessed a horrific global war, the unprecedented genocide of six million Jews, and the first use of a nuclear weapon, leading to the destruction of tens of thousands of civilians. New forms of modern communication, including the widespread exposure to television, dramatically transformed people's experience of the world around them.

For still others the council would serve as but another ecclesiastical tool for both condemning the evil forces at work in the world and purging the church of dangerous heretical movements. As preparations for the council proceeded over the three and a half years following the pope's shocking announcement, the likely outcome of the council was far from clear. The pope had handed over responsibility for the planning of the council to leading officials of the Roman Curia. Under this curial leadership, the preparatory commissions drew on the expertise of mostly "safe" theologians, and the draft documents they produced, with a few exceptions, did not advance topics beyond the status quo. The rules for the actual conduct of the council were not well developed, and the council was further hampered by the decision to have the entire council conducted in

The "Roman Curia" refers to various ecclesiastical departments in the Vatican that serve the pope and bishops in the exercise of their leadership over the universal church. These departments or "dicasteries" include congregations, councils, and tribunals.

Latin without the benefit of a translation service. As the actual opening of the council approached in the summer of 1962, some leading bishops and theologians feared the council was doomed to failure.

The reasons why the council did not, in fact, fail present a fascinating story that cannot be fully recounted here.[1] It is fair, however, to attribute the remarkable success of the council to the following factors. First, Pope John XXIII offered a remarkable address at the opening Mass of the council. In it he called for an *aggiornamento*, the task, that is, of bringing the church "up to date." He quite pointedly distanced himself from some negative voices in the church, including some of his closest advisers who were pessimistic about the state of both the world and the church itself. He called for a deeper penetration of church teaching in order to present its great wisdom in a manner intelligible to humanity today. He spoke of the need to replace the harsh medicine of condemnation with the "medicine of mercy." Catholics must learn to persuade others of the truth of the Catholic faith.

A second factor had to do with the representation on the conciliar commissions. On the first day of the council itself, the bishops needed to elect sixteen bishops to serve on each of ten conciliar commissions. There was some subtle pressure placed on the bishops to simply reelect those bishops who had served on the preparatory commissions. Through some shrewd parliamentary maneuvering, the bishops were able to arrange a recess in order to meet in five different language groups to propose their own slate of candidates. The result was a more ideologically and geographically balanced representation on these important commissions.

Third, for many of these bishops, the council provided a remarkable opportunity for their own ongoing education. Many of these bishops had not picked up a theology textbook since their priestly ordination. Now in Rome for several months each fall from 1962 to 1965, a total of four sessions, the bishops were able to attend evening lectures conducted by some of the world's leading scholars. Also, because the bishops were seated not geographically but in terms of seniority, they often had the opportunity to sit with bishops from other countries and even continents. This allowed them to considerably broaden their own ecclesial horizons. The well-known Vaticanologist Giancarlo Zizola tells the story of visiting Bishop Albino Luciani (the future Pope John Paul I) during the council where he was staying at a Roman *pensione* run by some Italian sisters. Luciani admitted that he tried to spend each afternoon in his room studying, because, as he put it, everything I learned at the Gregorian is useless now. I have to become a student again. Fortunately I have an African bishop as a neighbor in the bleachers in the council hall, who gives me the texts of the experts of the German bishops. That way I can better prepare myself.[2]

Fourth, many council bishops found ways to organize and communicate with one another to further discuss various proposals. One such group was called the *Domus Mariae*. This group consisted of only twenty-two bishops, all generally committed to the cause of conciliar reform. They met weekly to discuss topics being considered by the council. What was significant about this small group was their organizational structure. They sought out bishops who were connected to the various national episcopal conferences. The *Domus Mariae* group then served as a sort of clearinghouse for the consideration of various topics. They would debate issues and offer compromise proposals that would then be communicated to the bishops of the various conferences. In an age without e-mail or even widespread photocopying, this allowed for the rapid dissemination of ideas and proposals while providing a forum for individual episcopal conferences to raise their concerns.[3]

These and many other factors contributed to a dramatic reorientation of the council that surprised and often frustrated the minority group of bishops resistant to any agenda for ecclesial reform. By the end of the fourth and final session, the council would promulgate sixteen documents: four constitutions, nine decrees, and three declarations. The quality of the material, not surprisingly, was uneven. All four constitutions would make crucial contributions, as would the decrees on ecumenism, the office of the bishop, the apostolate of the laity, the missionary life of the church, and the ministry and life of priests. The declarations on religious freedom and the church's relationship to non-Christian religions would also be important. Other documents, however, suffered from being hastily composed and are rarely cited today.

Appropriating the council's teaching has proved to be a daunting task. There are several reasons for this. The first concerns the massive volume of the conciliar documents. The twenty-one ecumenical councils together produced 37,727 lines of text. Of those some 37,000 lines, Vatican II alone produced 12,179 (approx. 32 percent), whereas the Council of Trent, the next most prolific council, produced 5,637 lines of conciliar text. It is very difficult to digest and synthesize such a large body of material. We must add to this difficulty the lack of a common theological or philosophical foundation to the documents of Vatican II. This becomes clearer if we compare Vatican II to the previous two councils, Vatican I (1869–70) and the Council of Trent (1545–63). The documents of those two councils exhibit a relative conceptual precision, unambiguous definition of positions and unity of genre that cannot be found in the documents of Vatican II. Both Trent and Vatican I were grounded in a theological scholasticism that gave to each council a real, if limited, conceptual unity. By contrast, in Vatican II's texts we find biblical references alternating with historical expositions, analyses of contemporary issues, citations of previous councils (half

> Scholasticism refers to a broadly conceived approach to theology that emerged in the Middle Ages with the rise of the medieval university. It presupposed a clear distinction between human reason and divine revelation and sought to use the categories of rhetoric and philosophy to bring a certain conceptual rigor to the exposition of the Christian faith. This task was made possible, in large part, by the medieval rediscovery of the texts of early Greek philosophers. Scholasticism is most often associated with the contributions of Peter Abelard, St. Anselm of Canterbury, St. Albert the Great, St. Thomas Aquinas, and St. Bonaventure.

of them from Trent and Vatican I), and references to papal texts (half were to the texts of Pius XII).

Yet another difficulty in grasping the council's teaching has to do with a pastoral judgment of Pope Paul VI. Early in his pontificate, Pope Paul expressed a concern that some of the teachings of the council might create harmful church divisions. Consequently, though the rules of the council allowed a document to be approved with a two-thirds majority, Pope Paul made it known that he wished the documents to be approved by a much more significant majority among the bishops. A cursory review of the final voting suggests that the pope got what he desired; no document was opposed in the final vote by more than a handful of bishops. But there was a price to be paid for this high level of unanimity. Significant compromises were made. When achieving full consensus was unlikely, the support of opposing sides of an issue was often secured by juxtaposing, sometimes in the same paragraph, alternative formulations. Of course, to some extent this kind of compromise is evident at every council. It is why conciliar documents should never be read as if they were systematic treatises. Indeed, anyone who has ever served on a committee to draft a common document like a mission statement is aware of this fact. Nevertheless, because of the uniquely transitional character of Vatican II, juxtaposition played a more prominent role than usual. The use of juxtaposition ultimately enabled passage of sixteen documents. It also made it possible, however, for various ideological camps to appeal to certain passages that appeared to support their particular ecclesiastical agenda while excluding other texts. Any responsible approach to interpreting the council documents has to be aware of the danger of the kind of proof-texting that biblical fundamentalists often employ. The best way to avoid this tendency is to follow a more comprehensive approach to the interpretation of the council documents.

Ormond Rush contends that an adequate interpretation of Vatican II must incorporate three complementary strategies. The first will focus on how the texts of the council developed over time.[4] The focus here is on discovering what the council bishops meant in a particular passage by looking at the history of the text itself. We will want to ask, for example, how a text or passage changed from the preparatory documents to its final form. We will want to look at the teaching of the church prior to the council and ask how this text received that teaching: What principles continued to be asserted? What changes were made? Where was there development? Notes from the conciliar commissions that drafted and revised the texts will be important in arriving at an adequate interpretation of a text, as will the various speeches and debates that transpired during the council. An excellent example of this can be found in the voluminous scholarly literature that is dedicated to *Lumen Gentium* 8 and its teaching that the church of Jesus Christ *subsists in* the Roman Catholic Church. Numerous studies have focused on the use of the term "subsists" and have tried to discern the meaning of this word, in the council's intention, by carefully studying various council speeches and the notes from those who participated in the drafting of this text. Rush refers to this interpretive strategy as a "hermeneutics of the authors."

> "Hermeneutics" is the term for any theory of the interpretation of a text.

A second strategy will focus on the final form of a particular text or passage.[5] Here, special attention will be given to the genre of the text and the rhetorical style that is being employed. An excellent example of this can be found in the work of the Jesuit church historian John O'Malley. O'Malley has argued that one of the most overlooked features of the teaching of Vatican II is its distinctive rhetorical style.[6]

Most documents from prior councils fairly closely followed a more juridical or legal rhetorical style common to Roman law. We should remember that it was Emperor Constantine who actually convened the first Council of Nicea. Councils themselves were often viewed as judicial and legislative bodies that rendered judgments and issued decrees. Often included in these documents were penalties, known as canons, to be assigned to those who failed to comply.

For O'Malley, the most striking feature of Vatican II was its dramatic departure from this rhetorical style. Vatican II employed a literary genre taken from the ancient rhetorical tradition known as the epideictic genre, also known as "panegyric." According to O'Malley, a panegyric "is the painting of an idealized portrait in order to excite admiration and appropriation."[7] The key idea here is that this genre seeks to *persuade* the reader toward the emulation of an ideal. This new rhetorical approach is reflected in the council's distinctive terminology. In place of the harsh language of condemnations and penalties, the council makes considerable use of "horizontal" terms like "brothers and sisters," "people of God," "the priesthood of all believers," and "collegiality." O'Malley also notes the use of "terms of reciprocity" like "cooperation," "partnership," and "collaboration."[8] Third, he finds "humility-words" like "pilgrim" and "servant." Finally, he identifies "interiority words" like "charism," "conscience," and "joy and hope, grief and anguish." In O'Malley's view, attending to this linguistic shift is essential for arriving at an adequate appreciation of what the council was trying to communicate in its documents. What we encounter in these linguistic changes is nothing less than a new understanding of the church and a new way of communicating the Christian message.

Rush also considers within this second interpretive strategy (which he refers to as a "hermeneutics of texts") the need to attend carefully to the specific context of a passage, that is, how it fits in both the larger document in which it appears and how it relates to other conciliar texts. Here, one must ask, going back to the example of the *subsistit* passage, how the authentic meaning of this passage in *Lumen Gentium* 8 might be enriched and clarified by the Decree on Ecumenism (*Unitatis Redintegratio*) 3.

Finally, Rush claims that an adequate interpretation of the council's teaching must also look at what has happened in the almost five decades since the close of the council. How have people read the council's teaching? How has it been appropriated, developed, and/or reinterpreted in later church documents, canon law, church practices, and the lived faith of the church? This he refers to as a "hermeneutics of receivers."[9]

This slim volume cannot possibly provide a comprehensive interpretation of the council's teaching. Rather, our hope is to guide the reader into a direct engagement with the conciliar documents themselves. The difficulty is that the sheer volume of the council documents can overwhelm the reader. To address this problem we have identified twenty passages from the council documents that we believe provide interpretive "keys." Drawing on the considerable scholarship on Vatican II, including the fruit of all three of the interpretive strategies we have discussed above, we have identified twenty passages that can lead the reader to a greater appreciation for the larger vision of the council. These passages provide, we believe, an important entry point into the council documents and a lens for comprehending the council's overall teaching.

As one might imagine, identifying these passages has not been easy. To be honest, the selection process began as a kind of "five books you would take on a desert island" exercise. The first list included forty passages! We were able to pare down that list to twenty, largely because we realized that many other related passages could be considered in the process of exploring each of the twenty we have chosen. Both of the authors of this volume are ecclesiologists by training, that is, we specialize in theological questions related to the nature and mission of the church. Our interest in the theology of the church has doubtless influenced the passages we have selected. For example, the council documents have some very important things to say about the church's moral teaching that we were unable to explore in any detail.

It is our hope that this volume will serve not as a substitute for the documents of Vatican II but rather as a helpful guide to lead the reader into a more informed study of the council documents themselves. A majority of Catholics alive today have no personal recollection of the church before Vatican II or even of the crucial period that immediately followed the council when many of the council's teachings were first being implemented. For many of the students we teach, Vatican II is simply the last of twenty-one different ecumenical councils with little more relevance to their lives than the Third Council of Constantinople. It is our hope that this volume will help to remedy this regrettable situation. We are convinced that Vatican II remains the most important event in Roman Catholic history since the Protestant Reformation. At a time in our church when much of the council's teaching is being minimized, dangerously reinterpreted, or altogether ignored, an authentic and informed understanding of the council is more important than ever. We hope that these "keys" to the council will unlock a vision of the church that remains both challenging and liberating, a vision capable of guiding our church in the decades to come.

Notes

¹ Richard R. Gaillardetz, "What Can We Learn from Vatican II?," in *The Catholic Church in the 21st Century*, ed. Michael J. Himes (St. Louis: Liguori Publications, 2004), 80–95.

² Giancarlo Zizola, "He Answered Papal Summons to Journalism," *National Catholic Reporter* (October 4, 2002): 10.

³ A fascinating study of this group can be found in Melissa J. Wilde, *Vatican II: A Sociological Analysis of Religious Change* (Princeton: Princeton University Press, 2007).

⁴ Ormond Rush, *Still Interpreting Vatican II: Some Hermeneutical Principles* (New York: Paulist, 2004), 1–34.

⁵ Ibid., 35–51.

⁶ John W. O'Malley, *What Happened at Vatican II* (Cambridge: Belknap Press, 2008).

⁷ Ibid., 47.

⁸ Ibid., 49–50.

⁹ Rush, *Still Interpreting Vatican II*, 52–68.

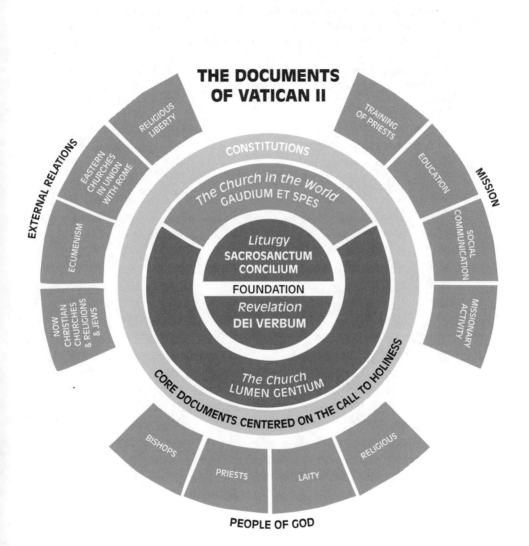

THE DOCUMENTS
OF VATICAN II

CONSTITUTIONS

The Church in the World
GAUDIUM ET SPES

Liturgy
SACROSANCTUM
CONCILIUM

FOUNDATION

Revelation
DEI VERBUM

The Church
LUMEN GENTIUM

CORE DOCUMENTS CENTERED ON THE CALL TO HOLINESS

EXTERNAL RELATIONS

RELIGIOUS
LIBERTY

EASTERN
CHURCHES
IN UNION
WITH ROME

ECUMENISM

NOW
CHRISTIAN
CHURCHES
& RELIGIONS
& JEWS

MISSION

TRAINING
OF PRIESTS

EDUCATION

SOCIAL
COMMUNICATION

MISSIONARY
ACTIVITY

PEOPLE OF GOD

BISHOPS

PRIESTS

LAITY

RELIGIOUS

Chapter One

Through Baptism We Are Implanted in the Paschal Mystery

(*Sacrosanctum Concilium* 6)

Just as Christ was sent by the Father so also he sent the apostles, filled with the Holy Spirit. This he did so that they might preach the Gospel to every creature (see Mk 16:15) and proclaim that the Son of God by his death and resurrection had freed us from the power of Satan (see Acts 26:18) and from death, and brought us into the Kingdom of his Father. But he also willed that the work of salvation which they preached they should enact through the sacrifice and sacraments around which the entire liturgical life revolves. Thus by Baptism men and women are implanted in the paschal mystery of Christ; they die with him, are buried with him, and rise with him.

Background

All of Christian faith hinges on the death and resurrection of Christ. The centrality of the paschal mystery in the life and prayer of the church is an important key to understanding the liturgical renewal proposed by the Second Vatican Council. This same insight informs the council's reflections on the sacraments, the life of holiness, the vocation of humanity, and the mission of the church in the world. For Catholics who lived through the period during and immediately following the Second Vatican Council, the changes brought about in the liturgy—the prayer of the church—were perhaps the most visible and immediate expression of the reforms the council effected. The Constitution on the Sacred Liturgy (*Sacrosanctum Concilium* [SC]) was the first major document debated during the council and one of the first to be promulgated at the end of the council's second session, on December 4, 1963. It was received more readily than some of the other draft documents presented

> Liturgy: The public worship of the church, from the Greek, *leitourgía*, which means, literally, "the work of the people." The liturgy is the ritual activity of the community, as distinguished from private prayer or pious practices.

1

to the bishops at the council, as it embodied more than others the direction laid out for the work of the council by Pope John XXIII: to bring the life of the church up to date (*aggiornamento*) while remaining faithful to the tradition. The Constitution on the Sacred Liturgy was the product of a protracted effort on the part of liturgists and other scholars to return to the ancient sources and, at the same time, to update and renew the pastoral dimension of the liturgy.

For over a century, a movement of liturgical renewal had been stirring in the church, especially in Germany and France. This movement was nourished by a renewed attention to Scripture, to early Christian writings, to the history of the early church, and to the renewal of monastic life and prayer. Its twentieth-century expression received its orientation from the Benedictine Dom Lambert Beauduin during a congress of lay Catholics in Malines, Belgium, in 1909. In 1940, the German bishops' conference established a study group to explore the renewal of the liturgy, and in 1943 the influential Centre National de Pastorale Liturgique (National Center for Pastoral Liturgy) was founded in Paris. Pope Pius XII undertook a series of initiatives that prepared the way for the more substantial reform that would follow at Vatican II. His 1947 encyclical letter, *Mediator Dei*, spoke in favor of liturgical renewal. During the pontificate of Pius XII, a new translation of the psalms was produced for use in a revised edition of the Liturgy of the Hours. From 1951 to 1956 the rites of the Easter Triduum were reformed, in particular, restoring the observance of the Easter Vigil on Holy Saturday night. Efforts were made to simplify rubrics and to update the calendar of feast days. Rules were relaxed for fasting before Mass, for the use of hymnody, and for some use

> **Liturgy of the Hours:** Hymns and prayers organized around the daily recitation of the psalms, especially at Morning and Evening Prayer. This prayer of the whole church is also known as the Divine Office or the Breviary. The celebration of the liturgy at various intervals throughout the day contributes to the sanctification of time. This very ancient form of the church's prayer was clericalized and began to be recited in private in the Middle Ages when its daily recitation was required of all clergy. The Second Vatican Council encourages a recovery of the communal celebration of the Hours so as to include the laity, especially in the office of Evening Prayer, on Sundays and solemn feasts (SC 100).

> **Triduum:** The period of three high holy days in the liturgical year that are marked by one continuous celebration of prayer in three "acts": Holy Thursday, Good Friday, and Easter Sunday.

of the vernacular, and experiments were authorized for the use of a more "dialogical" form of the liturgy.

Many protagonists of the liturgical renewal were named as members and consultants to the Preparatory Commission on Sacred Liturgy in the fall of 1960. They worked during the preparatory phase of the council to prepare the draft text that was presented to the bishops in October 1962. The Constitution on the Sacred Liturgy did not claim to be an exhaustive reflection on the prayer of the church. Rather, it sought to lay out a number of general norms and principles to be followed in a subsequent reform of the rites of the church—a task that would be carried out in the years that immediately followed the council.[1] The constitution opens with the recognition of the council's intention "to adapt more closely to the needs of our age those institutions which are subject to change" and recognizes "cogent reasons for undertaking the reform and promotion of the liturgy" (SC 1).[2] The relatively quick passage through the process of drafting, conciliar debate, and voting is an indication that the Constitution on the Sacred Liturgy was the fruit of a long process of maturation reaching back into the preceding century.

The Centrality of the Paschal Mystery in the Prayer of the Church

The first chapter of the Constitution on the Sacred Liturgy is a reflection on the nature of the liturgy and its importance in the life of the church. At the center of the church's prayer we find the heart of our faith, the source of our salvation, in the paschal mystery of Christ. The term "paschal" comes from the Greek *pascha*, which is, in turn, a translation of the Hebrew *pesach*, or Passover. In the feast of Passover the people of Israel recall the moment of salvation when they were set free from bondage in Egypt, thanks to God's intervention. Just as the blood of the Passover lamb protected the Jewish people from death, and the ritual eating of the

> Mystery: From the Greek term *musterion*, applied to Christ in the New Testament (Col 4:3). It refers literally to a reality that is hidden, veiled, beyond the complete grasp of human comprehension. God is utterly mysterious and incomprehensible yet freely discloses God's self to us through the humanity of Jesus Christ. In the early church the term "mystery" was also applied to the sacraments, visible signs that manifest the action of God.

lamb was for them a remembrance of Israel's passage from slavery into the freedom of the Promised Land (Exod 12:1-50), for the earliest Christians, Christ was the sign of a new Passover. In his first letter to the Corinthians

St. Paul writes, "our paschal lamb, Christ, has been sacrificed" (1 Cor 5:7). John's gospel draws a clear parallel between the liberation of Israel and the redemptive death of Christ by suggesting that Jesus was crucified at the very hour when the paschal lambs were being slaughtered in the temple for the Passover feast (John 19:31).

The paschal mystery refers to the mystery of God's saving work in the history of the world. To accomplish our redemption, God sent God's Son, who became incarnate in the human nature of Jesus of Nazareth—the long-expected Messiah, or Christ. Through Jesus' life, teaching, and ministry, and especially in his death and resurrection, the depth of God's love for humankind is revealed. For every Christian, the meaning of human history is manifested in this act of divine self-giving. Through his cross, Christ establishes a new covenant between God and humankind. It is through his passing through death to resurrection that we are freed from sin and death and born to new life. While Christ has died and is risen once and for all (Heb 9:25-26), the unrepeatable gift of his total self-giving on Calvary—the mystery of his love—is at work in our lives in and through the prayer of the church. It is manifested in our lives whenever we choose not to live for ourselves but to turn away from our inclinations to self-centeredness in order to love and serve others. In the liturgy, the council affirms, "'the work of our redemption takes place,' . . . enabling the faithful to express in their lives and portray to others the mystery of Christ and the real nature of the true church" (SC 2).

Sharing in the Paschal Mystery through the Sacraments

Our sharing in the mystery of Christ's death and resurrection begins from the moment of baptism. The prayers of the initiation rite draw clear parallels between the waters of baptism and the symbol of water in the great moments of salvation history, beginning from the dawn of creation:

> In baptism we use your gift of water,
> which you have made a rich symbol of the grace
> you give us in this sacrament.
> At the very dawn of creation
> your Spirit breathed on the waters,
> making them the wellspring of all holiness.
> The waters of the great flood
> you made a sign of the waters of baptism
> that make an end of sin
> and a new beginning of goodness.

Through the waters of the Red Sea
you led Israel out of slavery
to be an image of God's holy people,
set free from sin by baptism.
In the waters of the Jordan
your Son was baptized by John
and anointed with the Spirit.
Your Son willed that water and blood should flow from his side
as he hung upon the cross.[3]

The evocative image of the water and blood flowing from the side of Christ is an image of our rebirth through his death and resurrection. It symbolizes, as well, the water of baptism and the Blood of Christ that we receive in the sacrament of the Eucharist.

The mystery of God's self-gift to us in Christ continues to work in and through the sacramental life of the church. As the council teaches, "the liturgy of the sacraments and sacramentals sanctifies almost every event of their lives with the divine grace which flows from the paschal mystery of the passion, death and resurrection of Christ. From this source all the sacraments and sacramentals draw their power" (SC 61). In the sacraments we encounter the person of Christ whose loving self-gift, when we are properly disposed and open to receive it, transforms and draws us into the pattern of his self-giving.

It is especially in the Sunday Eucharist, the memorial of the death and resurrection of Christ, that we celebrate the paschal mystery. The council recalls that this weekly celebration of the Lord's Day is "the original feast day" of Christians. Indeed, every Sunday is a "little Easter," recalling the

> Sacramentals: Sacred signs authorized for use by the church that bring about some spiritual effect or occasion a personal encounter with the grace of Christ, apart from the seven liturgical signs of the church that have been designated as "sacraments." Examples include holy water, the sign of the cross, ashes, the rings exchanged by spouses to symbolize their marriage vows, or blessings. The Constitution on the Sacred Liturgy observes, "There is scarcely any proper use of material things which cannot . . . be directed toward people's sanctification and the praise of God" (SC 61).

central mystery of our faith in the risen Christ. In each celebration of the Eucharist the faithful gather to renew their baptismal commitment, "so that, by hearing the word of God and taking part in the Eucharist, they may commemorate the suffering, resurrection, and glory of the Lord Jesus, giving thanks to God who 'has given us a new birth into a living hope through the resurrection of Jesus Christ from the dead' (1 Pet 1:3)" (SC 106). In the Eucharist we join in the church's great prayer of thanksgiving for the gift of God's own self revealed to us in Jesus. In the eucharistic prayer we join the gift of our own lives to his sacrifice, in a response of gratitude. Through the sacramental signs of bread and wine we receive his body and blood—gifts that symbolize his life poured out for us—food and drink to nourish us on life's journey, where each day we are called to make an offering of our lives for others. In this ritual prayer of the church we are schooled in the most fundamental attitudes and habits needed for Christian living. The pedagogy of the paschal mystery comes to shape the logic of our daily lives.

The Paschal Character of the Liturgical Year

The Second Vatican Council sought to restore the "paschal character" of the Sunday liturgy and, indeed, of the entire liturgical year.[4] The celebration of memorials for saints and martyrs, which had accumulated through the centuries in the liturgical calendar, was no longer to obscure or take precedence over the Sunday memorial of Christ's death and resurrection (SC 111). As a result, the calendar of Sunday celebrations throughout the liturgical year and the revised Sunday Lectionary were ordered in such a way as to mark the mysteries of Christ's life and ministry throughout the year (SC 107), with the high point centered on the Easter Triduum, the "most solemn of all feasts" (SC 102). The commemoration of saints' days, then, was resituated in a proper relationship to the mysteries of our redemption that orient the liturgical seasons, inasmuch as the saints themselves point toward Christ, who alone is the source of saving grace: "[T]he church proclaims the paschal mystery in the saints who have suffered and been glorified with Christ" (SC 104). We honor and venerate the saints in the prayer of the church to the extent that their lives of holiness are an icon or image pointing toward Christ's own self-giving love. Their example inspires us in our own path to holiness.

The paschal character of the season of Lent, in particular, has been restored so that we mark it as a time to repent and deepen our baptismal covenant, which is properly renewed when we reaffirm our baptismal promises in the Easter liturgy. The restoration of the corporate dimension of penance on the Sundays of Lent and of the liturgical rites for catechumens (*Ad Gentes Divinitus* [AG] 14)—those who will be baptized into the faith on Easter night—help us to see the entire Lenten season as a journey toward the celebration of our redemption in the Triduum. Notably, it is through the liturgy itself, in the proclamation of the Word and the commemoration of the mysteries of salvation throughout the year, in particular through the season of Lent, that catechumens are to prepare for baptism:

> The catechumens should be properly initiated into the mystery of salvation and the practice of the evangelical virtues, and they should be introduced into the life of faith, liturgy, and charity of the people of God by successive sacred rites. . . .
> It is desirable that the liturgy of Lent and Paschal time should be restored in such a way that it will serve to prepare the hearts of the catechumens for the celebration of the Paschal Mystery, at whose solemn ceremonies they are reborn to Christ in baptism. (AG 14)

Through their attentive listening to the word of God and attending to the action of the liturgy, the lives of the catechumens are progressively transformed and converted until they become a living witness to the love of Christ. Through their baptism on Easter night, we celebrate the mystery of their rebirth and renew our own participation in the paschal mystery through the renewal of our baptismal promises.

New Life and the Vocation of Humanity

As Christians, we do not live as if this world were a kind of waiting room where we simply bide our time and place all our hope in the glory of a resurrection in the afterlife. If we take St. Paul at his word, our new life in the risen Christ has already begun: "Do you not know that all of us who have been baptized into Christ Jesus were baptized into his death? Therefore, we have been buried with him by baptism into death, so that, just as Christ was raised from the dead by the glory of the Father, so we too might walk in the newness of life" (Rom 6:3-4). Our resurrection is not something that we await beyond the moment of our physical death. Our new life has already begun. In baptism, we set aside our old self, the self that was "enslaved to sin" (Rom 6:6), and we are reborn. As Paul says, we must consider ourselves "dead to sin and alive to God in Christ Jesus" (Rom 6:11). Though we remain weak and sinful human beings, wounded by the consequences of sin in our lives, we know that sin, evil, and even death itself will not have the last word. While we await the fullness of the resurrection at the end of time, we already enjoy the firstfruits of that life here and now, as we respond to the invitation of Christ to share life in all its fullness. The redeeming love of God has been revealed to us in Christ, and, in and through the church, it continues to overturn the forces of sin in human history each time we forgive, bring healing, and redress the effects of injustice in the world. The church is the community of the baptized, a community of redeemed sinners, a sign of humanity reconciled with God.

The centrality of the paschal mystery is reflected in the Second Vatican Council's understanding of God's design for all humanity. This vision is laid out most clearly in the council's Pastoral Constitution on the Church in the Modern World (*Gaudium et Spes* [GS]), especially in this text's development of a Christian anthropology, a vision of the new humanity established through Christ. Christ himself is the embodiment of that new humanity, the "new Adam" who reveals to us the love of God and in so doing "fully reveals humanity to itself and brings to light its very high calling" (GS 22). This Christ-centered view of human history is at the heart of the church's conviction regarding the unequivocal dignity of the human person. Because the divine Word has entered into human history and taken up our human nature in Jesus Christ, all of history is changed and all of humanity is raised up. Every human person enjoys the offer of God's gift revealed in Jesus (1 Tim 2:4). His death and resurrection have overcome all that separates us from God and from one another. A new creation has begun. Christ, the new Adam,

> who is the "image of the invisible God" (Col 1:15), is himself the perfect man who has restored in the children of Adam that likeness to God which had been disfigured ever since the first sin. Human nature, by the very fact that it was assumed, not absorbed, in him, has been raised in us also to a dignity beyond compare. For, by his incarnation, he, the Son of God, has in a certain way united himself with each individual. . . . [H]e has truly been made one of us, like to us in all things except sin.
>
> As an innocent lamb he merited life for us by his blood which he freely shed. In him God reconciled us to himself and to one another. (GS 22)

Jesus invites his disciples to follow in his footsteps, to wash one another's feet (John 13:1-15), and to lay down their lives for one another in loving service (John 10:11-18). He calls us to reproduce the pattern of his dying and rising in our own lives, to pour out our lives for others. According to the Pastoral Constitution on the Church in the Modern World, this high calling is not reserved to Christians. It applies to "all people of good will in whose hearts grace is active invisibly" (GS 22). The vocation of humanity will be realized only when all people learn to live together in self-transcending love. All of humanity is called to share in the outpouring of divine love. By reproducing the pattern of the paschal mystery in our lives, we bring about God's plan for all the world: "For since Christ died for everyone, and since all are in fact called to one and the same destiny, which is divine, we must hold that the holy Spirit offers to all the possibility of being made partners, in a way known to God, in the paschal mystery" (GS 22).

Sharing in the Divine Life

All are called to become participants and sharers in the divine life. This mystery is expressed sacramentally in baptism where we are incorporated into Christ and drawn into the exchange of self-giving love among the three Divine Persons of the Trinity. This mutual exchange of love and of life is the gift that we call grace. Karl Rahner spoke of grace as the love of God outside the Trinity, the overflowing of God's self-giving in the exchange of love between Father, Son, and Spirit.[5] God sends the Son to reveal God's love for humanity. Jesus is faithful to his covenant of love with God, whom he calls *Abba*, "Father," even unto death. In love, the Father raises him up from death. Through his death and resurrection, Christ reconciles fallen humanity to God and opens up the path to new life. Jesus is guided and strengthened throughout his life by the Spirit, whom the tradition has understood to be the love between the Father and the Son. In baptism we are anointed by God's Spirit to become sons and daughters of God (Rom 8:12-17). The anointing of the Spirit makes us a priestly people (1 Pet 2:9) and enables us, as partners in the paschal mystery, to offer the sacrifice of our whole lives to God in gratitude and praise.[6] This offering is realized in the many ordinary acts of our everyday lives: in encounters with family and friends, with colleagues and strangers—at home, in schools and factories, in offices and places of commerce, in the many relationships that shape us and our lives with others wherever we live. In every meeting, in each decision, every moment of each day, we are called to be bearers of the divine life and artisans of a new creation. In each moment, we are called to witness to and proclaim the good news of God's saving love for us revealed in Jesus Christ. The paschal mystery that we celebrate in the liturgy shapes our daily living and makes us agents of transforming love in the world.

Notes

[1] For a detailed account of the revision of the Roman Rite through this period, see Annibale Bugnini, *The Reform of the Liturgy 1948–1975* (Collegeville, MN: Liturgical Press, 1990).

[2] Unless explicitly noted, all quotations from the council documents are taken from Austin Flannery, ed., *Vatican Council II: The Basic Sixteen Documents* (Northport, NY: Costello Publishing, 1996). Minor authorial changes in the translations are indicated by brackets.

[3] RCIA 222, in *The Rites of the Catholic Church*, vol. 1 (Collegeville, MN: Liturgical Press / Pueblo, 1990).

[4] In this discussion we are drawing from Josef A. Jungmann, "Constitution on the Sacred Liturgy," in *Commentary on the Documents of Vatican II*, 5 vols., ed. Herbert Vorgrimler (New York: Herder and Herder, 1967–69), vol. I, 1–87, at 72.

[5] See Karl Rahner, "Remarks on the Dogmatic Treatise 'De Trinitate,'" in *Theological Investigations*, vol. IV (New York: Seabury / London: Dartman, Longman & Todd, 1974), 77–102, at 96.

[6] See Paul Philibert, *The Priesthood of the Faithful: Key to a Living Church* (Collegeville, MN: Liturgical Press, 2005).

Chapter Two

Christ Is Always Present in His Church

(*Sacrosanctum Concilium* 7)

To accomplish so great a work Christ is always present in his church, especially in liturgical celebrations. He is present in the sacrifice of the Mass both in the person of his minister, "the same now offering, through the ministry of priests, who formerly offered himself on the cross," and most of all in the eucharistic species. By his power he is present in the sacraments so that when anybody baptizes it is really Christ himself who baptizes. He is present in his word since it is he himself who speaks when the holy scriptures are read in church. Lastly, he is present when the church prays and sings, for he has promised "where two or three are gathered together in my name there am I in the midst of them" (Mt 18:20).

Background

As we saw in chapter 1, the mystery of Christ's saving work continues to be accomplished through the liturgy, the public worship of the church. Article 7 of the Constitution on the Sacred Liturgy, which follows immediately on the same document's initial reflection on the paschal mystery, turns to the various ways in which Christ is present or to the diverse ways that we encounter him in the liturgy. Here, attention has shifted from the saving action of Christ in the history of salvation to the person of Christ himself. The action of the liturgy is an action of Christ himself and the transformative power of the liturgy has its source in the experience of encounter with Christ who comes to meet us in various ways, including through the ministry of the church, the sacramental signs, the proclamation of the Word, and in the gathered people of God. Before we consider these various expressions of Christ's presence in the liturgy, a word about the realism of the sacraments is in order.

The Catholic tradition is deeply marked by an incarnational or sacramental principle. This principle is rooted in the doctrine that the divine Word and Son of God became incarnate, took flesh in the human nature of Jesus of Nazareth, being born of the Virgin Mary. According to the

Council of Chalcedon (451), he is truly God and truly human, for in his person the divine and human natures are united. The humanity of Jesus is the principal sign through which God has chosen to reveal God's self to humankind. This mystery of the Christian faith gives rise to the profound conviction that the presence of the invisible God is mediated or disclosed through created realities that act as symbols. The sacraments function as visible signs or symbols of the divine mystery that effectively communicate the reality they signify.

Vatican II's treatment of the sacraments reflects the influence of the renewal in the study of the liturgy. By examining the sacramental life of the church from a liturgical perspective, Catholic theology in the twentieth century was able to move beyond an overly scholastic approach, which, especially since the Council of Trent (1545–63), had treated the sacraments under the more abstract and metaphysical categories of causality, matter and form, substance and accidents, or considered them from more formal juridical and rubrical perspectives. A return to the earliest sources of the church's life of prayer by twentieth-century theology through the study of ancient texts and writings led to a deeper appreciation of the ecclesiological, christological, and trinitarian foundations of sacramental life.

Rubrics: These are formal rules or laws that govern the proper performance of a church ritual.

Catholic teaching and theology maintained that through the sacraments the church, like a mother, begets its own children. Yet this affirmation was now balanced by the recognition that the church is itself brought into being by the sacraments. The source of her life is in Christ and in the divine life of the Trinity. The church, as the priestly people of God, in her life and ministry acts as an instrument and mediator of the grace of God, which comes through Christ and bestows the Holy Spirit. In and through the sacraments and sacramentals of the church, the grace of God is freely offered to those whose hearts are open to receive it. The source of the transforming power of the sacraments is not in any purely human agency, nor principally in the ministry of the church, but flows from the saving mystery of the death and resurrection of Christ. The risen Christ, through the power of the Spirit, continues to communicate this gift to us through the visible signs of creation, especially through the seven sacramental signs of the church.

In the mid-twentieth century, studies by Dom Odo Casel[1] and others focused on the presence and action of the mystery of God in the liturgy. They recovered the notion of liturgical memorial that was central to Jewish prayer and demonstrated its significance for our understanding of the sacraments. We saw in chapter 1 that for Christians, Christ is the new Passover (1 Cor 5:7). His saving action was prefigured in the liberation of the people of Israel from the slavery of Egypt, an event that continues to be celebrated today in the Jewish feast of Passover. During the Passover celebration, Jewish families gather to recall that fateful night when God spared Israel from death and slavery and led them safely through the waters of the Red Sea. The elder in each family recounts the event, not as a memory of the distant historical past, but as a living memory: "*We* were Pharaoh's slaves in Egypt, but the LORD brought *us* out of Egypt with a mighty hand. The LORD displayed before *our* eyes great and awesome signs and wonders against Egypt, against Pharaoh and all his household. He brought *us* out from there in order to bring *us* in, to give *us* the land that he promised on oath to our ancestors" (Deut 6:21-23; emphasis added). For the Jewish community, this moment of liberation is not simply a fact of history to be recalled nostalgically each year. Its effects are understood as present and active here and now, liberating all who share in God's covenant.

The first followers of Jesus were practicing Jews. They continued to gather in the synagogue, to worship in the temple at Jerusalem (Acts 2:46; 3:1; 5:20-26), and to observe the Jewish calendar of feasts. They came to understand the dying and rising of Jesus in light of the Passover motif. As a sign of the new covenant in Christ, they gathered together in their homes for the breaking of bread (Acts 2:46). In one of the earliest texts of the New Testament, Paul recounts the tradition that he himself received concerning the celebration of the Lord's Supper: "For I received from the Lord what I also handed on to you, that the Lord Jesus on the night when he was betrayed took a loaf of bread, and when he had given thanks, he broke it and said, 'This is my body that is for you. Do this is remembrance of me'" (1 Cor 11:23-24). The Gospel of Luke recounts the meal of the new covenant that Jesus shared with his disciples in the context of Passover (Luke 22:1-13) in similar terms, and repeats the command, "Do this in remembrance of me" (Luke 22:19).

Paul and Luke use the Greek term *anamnesis* or "memorial," the same term that was used in the Septuagint, the Greek version of the Old Testament Scriptures, to translate the Hebrew word *zicharon*, the term applied to Israel's memorial of the Passover. The breaking of the bread and the sharing of the cup in this ritual meal became for Christians symbols of the crucified body and shed blood of Christ upon the cross. The memorial of the Lord's Supper is a living memory, an actualization of the effects of Christ's saving death and resurrection. What happened then is made effective in the present. Early

Christians understood his dying and rising as the source of a new covenant, a new Passover, a liberation from the slavery of sin and from the power of death. Each time they broke bread and shared the cup of thanksgiving together, they "re-membered" the paschal mystery of Christ. Each Eucharist is a participation, here and now, in this saving event (1 Cor 10:16).

The recovery of these insights contributed to a deeper understanding of how Eucharist, the great thanksgiving prayer of Christians, is much more than a simple recollection of the historical death of Jesus. Through the sacramental ritual, we transcend historical time; his saving work is made actual in the here and now of our lives. The notion of memory was an important element of the treatment of the sacraments by Thomas Aquinas in the Middle Ages, who considered them as commemorative signs. Similarly, the Council of Trent continued to speak of the Eucharist as a memorial. The Constitution on the Sacred Liturgy builds on this long tradition to affirm the ways in which Christ is sacramentally present uniquely in the Eucharist, though not exclusively in this one sacrament.

In the mid-twentieth century the work of the Dominican Edward Schillebeeckx,[2] Karl Rahner,[3] and others brought the traditional understanding of the sacraments into dialogue with the approaches of contemporary philosophy in order to highlight the christological basis of the sacramental life of the church. They understood the event of salvation as an action brought about through the personal encounter between God and the human person. Their approach stood in sharp contrast to the dominant approach of Catholic theology on the eve of the council, often referred to as neoscholasticism, which presented the sacraments in abstract philosophical, juridical, and sometimes mechanistic terms. Rahner, Schillebeeckx, and others proposed a more relational and personalist model that understood the sacraments as privileged moments of communion with Christ. They insisted that sacraments were about more

Neoscholasticism: This theological approach depended on the philosophical and theological categories that emerged in the age of scholasticism, the twelfth through the fourteenth centuries that produced such luminous scholastic figures as St. Anselm, Abelard, St. Thomas Aquinas, St. Bonaventure, and Duns Scotus. Scholasticism was characterized by a strong emphasis on conceptual rigor through the use of philosophical concepts and categories. This scholasticism would be revived in the sixteenth century and again in the nineteenth and early twentieth centuries. Pope Leo XIII published an encyclical in 1879, *Aeterni Patris*, in which he called for all seminary education to give a privileged place to the philosophy of St. Thomas Aquinas.

than receiving grace, understood as a kind of quantifiable "thing." The sacraments are essentially about our encounter with a person—Christ. Christ is presented as the foundational sacrament, the ultimate sign and manifestation of God's love for the world. God is revealed to us in and through the sign of his humanity. The seven sacramental signs of the church flow from this unparalleled encounter with God through Christ and become occasions for this continuing encounter in the life of the church. In each of the sacraments we encounter Christ in different modalities: through the ministry of the church, through the sacramental signs, through the proclamation of the Word, and in the gathered assembly.

The Teaching of the Council

The council drew on these many new developments in an effort to move beyond the aridity and formalism of so many neoscholastic approaches to the liturgy. In particular, there was an effort to encourage the faithful to broaden their appreciation of the diverse ways in which Christ can be encountered in the liturgy. The council explicitly affirmed that there were multiple modes through which Christ was to be encountered.

Christ Is Present through the Ministry of the Church

The Constitution on the Sacred Liturgy understands that while it is the Spirit of Christ that makes the liturgical life of the church effective, at the same time the liturgy is seen as the work of the people. The council presents the whole gathered assembly as the agent of liturgical life. It acknowledges the distinctive role of the presider within that community, who represents Christ in a unique manner. The Dogmatic Constitution on the Church (*Lumen Gentium* [LG]) affirms that all those who are baptized into Christ participate in the threefold office of Christ as priest, prophet, and king. Some are called from within the priestly people of God to serve within the ordained priesthood. Their task is to enable all the baptized to live out their priestly vocation in the offering of their lives in the world.

In article 7 of the Constitution on the Liturgy, the council builds upon a key insight that has come down to us from St. Augustine, who wrote in the fifth century that when anyone baptizes, it is Christ who baptizes.[4] Augustine proposed that Christ is the minister of the sacraments, the high priest (Heb 9:11) and one mediator (1 Tim 2:5; Heb 9:15) between God and humankind. It is Christ that we encounter. In the sixteenth century, the Council of Trent applied this understanding in its teaching on the sacrifice of the Eucharist when it said, "it is one and the same victim here offering himself by the ministry of his priests, who then offered himself on the cross."[5] While the unique sacrifice of Christ cannot be repeated (Heb 9:25-26), the risen Christ continues to offer us the possibility of taking part in the saving effects of that event through the agency of those who preside over the prayer of the community.

The Second Vatican Council builds on the teaching of Pope Pius XII, who, in his 1947 encyclical letter On the Sacred Liturgy, *Mediator Dei*, taught that among the ways that we encounter Christ in every liturgical action, he is present with the church "in the person of the minister." He qualified this affirmation further to indicate that in the liturgy the priest plays a mediating role. He functions as a "go-between" linking God and the gathered community, at once repeating the words of Christ to his disciples and expressing the prayer of the whole people to God. Pius XII wrote that by virtue of their ordination, priests "represent the person of Christ before the people entrusted to them and represent the people themselves before God" (*Mediator Dei* 40). Therefore the priest acts as a representative of Christ, acting in his name or in his person (*in persona Christi*). Yet at the same time, he remains a member of the priestly people of God and acts in their name, in the person of the church (*in persona ecclesiae*).

The Constitution on the Sacred Liturgy holds together the twofold mediating role of the priest when it teaches that "the prayers addressed to God by the priest who, in the person of Christ, presides over the assembly, are said in the name of the entire holy people and of all present" (SC 33). In its insistence that Christ is present and active in and through the ministry of the priest, the Second Vatican Council helps us to see that ministry is always in the service of Christ and his people. It is never to be considered a privilege or power to be lorded over others; it exists only for the community of Christ. The model for all ministry in the church remains Christ himself who laid down his life for his friends (John 10:17-18).

Christ Is Present in Sacramental Signs

Seven liturgical actions of the church have been designated as sacraments, visible signs through which we encounter the saving power of the risen Christ. Just as God chose to reveal God's love to us through the humanity of Jesus Christ, God makes use of the ordinary material reality of creation—bread, wine, water, oil—to communicate that same love to us today. God addresses us through the concrete embodied reality of human experience—through our senses of sight, hearing, taste, touch, and smell.

The all transcendent and infinite Creator of the universe comes to meet us in the finitude of human experience.

Christ is present and active especially in the Eucharist, where the Christian community gathers to celebrate the source of our salvation in the paschal mystery of Christ. *Sacrosanctum Concilium* presents the Eucharist as a "memorial," though in much richer terms than did the Council of Trent. The memory of Christ's death and resurrection is actualized each time we take part in the paschal meal by eating and drinking the bread and wine of the Eucharist. The anamnesis or eucharistic memorial transcends the bounds of time. We recall Christ's unrepeatable sacrifice on Calvary, we celebrate the presence of the risen Christ with us now, and we anticipate the future fulfillment of God's kingdom by partaking in a meal that prefigures the heavenly banquet of the Lamb (Rev 19:6-9; SC 47).

In the bread and wine of the Eucharist we receive the Body and Blood of Christ, signs of his life given for us. Catholic theology has spoken of Christ's presence in the signs of bread and wine as a "Real Presence" to express the conviction that through the action of God's Spirit, the bread and wine are changed to become the Body and Blood of Christ. In the Middle Ages, the term "transubstantiation" was introduced to convey the notion that while the appearances of bread and wine (the "species") remain, the underlying reality or "substance" is truly changed into the Body and Blood of Christ. Employing a set of metaphysical categories drawn from the world of philosophy, Catholic theology sought to affirm the presence and action of the risen Christ in the Eucharist. He becomes sacramentally present in the signs of bread and wine. He is not present physically, but metaphysically (beyond the physical reality), or personally, in his glorified humanity. As one contemporary scholar of the liturgy has put it, "The body of Christ offered to Christians in consecrated bread and wine is not some*thing* but some*one*. In the Eucharist Christ is present not as an 'object' to be admired, but as a person (a 'subject') to be encountered."[6] In the Eucharist, more than any other sacrament, the sign and the reality signified are one and the same: bread and wine *become* the Body and Blood of Christ. He gives his very self to us in these sacramental signs.

Christ is present and active in and through the other sacramental signs of the church. In the waters of baptism we are cleansed from sin, born into new life, incorporated into Christ and into his Body the church. In confirmation we are anointed with the oil of chrism, the seal of our messianic vocation and participation in the priestly, prophetic, and royal offices of Christ. In the sacrament of reconciliation, we encounter the compassion and forgiveness of Christ acting in and through the ministry of the church.

Through the anointing of the sick we encounter the healing power of Christ, who strengthens us in the face of serious illness, disability, or the approach of death. In the sacrament of Christian marriage, spouses come to embody the faithful covenant love of Christ in the daily living out of their self-giving love for each other. Through the laying on of hands in the sacrament of ordination, the ministers of the church (deacons, priests, bishops) are called to follow Christ in a humble ministry of service within the Christian community, and be his ambassadors in the public actions of the church.

Christ Is Present in the Proclamation of the Word

As the Constitution on the Sacred Liturgy suggests, Christ, the incarnate Word of God, continues to speak to us each time the Scriptures are proclaimed in the church. One of the principal concerns of Vatican II, as it sought to renew the prayer, theology, and teaching ministry of the church, was to restore the proclamation and study of the word of God to its central place in the life of the church. Indeed, the Constitution on Divine Revelation (*Dei Verbum*) recalls that the same reverence that Christians accord to the sacrament of Christ's presence in the Eucharist is due to the Scriptures, in particular to the Book of the Gospels: "The church has always venerated the divine scriptures as it has venerated the Body of the Lord, in that it never ceases, above all in the sacred liturgy, to partake of the bread of life and to offer it to the faithful from the one table of the word of God and the Body of Christ" (DV 21). This veneration is expressed in the reverence shown for both the Book of the Gospels and for the consecrated bread and wine in the celebration of the Eucharist. The faithful are nourished equally through the proclamation of the Word in the Scriptures and by partaking in the Body and Blood of Christ. The council's teaching gave rise to the notion of "two tables," namely, the "table of God's Word" (SC 51) and the "table of the Lord's Body" (SC 48), to refer to the way that the faithful are nourished in the ministry of Word and sacrament. These two interdependent movements, the liturgy of Word and the liturgy of sacrament that make up the liturgy of the Eucharist, "are so closely connected with each other that they form but one single act of worship" (SC 56).

To make the central role of the Word more evident in the prayer of the church, the council directed that the Lectionary be revised in order to provide for a more ample selection of readings for use in the Sunday and weekday celebrations of the Eucharist, for the other sacramental rites, and for the Liturgy of the Hours (SC 92). As a result of the liturgical reform called for by the council, the Sunday Lectionary contains the Sunday readings organized on a three-year cycle and following the seasons and principal feasts of the liturgical year. Readings for each Sunday or feast day are chosen from the Old Testament, psalms, epistles, and gospels. The weekday Lectionary is organized according to a two-year cycle of more or less continuous readings. The revised Lectionary for Sunday readings was organized according to a cycle of three years to ensure that "the more significant part of the sacred Scriptures" would be proclaimed to the people (SC 51).[7] This pattern of organizing the Sunday readings was largely adopted, with some minor revisions, by many other Christian traditions as they too reformed their liturgical rites in the wake of Vatican II.[8] This has had an important effect in the development of a common pattern of prayer and worship, which in turn is helping the separated churches grow together in unity.[9] Besides this unforeseen aspect of recovering the central role of the Scripture in the prayer of the church, the council encouraged Catholic scholars to collaborate with biblical scholars from other churches whenever possible, in the preparation of common translations of the Scriptures in order that all Christians might benefit from the results of the very best scholarship and have access to texts of the highest quality (DV 22).

The renewal of the preaching of the Word is another vital aspect of Vatican II's effort to ensure that the life of all the baptized be nourished and informed by the wisdom of the Scriptures. This is accomplished through a homily, an essential element of every liturgy, where "the mysteries of the faith and the guiding principles of the christian life are expounded from the sacred text" (SC 52). The homily is to be based upon the word of Scripture proclaimed in the liturgy, "for in them is found the proclamation of God's wonderful works in the history of salvation, the mystery of Christ ever made present and active in us" (SC 35). In order to carry out this ministry of preaching responsibly, all those engaged in the ministry of the Word—teachers, catechists, deacons, priests, theologians, and others—are exhorted by the council to "immerse themselves in the scriptures by constant spiritual reading and diligent study" (DV 25). Echoing Augustine, the Dogmatic Constitution on Divine Revelation insists, "it must not happen that any of them become 'empty preachers of the word of God to others, not being hearers of the word in their own hearts'" (ibid.).[10] Indeed, all the baptized faithful are urged to grow in their knowledge of Christ through frequent reading and prayer with the Scriptures.

Christ Is Present in the Gathered Assembly

Christ is present in the midst of those who gather in his name, as we learn in the Gospel of Matthew (18:20). In baptism, the baptized faithful are incorporated into Christ and bound to one another in his body, the church. We have already seen that the action of the liturgy is an action of Christ who continues to offer us a share in the divine life through the sacramental life of the church. When those who are called together in the church sing and pray, offering praise and thanksgiving for the gifts of God, their offering is joined to that of Christ. In this sense, the gathered people of God is the primary subject and agent of the liturgy. This is most evident in the eucharistic prayer, which is, above all, a sacrifice of praise. Through their participation in this great prayer of the church, the people of God join the offering of their lives to the unique offering of Christ's life for us. Through the celebration of his death and resurrection, our lives are taken up into the life of Christ. Saint Paul reflects on this reality when he writes to the church at Corinth: "For while we live, we are always being given up to death for Jesus' sake, so that the life of Jesus may be made visible in our mortal flesh" (2 Cor 4:11). The liturgy is not a repetition of Jesus' death on Calvary, but that great historical event becomes present now in a sacramental way, so that we may receive what he accomplished for us once and for all.

The Constitution on the Sacred Liturgy points to this reality when it says, "They should give thanks to God. Offering the immaculate victim, not only through the hands of the priest but also together with him, they should learn to offer themselves. Through Christ, the Mediator, they should be drawn day by day into ever more perfect union with God and each other, so that finally God may be all in all" (SC 48). In baptism, the faithful are raised to the dignity of a chosen race, a royal priesthood, a holy nation, and a people of God's own choosing (1 Pet 2:9). As participants in the priesthood of Christ they are called to offer their lives for others in imitation of his self-giving love. Saint Paul understands a life of witness and service to be part of our "worship" of God, as he writes to the early Christians of Rome, "present your bodies as a living sacrifice, holy and acceptable to God, which is your spiritual worship" (Rom 12:1). As the Body of Christ, the whole people of God is an instrument of Christ who is active and present in the prayer of the church. In this sense, we can say that the whole church makes the Eucharist. At the same time, we must affirm that the Eucharist makes the church, for it is a sign of what we are and are called to be: images of Christ and of his self-giving love for all of humanity.

The bond of communion with Christ and with all those who belong to Christ's Body, the church, is one of the principal effects of the Eucharist. By their love for one another and by their unity, the ecclesial Body of Christ is a sign and sacrament of the new humanity transformed by Christ. A heightened awareness of the corporate dimension of the life and prayer of the church is rooted in the council's profound concern to promote the full participation of all the faithful in the prayer of the church, a subject to which we now turn.

Notes

[1] Odo Casel, *The Mystery of Christian Worship* (Westminster: Newman Press, 1962).

[2] Edward Schillebeeckx, *Christ the Sacrament of Encounter with God* (New York: Sheed and Ward, 1963).

[3] Karl Rahner, *The Church and the Sacraments* (New York: Herder and Herder, 1963); "Considerations on the Active Role of the Person in the Sacramental Event," in *Theological Investigations*, vol. 14 (New York: Seabury, 1976), 161–84.

[4] Augustine, *In Ioannis Evangelium (On John's Gospel)*, VI, chapter 1, 7.

[5] Council of Trent, *Session 22. Teaching and Canons on the Most Holy Sacrifice of the Mass*, in *Decrees*, II, chapter 2, p. 733. This same teaching is repeated in the context of SC 7.

[6] Nathan Mitchell, "Who Is at the Table: Reclaiming the Real Presence," *Commonweal* 122 (January 27, 1995): 12.

[7] See Normand Bonneau, *The Sunday Lectionary: Ritual Word and Paschal Shape* (Collegeville, MN: Liturgical Press, 1998).

[8] Consultation on Common Texts, *The Revised Common Lectionary* (Nashville: Abingdon, 1992).

[9] See Horace T. Allen, "The Ecumenical Import of Lectionary Reform," in *Shaping English Liturgy: Studies in Honor of Archbishop Denis Hurley*, ed. Peter C. Finn and James M. Schellmann (Washington, DC: Pastoral Press, 1990), 361–84. Ecumenical collaboration in the production of common translations of the Scriptures is encouraged in DV 22. For a fuller presentation of the ecumenical significance of liturgical renewal, see James F. Puglisi, ed., *Liturgical Renewal as a Way to Christian Unity* (Collegeville, MN: Liturgical Press, 2005).

[10] Augustine, *Sermon 179*.

Chapter Three

Full, Conscious, Active Participation in the Liturgy

(*Sacrosanctum Concilium* 14)

> It is very much the wish of the church that all the faithful should be led to take that full, conscious, and active part in liturgical celebrations which is demanded by the very nature of the liturgy, and to which the Christian people, "a chosen race, a royal priesthood, a holy nation, a redeemed people" (1 Pet 2:9, 4-5) have a right and to which they are bound by reason of their Baptism.
>
> In the restoration and development of the sacred liturgy the full and active participation by all the people is the paramount concern, for it is the primary, indeed the indispensable source from which the faithful are to derive the true Christian spirit. Therefore, in all their apostolic activity, pastors of souls should energetically set about achieving it through the requisite formation.

Background

When Catholics today speak of the reform of the liturgy, many mistakenly imagine that the key reforms inaugurated by Vatican II came "out of the blue," as it were. However, at the heart of the liturgical renewal was its call for fuller participation on the part of all the baptized in the liturgy, a call first made by Pope Pius X, in a 1903 *motu proprio* titled *Tra le Sollecitudini*. The primary focus of this text was the renewal of sacred music, especially the use of Gregorian chant in the celebration of the Mass. "In order that the faithful may more actively participate in the sacred liturgy," Pius X urged, "let them be once again made to sing Gregorian chant as a congregation" (3). The pope was well aware that for many Catholics the Mass had become more an occasion for private devotion than active participation in the Eucharist. Pius X saw himself as a reformer and encouraged the laity to receive the Eucharist with greater frequency. He revised the traditional order of the sacraments of initiation, permitting children who had reached the age of reason (age seven) to make their First Communion before being confirmed so their participation in the Eucharist would not be unduly delayed.

Dom Lambert Beauduin, a Belgian monk of the Benedictine Abbey of Mont César, was also much concerned about the torpor that had overtaken Catholic worship. He spoke to a congress of the Catholic Action movement in 1909 at the invitation of Cardinal Mercier of Malines. Beauduin was deeply imbued with the renewed study of the prayer of the early church. He transposed Pope Pius X's desire for fuller participation in the prayer of the church into a far-reaching vision for the renewal of what he saw as a rather soulless prayer of the church. For Beauduin, the meaning of the liturgy was no longer apparent to the people. His speech, which emphasized the full participation of all the baptized in the celebration of the liturgy, is regarded by many historians today as the beginning of the contemporary movement for liturgical reform. Beauduin was deeply influenced by the works of Dom Columba Marmion (1858–1923) and Dom Prosper Guéranger (1805–75), both of whom had sought to contribute to a renewed life of monastic prayer in the Benedictine tradition. An experienced chaplain of the working class, he sought to combine the fruits of liturgical scholarship with a profound pastoral concern to renew the vitality of parish life and make the meaning of the liturgy more intelligible for ordinary Catholics. Beauduin wanted to restore the liturgy to its rightful place in the life of the church. For too long, he was convinced, it had been the prerogative of a religious elite (monks, clergy, and religious). The liturgy must be returned to its proper role as the principal prayer and formative influence in the life of all the baptized. A brief consideration of his concerns can help us to appreciate the state of Catholic liturgical life in the early twentieth century.

Since the Middle Ages, the celebration of the liturgy had become largely the concern of clergy and religious. The laity attended Mass as silent and devout, yet passive, spectators. The form of the Eucharist celebrated up until the Second Vatican Council was the Roman Rite established in the *Missale Romanum* of Pope Pius V in 1570. It was derived from a form of the medieval "papal" Mass, a shortened form of the liturgy in use in the papal chapel in Rome and spread through the influence of the Franciscan Order. Like many forms of the medieval Western liturgy, it suffered from numerous additions and repetitions, including an accumulation of votive prayers for the dead, the saints, and the Blessed Virgin Mary. The liturgy was celebrated in Latin, a language introduced into the public prayer of the church in the city of Rome as late as the fourth century, where it was the vernacular language of the people. Elsewhere, early Christians worshiped in a variety of local languages, including Greek, Coptic, and Syriac. Long before the twentieth century, Latin had become quite foreign to most members of the Roman Catholic Church.

Chief among Beauduin's criticism of the state of the liturgy in the early twentieth century was that an excessive interest in individual forms of devotion now substituted for genuine participation in the action of the liturgy, often at the encouragement of pious associations.[1] Private devotional practices had begun to obscure the primary role of the corporate and public worship of the church. It was not unusual for laypeople to spend the hour of the Sunday liturgy reciting the rosary, praying the Stations of the Cross, or reading from a proliferation of devotional books containing collections of pious prayers. Few actually received Communion. Many considered the highest form of worship to be the adoration of the exposed Blessed Sacrament. One image of what was going on in much of Catholic worship is that of a church full of parishioners in their own phone booths, with independent phone lines all connecting to the altar and then shooting up to God. The sense of common worship was minimal.

Beauduin promoted the recovery of an ancient understanding of the liturgy as the priestly offering and work of Christ, and of his Mystical Body on earth, the church. He rightly held that the full, conscious, and active participation of all the faithful in the church's sacrifice of praise flowed from the very nature of the liturgy and of the church. To encourage the active participation of all the faithful, he asked that the assembly be permitted to respond to the priest together with the acolyte, who alone took the part of the people, and he encouraged the use of dialogical prayers. He argued that the faithful ought to receive Communion each time they took part in the liturgy, that they ought to receive both the bread and the cup, and that they ought to receive Communion in the hand while standing, rather than on the tongue while kneeling. He encouraged the common celebration of the Liturgy of the Hours, especially the offices of Morning and Evening Prayer. He suggested a simplification of the calendar of saints and a clearer ordering of the liturgical year to make the meaning of each celebration more accessible to all. Finally, he argued for greater simplicity in the appointment of places of worship so the focus of the gathered assembly would be more easily directed to a single, unencumbered altar. The many ideas advanced by Beauduin prior to the First World War were embraced by many others in the liturgical renewal movement and they were received as the guiding principles of the liturgical reform undertaken by the Second Vatican Council.

The Guiding Principle for the Reform of the Liturgy

The principle of the full, conscious, active participation of all the faithful in the celebration of the liturgy is the first and overarching principle intended to orient all of the council's efforts to renew the public prayer of the church. The affirmation that the active participation of the faithful is an inherent "right" of all "by reason of their Baptism" is an indication that this participation is rooted in a renewed understanding of the nature of the church. It follows from a renewed appreciation of the dignity of all the baptized faithful as members of the priestly people of God. The call for full participation has rightly been called "the refrain" of the Constitution on the Sacred Liturgy, as the term "participation" occurs sixteen times in all (SC 12, 14, 19, 26, 27, 30, 41, 50, 55, 79, 114, 121, 124). The primary aim of the reform of the eucharistic liturgy and all the other rites of the church is "that devout and active participation by the faithful may be more easily achieved" (SC 50). The council sought to lead the baptized faithful not simply to a more active engagement in the exterior ritual action of the liturgy but to bring about a fuller participation in the paschal mystery of Christ celebrated in the eucharistic memorial, the source of all Christian living:

> The church, therefore, spares no effort in trying to ensure that, when present at this mystery of faith, Christian believers should not be there as strangers or silent spectators. On the contrary, having a good grasp of it through the rites and prayers, they should take part in the sacred action, actively, fully aware, and devoutly. They should be formed by God's word, and be nourished at the table of the Lord's Body. (SC 48)

In order to ensure that the participation of all the baptized is "conscious," that is, knowing, responsible, informed, and fully understanding the meaning of the rites and gestures of each celebration, *Sacrosanctum Concilium* recognizes the necessity for liturgical formation. More than comprehending the words and gestures intellectually, the baptized faithful ought to be led to grasp the depth of the "mysteries" being celebrated and orient their lives by them. The Second Vatican Council envisions a commitment to liturgical formation not only for seminarians, diocesan liturgical commissions, members of parish liturgy committees or those mandated to carry out the various liturgical ministries (acolytes, lectors, ministers of communion) but it also calls for the liturgical instruction of *all* the faithful to foster "their active participation, internal and external, in the liturgy, taking into account their age, condition, way of life and standard of religious culture" (SC 19). A sound liturgical formation is an integral aspect of all catechesis and formation for Christian living.

The Communal Nature of the Liturgy

The conciliar reform is grounded in a renewed awareness of the liturgy as the action of Christ and his Spirit in and through his ecclesial Body, the church. A new consciousness of the agency of the church in turn inspired a more profound insight into the communal nature of the liturgy. Participation in the liturgy flows from our belonging to the community of disciples gathered together in Christ. This means that liturgical participation cannot be properly conceived as the sum of the acts of private prayer on the part of those individuals who happen to be gathered in the same church on a given day (the "collection of phone booths" we mentioned before). While the celebration of the liturgy may touch each of those gathered in different ways, the action of the liturgy is the action of the "whole church."

The council insists that liturgical celebrations "are not private functions but are celebrations of the church" (SC 26). For this reason, when the revised rites were introduced for use following the Second Vatican Council, the faithful were discouraged from carrying on their private devotional prayer (e.g., reciting the rosary, reading pious devotional prayers and meditations) during the actual celebration of the liturgy. As the prayer of the whole community, the action of the liturgy would be less than complete without the attentive participation of all those gathered. All are "encouraged to take part by means of acclamations, responses, psalms, antiphons, hymns, as well as by actions, gestures and bodily attitudes." Another essential means of taking part in communal prayer is through the observance of "a reverent silence" at appropriate moments in the liturgy (SC 30). Silence provides a space to recollect ourselves; to prepare ourselves to listen to the proclamation of the Word; to reflect on the words and gestures; to prepare our own expressions of humble contrition, intercession, grateful thanks, or joyful praise in accord with the rhythm of each rite.

In light of the communal nature of liturgical prayer, the practice of so-called "private" Masses is discouraged by the Second Vatican Council. The Constitution on the Sacred Liturgy "emphasize[s] that rites which are meant to be celebrated in common, with the faithful present and actively participating, should as far as possible be celebrated in that way rather than by an individual and quasi-privately" (SC 27). The practice of priests celebrating the Eucharist without the presence of an assembly began among monastics in the early Middle Ages. Side altars were built in larger churches to provide a space for the multiple celebrations of these "private" Masses. Ecclesiastical decrees were issued requiring that one or two acolytes be present to serve at the altar and to say the responses of the people—a continuing recognition, however minimal, of the liturgy's inherently communal character. In recognition of the public and communal character of the church's prayer, Catholic teaching no longer uses the term "private" Mass. The present Code of Canon Law reiterates that the public and communal celebration of the liturgy should be the norm when it says, "Except for a just and reasonable cause, a priest is not to celebrate the eucharistic sacrifice without the participation of at least some member of the faithful" (CIC 906).

It may be challenging in contemporary Western society to think of ourselves as belonging to this wider reality, the church, which is manifested in the gathered assembly of the people of God. Many Catholics today identify far more loosely with the church as a community than they did in the past. In recent years we have witnessed a trend toward increasingly large parish communities. Especially in large urban centers, the same sense of anonymity and impersonality that permeates our culture has crept into the culture of parish communities. Our community of worship may not be in the neighborhood where we live, work, or go to school, with the result that we know very few of those who belong to the parish community. The experience of social fragmentation or compartmentalization may make it harder for us to conceive of the corporate dimension of prayer.

Yet perhaps our experience of the church in the present moment of social change and transformation can also be seen as an opportunity to deepen our understanding of both the nature of the church and the communal nature of its prayer. Fewer and fewer Catholics now, or in the future, will take part in the life of the church from a sense of social convention or obligation. In the space of a generation, it has become much more of a free, voluntary association. At the same time, parish communities have come to reflect more than ever the diversity of the world in which we live—ethnically diverse, bringing together men and women of differing social class and background. The "catholicity" of the people of God is reflected in a community that is inclusive of "all nations." The members of the people of God share in the same dignity and call to holiness, regardless of their social location, income, education, ethnicity, and skin color. The fact that many contemporary parishes are a reflection of the *cosmopolis* in which we live may help us to become more aware of the fact that what binds us together is a bond beyond the familiarity of neighbors and friends. The basis of our community lies in Christ. This calls us to recognize his image on the face of all those around us who gather to sing praise and give thanks. Each eucharistic community is, in microcosm, a sign of the whole church at prayer (SC 41).

The Noble Simplicity of the Roman Rite

Another important principle that was to guide the reform of the liturgy and enable a fuller, more conscious participation in the prayer of the church was a desire to return to the "noble simplicity" that had characterized the Roman Rite in earlier times. For this reason, the liturgy constitution states, "The rites should radiate a noble simplicity. They should be short, clear, and free from useless repetition. They should be within the people's powers of comprehension, and normally should not require much explanation" (SC 34). Simply put, the meaning of the actions, symbols, and words of the liturgy should be apparent to all who take part in them. Thus, the council authorized a revision of the eucharistic rite "in such a way that the intrinsic nature and purpose of its several parts, as well as the connection between them, may be more clearly shown, and that devout and active participation by the faithful may be more easily achieved" (SC 50). The model for the new, revised rites is found in some of the most ancient rites of the church, including the eucharistic prayer of the third-century *Apostolic Tradition*, and the fourth-century Divine Liturgy of St. Basil the Great. The essential structure of gathering, listening to the Word, responding through the thanksgiving prayer of the Eucharist, and sending out on mission was restored. Many prayers were simplified, with "due care being taken to preserve their substance" (SC 50). Duplications were omitted and some important aspects of the liturgy that had been lost from view over the course of the centuries were restored to their rightful place. Among these were the *epiclesis* or the invocation of the Holy Spirit over the gifts of bread and wine and over the gathered assembly, the prayers of the faithful, and the reception of both the bread and the cup of Communion by all the faithful. The revision of the liturgical calendar was guided by a desire to simplify the accumulation of feasts and to give pride of place to the mysteries in the life of Christ in the cycle of the year.

This same spirit of simplicity is to characterize the art, architecture, and furnishings of churches and other places of worship. While the church welcomes many styles and expressions of art as contributing to our common praise, *Sacrosanctum Concilium* suggests that "sacred art" is distinguished by "noble beauty rather than sumptuous display" (SC 124). This same spirit is to be reflected in the style of liturgical vestments, and extends to the statuary of individual churches. "The practice of placing sacred images in churches for people to venerate is to be maintained. Nevertheless they should be restricted in number and their relative positions should reflect right order, lest they cause confusion among the christian people, or foster devotion of doubtful orthodoxy" (SC 125). This suggests the need for great care in the selection and positioning of statues, icons, paintings, and stained glass. These elements should not be multiplied or arranged in such a way that they might distract the attention of the gathered faithful from the central action of the liturgy, which takes place on the two tables of the ambo and the altar. The altar is to be placed in a central location where it can be surrounded by the ministers and people. Similarly, the ambo should be clearly visible to all, so that all may see and

> **Ambo:** From the Greek term meaning "reading table," a raised area with a stand from which the gospel is proclaimed.

hear the proclamation of the Word. While statues and icons may become objects of veneration, as an expression of the honor we bear toward the saints whom they represent, such devotion is not to detract in any way or to diminish the adoration that we owe to God alone, and is offered through Christ to the Father, in the power of the Spirit (LG 51). For this reason, the focal point of our attention should always be the ambo and altar, where the community listens to God's Word and commemorates the paschal mystery of Christ.

The Needs and Customs of Different Regions

Karl Rahner has commented that at this council, the Catholic Church developed an awareness of itself as a "world church" for the first time in its history.[2] Where previous ecumenical councils were primarily gatherings of bishops from the continent of Europe and the Mediterranean region, the Second Vatican Council gathered together more bishops than ever before, including men from every continent and indigenous bishops from Asia, Africa, and Oceania. These bishops were deeply aware of the pastoral challenges of attempting to celebrate the Christian faith using forms of worship that were developed in a distant culture and celebrated in an alien language. They spoke passionately of the need to adapt to the customs and local cultures of the peoples they served.

In recognition of this pastoral imperative, the Second Vatican Council recognized that the local bishops were most competent and qualified to determine whether it would be appropriate to celebrate the liturgy in the vernacular language, that is, to replace the use of Latin with the language of the local people (SC 35). They were authorized to prepare suitable translations of the prayers of the church and of the Scriptures for liturgical use (SC 35). As part of the council's wide-ranging acceptance of the need for a greater inculturation of the liturgy, the council encouraged the bishops of each region to commission architects, artists, and musicians to design churches and to promote the creation of works of sacred art and the composition of sacred music that would reflect the talents, gifts, and endowments of their local culture (SC 44–46, 119, 127)—all with a view to bringing about the active participation of the whole gathered assembly in each place. Since the council, there have been important efforts to develop forms of worship that are better adapted to the local cultures of the people, in particular in the Congo, India, and the Philippines. Yet liturgical scholars contend that much more remains to be accomplished to bring about a more adequate inculturation of the prayer of the church.

Through our full, conscious, and active participation in the prayer of the church we become more fully disposed to encounter Christ as he comes to us in the Word of God, in the sacraments, through the ministry of the church, and in the community of all the baptized faithful. When we get together to spend quality time with friends, we turn off our cell phones and other electronic devices to give them our undivided attention, to truly listen to their concerns, and to receive what they have to offer. So in the liturgy, we want to give our undivided attention to growing in friendship with God and communion with one another. When we take part in the liturgy, we not only participate in the ritual activity of the Christian community but we also enter more deeply into relationship with Christ. The liturgical reforms of the council are aimed at directing our attention to this relationship with the person of Christ who is at the heart of the church's prayer. For in and through him, the love of God is revealed to us. As we shall see in the next chapter, the same renewed attention to our encounter with Christ in the liturgy can be found in the council's personalist approach to understanding the Word of God in the Scriptures.

Notes

[1] Lambert Beauduin, *Liturgy and the Life of the Church* (Collegeville, MN: Liturgical Press, 1929).

[2] Karl Rahner, "Basic Theological Interpretation of the Second Vatican Council," in *Theological Investigations,* vol. 20 (New York: Crossroad, 1981), 78.

Chapter Four

A Theology of Divine Revelation

(*Dei Verbum* 2)

> *It pleased God, in his goodness and wisdom, to reveal himself and to make known the mystery of his will (see Eph 1:9), which was that people can draw near to the Father, through Christ, the Word made flesh, in the holy Spirit, and thus become sharers in the divine nature (see Eph 2:18; 2 Pet 1:4). By this revelation, then, the invisible God (see Col 1:15; 1 Tim 1:17), from the fullness of his love, addresses men and women as his friends (see Ex 33:11; Jn 15:14-15), and lives among them (see Bar 3:38), in order to invite and receive them into his own company. The pattern of this revelation unfolds through deeds and words which are intrinsically connected: the works performed by God in the history of salvation show forth and confirm the doctrine and realities signified by the words; the words, for their part, proclaim the works, and bring to light the mystery they contain. The most intimate truth thus revealed about God and human salvation shines forth for us in Christ, who is himself both the mediator and the sum total of revelation.*

Background

In the century prior to the Second Vatican Council, the dominant theological method in Catholic theology was neoscholasticism. This neoscholastic approach to theology was communicated through the theological genre of the dogmatic manual. These were seminary manuals produced to equip the cleric to expound and defend the fundamental truths of the Catholic faith, particularly against the attacks of Protestantism and the Enlightenment. The manual was structured around the assertion of a doctrinal thesis or statement of belief (e.g., "Jesus Christ is True God and True Son of God"[1]). After the articulation of the thesis would often appear a brief description of the various heretical "counter-propositions." This would be followed by various proofs from Scripture and tradition aimed at rebutting contrary views and then perhaps a more speculative exposition of this thesis's connections with other doctrines of the church.

This approach to theology and Christian faith was understandable at a time when the Catholic faith was thought to be under attack and in need of vigorous intellectual defense. For almost four centuries the church felt itself under attack from first the Reformers, then the rise of modern science, Enlightenment philosophy, and so on. This defensive posture put a premium on clear expressions of the faith of the church. Unfortunately, the dogmatic manuals, and the catechisms that were derived from those manuals, often gave the impression that divine revelation was little more than a collection of distinct truth statements. This is sometimes referred to as a "propositional model" of divine revelation. Although these truth statements had their remote origin in Scripture and tradition, their immediate source of authority was the magisterium that had formally proposed them as doctrine. This meant that it was the magisterium, not Scripture and tradition, that was the *proximate* rule of faith

Magisterium: Refers to the teaching authority of the whole college of bishops in communion with its head, the pope, when it teaches on a matter of faith and morals.

for ordinary Catholics. These manuals saw Scripture as merely the *remote* rule of faith, a rule that could not be relied upon without the guidance of the magisterium. Since revelation was presented as a collection of propositional truths, faith was conceived as an intellectual assent to those truths.

During the preparations for the Second Vatican Council, among the many draft documents that were prepared for the bishops' consideration was a draft document on divine revelation. This document was mostly a rehash of the neoscholastic theology found in the dogmatic manuals. Its view of revelation was propositional and it made little use of the biblical renewal movement that had begun to flourish in the decades prior to the council. In 1943 Pope Pius XII had issued an important encyclical, *Divino Afflante Spiritu*, which permitted Catholic biblical scholars to make use of the tools of historical criticism in their interpretation of Scripture. Yet the fruit of that scholarship was strikingly absent from the draft.

During the council debate on the draft a number of bishops complained about the schema's substantial failings. Indeed, a vote was taken to have the schema removed entirely. Through some shrewd parliamentary maneuvering, it was determined that a two-thirds majority would be required to remove the schema and start over. Although a clear majority of the bishops wished to reject the schema, they came just short of the two-thirds majority required. However, the next day Pope John XXIII decreed, on his own authority, that the schema be removed and that a new commission was to be created. It would have cochairs, a leading proponent of the first draft (Cardinal Alfredo Ottaviani, prefect for the Holy Office) and a leading opponent (Cardinal Augustin Bea, president of the Secretariat for Promoting Christian Unity). The final text was the result of the work of this commission and significant later amendments.

Dei Verbum Offers a Personalist and Trinitarian View of Divine Revelation

The key text for this chapter, *Dei Verbum* 2, demonstrates the overall theological shift in the document away from the propositional model that was so pronounced in the preparatory draft. The passage begins with a remarkable assertion: God does not reveal to us a collection of information; rather, God shares God's very self with us. What we see here is a more personalist model of divine revelation. God comes to us as a person, Jesus Christ, who is *"both the mediator and the sum total of revelation"* (emphasis added).

To appreciate this we might consider two different levels of communication, the informational and the interpersonal. First, imagine that you and a friend are attending a basketball game when you see in the crowd on the other side of the arena an old high school teacher of yours. You try to point her out to your friend by directing his gaze to the area where she is sitting. You then describe the clothes she is wearing and other distinctive features as best you can. Finally, your friend identifies your teacher. You communicated to your friend some information that helped him recognize her. But of course your friend really hasn't gotten to know your teacher as a *person*. That could only happen if he engaged her in relationship. Personal identity is only revealed in the context of relationship. This is a different form of communication altogether.

Getting to know someone as a person can only come through regular, authentic encounters with that person. By analogy, so it is with God. God doesn't just want us to master a body of information about God; God wants to share the divine life with us. Article 2 of the constitution tells us that revelation is primarily a matter of God inviting us into a relationship: "the invisible God . . . , from the fullness of his love, addresses men and women as his friends . . . , and lives among them . . . , in order to invite and receive them into his own company." As Joseph Ratzinger (now Pope Benedict XVI) observed in his commentary on *Dei Verbum*:

> The Council's intention in this matter was a simple one. . . . The fathers were merely concerned with overcoming neo-scholastic intellectualism, for which revelation chiefly meant a store of mysterious supernatural teachings, which automatically reduces faith very much to an acceptance of these supernatural insights. As opposed to this,

the Council desired to express again the character of revelation as a totality, in which word and event make up one whole, a true dialogue which touches man (sic) in his totality, not only challenging his reason, but, as dialogue, addressing him as a partner, indeed giving him his true nature for the first time.[2]

We should also note the trinitarian structure of divine revelation reflected in this text.

For too many of us the Trinity is an insolvable arithmetic problem: how can three equal one? Or worse, we may think of God as three individual "somethings" in a heavenly community—two men and a bird! But in this passage we encounter a much deeper understanding of the Trinity. The doctrine of the Trinity teaches us that God is radically personal and relational. The God who wishes to share the fullness of the divine life with us speaks a definitive, unsurpassable Word of love in Jesus Christ. This Word, Christ, is "the sum total of revelation." All that God wishes to offer us of God's self is offered in Christ. The doctrine of the Trinity helps us understand our God as an eternal event of perfect divine self-communication.

But what of the Holy Spirit? If God communicates God's self to us in the Word, it is the Holy Spirit that is God at work in our hearts enabling us to receive that Word. In article 5 of *Dei Verbum* the council writes that it is the Holy Spirit "who moves the heart and converts it to God, and opens the eyes of the mind and 'makes it easy for all to accept and believe the truth.'" Divine revelation is not some abstract divine act; it is personal. God wishes to communicate *to us* and does so by the power of the Spirit.

The personalist character of divine revelation is reinforced by *Dei Verbum* 2's reference to "the most intimate truth" communicated by God. This is a departure from the traditional Catholic stress on the "truths" or "mysteries" of the faith. The council is reminding us that revelation is not a collection of statements, theses, or teachings, but the single "intimate truth" of God's love for us in Christ by the power of the Spirit. This, of course, does not exclude Scripture, tradition, or church dogma from our understanding of divine revelation. God's revelation to us must be mediated in some way. Let's explore this further.

God is infinite, incomprehensible mystery, and we are finite creatures. Consequently, God's communication of God's self to us cannot be like communicating a bus schedule to a friend. Surely as limited creatures we cannot receive God as God is. If God really wishes to communicate with us, God must communicate God's self to us in a manner appropriate to our status as finite, embodied creatures. This is reflected in a medieval dictum, "that which is received is received according to the mode of the receiver" (*quidquid recipitur, recipitur ad modum recipientis*). God comes to us in a manner appropriate to our natures as finite, embodied creatures. As embodied creatures, the primary way in which we come to know our world is through symbols. We learn through language, concepts, images, and metaphors. It is through these symbols that God is able to "mediate" the sharing of divine life that is the substance of revelation. Avery Dulles referred to this understanding of revelation as "symbolic mediation."[3] These symbols mediate or make present God's self-gift. God comes among us in ways that we can grasp, in deeds great and small and in a special way in the testimony of Scripture.

The Role of Scripture

Within all Christian traditions Scripture is given pride of place as a mediation of divine revelation. Many Christians popularly refer to the Bible as the word of God and while this is not incorrect, it can be misleading. If we start with the council's personalist and trinitarian understanding of revelation in which God offers us the divine Word who in the fullness of time became incarnate as Jesus of Nazareth, then it is more accurate to speak of Scripture as the inspired *testimony* to the living word of God. Scripture is the privileged, inspired witness to what God has revealed to us. The Bible is not to be equated with revelation insofar as God had been communicating to God's people even prior to the creation of the Bible (e.g., God's encounter with Abraham).

According to the council, Scripture is God's word mediated through the testimony of human authors: "God chose certain men who, all the while he employed them in this task, made full use of their powers and faculties so that, though he acted in them and by them, it was as true authors that they consigned to writing whatever he wanted written, and no more" (DV 11). In this passage the council was embracing the use of modern historical criticism that was encouraged by Pope Pius XII. If we are to consider the intentions of the human biblical authors, then we must consider their use of diverse literary genres and metaphorical language as well as the various ways in which they were influenced "by their time and culture" (DV 12).

The council's personalist and trinitarian theology of revelation is also reflected in its treatment of the thorny question of biblical inerrancy. The early draft of the schema perpetuated the preconciliar view that Scripture was totally without error in all matters, religious and profane. Today we associate such a view with biblical fundamentalism. At the council many bishops recognized the growing difficulties with this approach; it left no room to deal with historical inconsistencies evident in the biblical text. The classic example often cited was Mark 2:26, which recounts David entering the house of God under the high priest Abiathar when, according to 1 Samuel 21:1ff., David did so not under Abiathar but under his father Ahimelech. One might also mention discrepancies in the gospels regarding at what point in Christ's ministry (at the beginning or the end) the so-called "cleansing of the temple" took place, or the disagreement among the gospels regarding whether or not Christ's Last Supper occurred on Passover. The bishops were generally in agreement that any theory of biblical inspiration needed to account for these difficulties. At the same time, they wished to avoid any sense that only "parts" of Scripture were inspired.

The solution was to focus on God's intention in inspiring Scripture in the first place. In *Dei Verbum* 11 the council taught that *all* Scripture was inspired, but inspired with a view toward the faithful communication of God's saving offer, not with a view to historical or scientific accuracy. The scientific and historical framework of biblical texts was to be read as a medium for the communication of God's offer of salvation. The council's perspective was carefully crafted to admit the possibility of human limitations, deficiencies, and even errors entering into the authorship of the sacred texts, but in such a way that God's saving truth was still faithfully communicated through the medium of the entire biblical testimony.

A consistent theme throughout the council documents is the need for the church to renew its commitment to the priority of Scripture in the life of the church. As we saw in chapter 2, *Sacrosanctum Concilium* emphasized the centrality of Scripture in the liturgy (SC 24) and called for an expanded liturgical Lectionary so that the faithful would have a broader exposure to Scripture through the liturgical readings (SC 51). Seminarians were to be taught that Scripture "was the very soul of all theology." So, in the Decree on the Training of Priests (*Optatam Totius*), the council writes, "After a suitable introduction, let them be carefully initiated into exegetical method, study closely the main themes of divine revelation and find inspiration and nourishment in daily reading of the sacred books and meditation on them" (OT 16). Finally, in *Dei Verbum* the council taught that all the Christian faithful were to be encouraged to "a frequent reading of the divine scriptures" (DV 25).

Although Scripture stands as the privileged medium of divine revelation, the same word of God revealed in Scripture would also be mediated in tradition, that is, in the church's liturgy, theological reflection, doctrinal pronouncements, and daily insight of ordinary believers. The Bible, liturgy, creeds, doctrinal pronouncements, and personal testimony—each in its unique fashion represents diverse expressions or mediations of the one revelation of God in Christ through the power of the Holy Spirit.

The Role of Church Dogma

Among the many "mediations of divine revelation" church dogma plays a special role. It is the normative expression of divine revelation as taught by the magisterium. Dogmatic teaching serves as an authoritative benchmark, the standard against which all other expressions will be measured. The terms *doctrine* and *dogma* are used in different ways in the Catholic tradition. In general, the term "doctrine" represents a broader category. Among the many doctrinal teachings of the church there is a smaller category of teachings that are called "dogmas." All dogmas are doctrines but not all doctrines are dogmas. However, we cannot treat church dogma as if it were identical with divine revelation. There is always more to God than can be expressed even in a dogma of the church. This is why, as St. Thomas pointed out, the object of our faith is not a propositional statement but the divine reality of God to which that proposition leads us.[4] Formal church teachings communicate something essential about God's saving offer, but they do not exhaust what God wishes to communicate to us. The point of church dogma is to draw us into a relationship with God.

> Doctrine: Any authoritative or normative formulation of a belief of the church, whether revealed or not. A church doctrine is intended to articulate a formal belief of the church that it draws in some fashion from its reflection on divine revelation, even if it may not itself be divinely revealed.
>
> Dogma: Any authoritative formulation, (1) the content of which is divinely revealed; and (2) that is proposed as such by the magisterium, either through a solemn definition of a pope or council, or by the teaching of the college of bishops in their ordinary and universal magisterium.

Since dogma can authentically mediate divine revelation while not exhausting it, these teachings can always be reformulated. In his influential address at the opening of the council Pope John distinguished between the substance of church teaching and its concrete formulation. The council incorporated this in the Pastoral Constitution on the Church in the Modern World (*Gaudium et Spes*): "Furthermore, theologians are now being asked, within the methods and limits of theological science, to develop more efficient ways of communicating doctrine to the people of today, for the deposit and the truths of faith are one thing, the manner of expressing them—provided their sense and meaning are retained—is quite another" (GS 62).[5] The council understood that even a dogma that has been taught infallibly can be subject to reformulation without being wrong. To say that a dogma has been taught infallibly means that we can trust that it will not lead us away from the path of salvation; it does not preclude our finding better ways to communicate its abiding truth. Further study and theological reflection can improve and refine the way we articulate church teaching. In Pope John XXIII's opening address he emphasized that there was no need for a council if its only task was to repeat church teaching. Rather, he insisted, it was necessary to pursue a deeper understanding of the faith of the church and more effective ways to present that teaching to the modern world.

In this chapter we have focused on an essential "key to the council." *Dei Verbum* 2 introduces us to the council's shift away from a propositional model of revelation to a theology of revelation that is both personalist and trinitarian. It is a theology of revelation that begins with the remarkable belief that God wishes to offer God's very being to us in a life of friendship and love. This more dynamic theology of revelation, in turn, led to a renewed theology of tradition, the topic of our next chapter.

Notes

[1] Ludwig Ott, *Fundamentals of Catholic Dogma* (St. Louis: Herder, 1955), 127.

[2] Joseph Ratzinger, "Dogmatic Constitution on Divine Revelation, Origin and Background," in *Commentary on the Documents of Vatican II*, 5 vols., ed. Herbert Vorgrimler (New York: Herder and Herder, 1967–69), vol. III, 155–98, at 172.

[3] For a fuller development of this understanding of revelation, see Avery Dulles, *Models of Revelation* (Garden City: Doubleday, 1983), 131–54.

[4] Thomas Aquinas, *Summa Theologiae* II-II, Q.1, a.3, ad 2.

[5] This same insight reappears in the Decree on Ecumenism (*Unitatis Redintegratio*), 6.

Chapter Five

A Theology of Tradition

(*Dei Verbum* 8)

> *The tradition that comes from the apostles makes progress in the church, with the help of the holy Spirit. There is a growth in insight into the realities and words that are being passed on. This comes about through the contemplation and study of believers who ponder these things in their hearts (see Lk 2:19 and 51). It comes from the intimate sense of spiritual realities which they experience. And it comes from the preaching of those who, on succeeding to the office of bishop, have received the sure charism of truth. Thus, as the centuries go by, the church is always advancing towards the plenitude of divine truth, until eventually the words of God are fulfilled in it.*

Background

The word "tradition" comes from the Latin *traditio*, which in turn is a translation of the Greek word *paradosis*. Both terms mean "to hand on" or "transmit." Early Christians understood these terms to refer both to the substance of the Christian faith that was handed on from generation to generation and to the process by which they handed on their faith. These two basic uses of the term "tradition" have long and complicated histories.

We have already discussed the propositional model of revelation that dominated Catholic theology in the decades prior to the Second Vatican Council. This model of revelation influenced the understanding of church tradition common at the time. The content of tradition was generally conceived less as a dynamic reality than as a collection of customs, laws, and doctrinal pronouncements that were in some sense added to what was revealed in Scripture. Neoscholastic theology treated doctrinal formulations as static and unchanging. It was generally held that the only way doctrine could develop was if there were new propositional statements that were logical developments of already established doctrines. Doctrine developed simply by moving from the implicit to the explicit.

Many theologians subscribed to the "two source theory," viewing Scripture and tradition as two distinct sources of divine revelation. In other words, the origins of some doctrines could be traced to Scripture and others to tradition. In fact, many medieval and baroque theologians wrote only of "traditions" in the plural. There was little sense of tradition as a dynamic living reality. The second way of understanding tradition, namely, as the process by which the one Christian faith was handed on, often focused on the magisterium as the principal organ for handing on the faith of the church.

The preparatory draft on divine revelation first presented for the council's deliberation included these reductive and even misleading understandings of tradition. That document made the "two source theory" the center piece of its theology of revelation and presented the magisterium as the privileged organ of tradition. Many bishops roundly criticized the draft, noting that while theologians had often assumed the theory of two sources, it had never been proposed as the authoritative teaching of the church.

Dei Verbum's Dynamic Theology of Tradition

The Second Vatican Council recognized the inadequacies of the dominant understanding of "tradition" enshrined in the preparatory draft. The Secretariat for Christian Unity also played an important role in sensitizing the drafters to the ecumenical implications of their work, particularly regarding the question of the relationship between Scripture and tradition.

Regarding the content of tradition, the council affirmed that tradition included "everything that serves to make the people of God live their lives in holiness and increase their faith. In this way the church, in its doctrine, life and worship, perpetuates and transmits to every generation all that it itself is, all that it believes" (DV 8). This passage conceives of tradition as a living reality, the lifeblood of the church. It includes doctrine, customs, and laws, but it also includes many theological and spiritual traditions, the church's worship, its distinctive practices and diverse paths to holiness.

> Although the council never explicitly makes use of the distinction, implicit in the text is a distinction between *tradition* (in the singular), which refers to the dynamic faith of the church in its entirety, and *traditions* (in the plural), which refers to different elements of tradition, some of which will have enduring value and others which will not.

The council carefully avoided the two source theory, teaching instead that "[t]radition and scripture make up a single sacred deposit of the word of God, which is entrusted to the church" (DV 10). Once the council shifted from a propositional view of revelation to one that centered on the living Word Incarnate as Jesus of Nazareth, it became possible to orient both Scripture and tradition as distinct but interrelated mediations of the same living Word.

This brings us to the key text with which we opened this chapter: "The tradition that comes from the apostles makes progress in the church, with the help of the holy Spirit. There is a growth in insight into the realities and words that are being passed on" (DV 8). This merits more in-depth consideration.

Tradition Progresses

In popular usage, any reference to "tradition" evokes some revered past that stands as the norm of all we do today. This sense of tradition is captured in the oft used phrase "that is the way we have always done it." There is a tendency for us to think of tradition as invariant, "etched in concrete." As we saw above, neoscholasticism generally had little place for genuine change or development in church doctrine. Vatican II dramatically departed from this static approach to tradition and church doctrine. Since tradition is a living reality, it grows and develops. Certain customs, practices, laws, theological approaches, and even certain doctrinal formulations may change and sometimes even outgrow their usefulness to the church. The council's reference to the "progress" of tradition speaks to an important theological question: can doctrine change and develop?

In the nineteenth century a small number of theologians reconsidered the issue by stepping outside of the propositional approach of neoscholasticism. Theologians like John Henry Newman, Johann Adam Möhler, and, in the early twentieth century, Maurice Blondel, started with a view of revelation quite close to the one adopted at Vatican II. For them, revelation could not be exhausted by church doctrine. Doctrines were authentic but still imperfect and even partial expressions of divine revelation. This is reflected in the council's adoption of the distinction between the "deposit of faith" itself and the concrete manner in which a particular doctrinal statement "expresses" the deposit of faith (GS 62). Church doctrine, and therefore tradition, progresses or develops as the church grows in its consciousness of the depth and breadth of God's self-communication.

The council did not just offer a new understanding of the development of doctrine; its own teaching is also an example of it. Many of Vatican II's teachings can best be understood as a genuine development or growth in church doctrine: its teaching on religious liberty, Catholicism's relationship to other Christian traditions, episcopal collegiality. The council's treatment of each of these topics brought about a substantive change in church teaching.

The Whole Christian Faithful Share Responsibility
for the Development of Tradition

Dei Verbum 8 also represents a decisive break from the view that the magisterium is the exclusive organ of tradition: "This comes about through the contemplation and study of believers who ponder these things in their hearts. . . . It comes from the intimate sense of spiritual realities which they experience. And it comes from the preaching of those who, on succeeding to the office of bishop, have received the sure charism of truth." The text does mention the necessary role of the bishops but not before it first cites the contributions of believers who, through contemplation, study, and intimate experience, allow church tradition to progress. What is striking is the vision of the bishops and the lay faithful cooperating in this "traditioning" process. This shared responsibility presupposes that all Christians have a spiritual gift for discerning God's word that enables them to contribute to the "progress" of tradition. In the Dogmatic Constitution on the Church (*Lumen Gentium*), the council refers to this spiritual gift as the *sensus fidei*, the sense or instinct for the faith:

> By this sense of the faith, aroused and sustained by the Spirit of truth, the people of God, guided by the sacred magisterium which it faithfully obeys, receives not the word of human beings, but truly the word of God . . . , "the faith once for all delivered to the saints." . . . The people unfailingly adheres to this faith, penetrates it more deeply through right judgment, and applies it more fully in daily life. (LG 12)

Each believer, by virtue of baptism, has a supernatural instinct or sense of the faith (*sensus fidei*) that allows each to recognize God's word and to respond to it. The individual exercise of this instinct is not, of course, infallible. Nevertheless, this spiritual instinct makes an important contribution to building up the faith of the church.

In addition to the spiritual sense given to each believer at baptism, we can also speak of the sense of the whole faithful (*sensus fidelium*), namely, that which the whole people of God in fact believe. This is not always easy to determine, and there will be instances when there is, at a given point in time, no consensus in belief among the faithful. This is more likely to be the case when the church is considering new and emerging issues or older questions in new contexts. When the faithful are united in their belief, manifesting a true consensus, we can speak of a *consensus fidelium*. According to Vatican II, when the whole people of God are in agreement, when they have achieved a *consensus*, the Holy Spirit is so active in them that they are protected from error; their judgment of belief is infallible.

The sense of faith given to each believer in baptism may be understood in two ways.[1] First, it can refer to a capacity of individual believers to understand God's revelation addressed to them in love. In this regard we might think of the sense of faith as a kind of spiritual instinct or sixth sense. It is this capacity that allows a believer, almost intuitively, to discern what is of God and what is not. But the sense of faith might also be thought of, not only as a capacity, but also as an actual perception or imaginative grasp of divine revelation.

The best analogy may come from our appreciation of art. When we encounter a piece of art like a beautiful sculpture or a moving musical composition, it has an effect on us; we apprehend the art from our own particular perspective. Our own life story, our storehouse of life experiences, inclines us to understand the work of art in a particular way. The work of the artist is completed in our viewing or hearing of the work. We bring something of ourselves to the work of art. The *sensus fidei* functions similarly. As Christians we encounter some story, event, or symbol from Scripture or tradition and it works on our religious imaginations. We ruminate over a biblical parable; we allow the power of a hymn to move our hearts; we meditate before a crucifix and ponder our sinfulness and the enormity of God's mercy. The fruit of these reflections, when shared, contributes to the living tradition of the church. Yet this is not a solitary process.

Infallibility: This is a gift of the Holy Spirit that is given to the whole church. It is exercised in diverse ways. The most basic form of exercise is in the common belief of the whole people of God. When all believers are in agreement on a matter of faith and morals, they cannot be mistaken in their belief. The gift of infallibility is also exercised by those called to be authoritative teachers of the faith, the whole college of bishops in communion with the Bishop of Rome. The college of bishops can teach infallibly through a solemn definition issued by an ecumenical council or in their ordinary teaching when, while dispersed throughout the world, they are in agreement that a teaching pertaining to faith and morals is to be held as definitive (LG 25). Finally this gift of infallibility can be exercised by the Bishop of Rome, who, in communion with his fellow bishops, can issue a solemn definition *ex cathedra*, "from the chair." Infallibility is a fundamentally negative concept insofar as it claims only that the judgment of belief or a teaching judgment *is not wrong*. In other words, when the church teaches on a matter infallibly, believers can be confident that this teaching will not lead them astray. Because a teaching has been taught infallibly, however, such a teaching can still be improved upon and reformulated in ways that better express the deep truth of the teaching.

Christians encounter God's divine revelation in the context of a community of faith. We hear the Scriptures preached to us as a community; we celebrate the liturgy as a community; we meditate before the crucifix on Good Friday as a community. Yet each of us uniquely encounters that one revelation. And when we give testimony to our personal encounters with God's revelation, received and interpreted within the unique stories of our lives, the community is enriched by our testimony. In our testimony the church receives the one revelation of God's love, incarnate in Christ by the power of the Spirit, as something fresh and vital. Consequently, as the council observed, all believers contribute something to the faith consciousness of the church, not only through the faithful acceptance of church doctrine, but also by offering their own imaginative construal of the divine self-gift they have received within the distinctive framework of their own life stories.

The Second Vatican Council taught that this *sensus fidei*, when exercised individually, is not infallible. It is always to be exercised in communion with the whole church and in a way that shows due respect to the authoritative teachers of the church, the bishops. The council affirmed the unique and necessary role of the magisterium as the authoritative interpreter of Scripture and tradition, yet it insisted that the "magisterium is not superior to the word of God, but is rather its servant. It teaches only what has been handed on to it. At the divine command and with the help of the holy Spirit, it listens to this devoutly, guards it reverently and expounds it faithfully. All that it proposes for belief as being divinely revealed it draws from this sole deposit of faith" (DV 10).

The magisterium exercises its authority in diverse ways. Rarely, there can be an exercise of the *extraordinary magisterium* in which either the whole college of bishops, or the Bishop of Rome individually (yet always in communion with the bishops), can issue a solemn definition that is protected from error by the charism of infallibility. More commonly the pope and bishops will exercise their *ordinary magisterium* and teach with the assistance of the Holy Spirit but without the gift of infallibility. Catholics owe to the pope and bishops, in this latter case, the presumption of truth, but they must be aware that in these exercises of teaching authority there remains a remote possibility of error.

One often hears the statement "the church is not a democracy," and it is true. Equally true, however, is the fact that the church is not a monarchy (the rule of the one over the many), an oligarchy (the rule of the few over the many), or an aristocracy (the rule of an elite class over the many). The church's deepest reality cannot be grasped by way of political analogues.

The church is the people of God, a spiritual communion, the temple of the Holy Spirit. Unlike a democracy, the church is not governed by a desire to achieve majority rule where the majority is determined by the popularity of a given position or opinion. In a majority I have a right to further my own views and preferences and to persuade others to my viewpoint as much as possible. In the church, as a spiritual communion, all the church's members have an obligation not to further their own views but to submit themselves before the will of God discerned by attending to the promptings of the Holy Spirit. This is far removed from the political logic of a liberal democracy. As such, all of its members have an obligation not to further their own ideological agendas but to submit to a pedagogy of the Spirit. What they offer in their testimony should be their hearing of God's word and the Spirit's promptings in their hearts. All church members, from the pope to the newly baptized, share this obligation to listen to God's word and to discern God's will. All Christians, from the pope to the newly baptized, must be open to have the Holy Spirit work on their minds and hearts and bring about a conversion in viewpoint. Only within such a spiritual perspective can we see the sense of the faithful and the teaching authority of the bishops cooperating rather than competing with one another.

Eschatological Character of Divine Revelation

There is one final insight to note in the key passage headlining this chapter. The Dogmatic Constitution on Divine Revelation, in article 8, teaches that "the church is always advancing towards the plenitude of divine truth." Here again we encounter a shift from the propositional model of revelation to a personalist and trinitarian one. Revelation, divine truth, is not something that the church ever really possesses. If revelation is a share in the divine life, then it is perhaps better to say that divine truth possesses us. The church can only "advance" toward the "plenitude" or fullness of divine truth because we will only be able to *fully* apprehend this truth in the eschaton, the culmination of all human history in God. We are called to live in the truth of God's love for us but divine truth is always greater than our apprehension of it. This passage stands as a bold repudiation of various forms of Catholic fundamentalism that absolutize church dogma by suggesting that once one has mastered church teaching one has somehow mastered God.

> Eschatology: This term refers to that sphere of theology concerned with the final destiny of individual humans, humankind, the church, and the entire cosmos.

This eschatological view of revelation also calls forth a certain humility regarding what the church can offer the world. The council wrote: "The church is guardian of the deposit of God's word and draws religious and moral principles from it, but it does not always have a ready answer to every question. Still, it is eager to associate the light of revelation with the experience of humanity in trying to clarify the course upon which it has recently entered" (GS 33). The bishops believed in the precious gift of the good news of Jesus Christ to the world, but they did not believe that knowing Christ meant always knowing how to respond to difficult social issues.

We have already discussed Pope John XXIII's commitment to *aggiornamento*, bringing the church up to date. However, another important aspect of the council's work involved a creative retrieval of neglected elements from the church's great tradition. This process was often referred to by the French term *ressourcement*, a "return to the sources." This "key to the council," *Dei Verbum* 8, presents a dynamic theology of church tradition that undergirds the council's ongoing return to the sources. By seeing tradition as a dynamic and living reality, the council offered a theology of tradition that acknowledged the active role of all the baptized in handing on the faith. The church that gives witness to this living tradition offers itself as a tangible sign and instrument of God's saving love to the world; it is, in short, a sacrament. We shall explore more deeply the sacramental reality of the church in chapter 6.

Notes

[1] For this treatment of the *sensus fidei*, see Ormond Rush, *The Eyes of Faith: The Sense of the Faithful and the Church's Reception of Revelation* (Washington, DC: Catholic University of America Press, 2009).

The Church Is Like a Sacrament

(Lumen Gentium 1)

> *Christ is the light of the nations and consequently this holy synod, gathered together in the holy Spirit, ardently desires to bring to all humanity that light of Christ which is resplendent on the face of the church, by proclaiming his Gospel to every creature (see Mk 16:15). Since the church, in Christ, is [like] a sacrament—a sign and instrument, that is, of communion with God and of the unity of the entire human race—it here proposes, for the benefit of the faithful and of the entire world, to describe more clearly, and in the tradition laid down by earlier councils, its own nature and universal mission.*

Background

The Dogmatic Constitution on the Church, *Lumen Gentium*, is an attempt to express in broad strokes the doctrinal self-understanding of the Catholic Church. This opening paragraph of the constitution, which begins the first chapter titled "The Mystery of the Church," sets the tone for all that will follow. As we saw in chapter 1, the term "mystery" is drawn from the New Testament. Saint Paul used the same word (*musterion* in Greek) to refer to the self-revelation of God in Jesus Christ. In the letter to the Colossians Paul writes that his mission is "to make the word of God fully known, the mystery that has been hidden throughout the ages and generations but has now been revealed to his saints"—the mystery that is Christ (Col 1:25-27; 2:2-3; 4:3). The term "mystery" carries with it the connotation of something that cannot be entirely explained or understood. Something about it always remains hidden, veiled, exceeds the grasp of our intelligence. Yet, St. Paul insists, the very mystery of God and of the divine love for humankind has been revealed; the divine Word has been spoken for us in a definitive way in Jesus Christ. Through him the mystery of God's very self has been made known. Even this real glimpse into the life of God, which we see with the eyes of faith, defies our efforts at explanation. Words can never adequately define or express the reality of God or of God's boundless love.

Paul's teaching is developed further in his letter to the Ephesians. He tells us that in the death and resurrection of Christ we have received forgiveness and been reconciled to God as God's adopted sons and daughters. In his paschal mystery Christ has revealed God's plan from all eternity to gather together the whole human community. "With all wisdom and insight he has made known to us the mystery of his will, according to his good pleasure that he set forth in Christ, as a plan for the fullness of time, to gather up all things in him, things in heaven and things on earth" (Eph 1:8-10). The mystery of God's reconciling love—a love that has broken down the dividing walls and hostility between Israel and the nations (Eph 2:14)—has been revealed to us through God's Spirit. The hope proclaimed by the prophets and the apostles is realized and we are now called to be witnesses to God's reconciling love before all peoples.

It was a short step from Paul's use of the term "mystery" with reference to God's plan of salvation revealed in Christ, to its application by early Christian writers to the sacramental life of the church. The mystery that we celebrate in the liturgical actions of the church is nothing other than our participation in the paschal mystery, the mystery of our redemption in Christ. Latin translations of the Bible and other Latin authors used the words *mysterium* or *sacramentum* interchangeably to translate the Greek *musterion*. By the fourth century, Christian authors began to use this language to speak about the ritual celebrations of the church. One such example can be found in the *Mystagogical Catechesis* of Cyril of Jerusalem. This work is a collection of teachings or catecheses given by the bishop of Jerusalem to newly baptized Christians in the days immediately following Easter. Cyril explains the mysteries that these new Christians have celebrated in the Easter liturgy—recalling their passage through death and resurrection to be reborn with Christ in baptism, and their sharing in his Body and Blood in the Eucharist. He refers to both baptism and Eucharist as "divine mysteries." Their deepest meaning, Cyril insists, cannot be discerned in outward appearances. Christian faith invites us to penetrate beyond the visible appearances of the sacraments in order to grasp the sacred realities that they signify.

During the Middle Ages Catholic theology began to apply the category of mystery, long understood to refer to the Mystical Body of Christ in the Eucharist, to the Mystical Body of Christ that is the church. The medieval authors understood that the fruit of participation in the Eucharist is unity, the communion with God and with one another that constitutes the very foundation of church. Yet this theology was somewhat abstract and largely ignored the historical and human face of the church. Many of these ideas lay dormant for many centuries, especially after the crisis of the Protestant Reformation in the sixteenth century. Protestant Reformers, who argued that the church had drifted so far from the Gospel as to deviate from God's divine intention in founding it, insisted in sometimes polemical terms that the visible church had been reduced to a remnant or a ruin. For them, the true church of Christ was no longer visible but was now hidden from view, and ought to be understood as more of a spiritual reality known only to God. In reaction to this, Catholic theology, led by the Jesuit theologian Robert Bellarmine, placed a strong emphasis on the continuity between the visible reality of the institutional church and the true church established by Christ. Cardinal Bellarmine's ideas, in particular his understanding of the church as a visible and "perfect" society, equipped with everything necessary for the salvation of its members, dominated in Catholic manuals of theology down into the early twentieth century. The teaching of Vatican II is an effort to restore a balance between understanding the inner, spiritual dimensions of the church and its concrete, historical, and visible human reality. To accomplish this, the council returns to the theology implied in the biblical and patristic understanding of *musterion*, which grounds a more incarnational theology of the church and the sacraments.

The Nineteenth- and Twentieth-Century Renewal of Ecclesiology

Already in the nineteenth century, Johann Adam Möhler (1796–1838) began to search for a deeper understanding of the church in all its dimensions. Under the influence of romantic idealism at the University of Tübingen, he turned back to the writings of Paul and the early church fathers to rediscover a more holistic understanding of the church as a dynamic and living reality, a complex human community imbued with the gift of God's Spirit. He advanced an understanding of the church as the continuation of the incarnation of Christ in human history.[1] As Edward Hahnenberg rightly observes, Möhler's genius "was to consider the Church not simply as the bearer of the mystery of faith, but as itself an aspect of this mystery."[2] Under the influence of Möhler, and later Matthias Scheeben,[3] the idea of church as a "mystery" began to gain ground in the latter half of the nineteenth century.

> Ecclesiology: A branch of theology dedicated to reflection on the "ecclesia," that is, the church, with its mission, structures, and ministries.

An early draft for a constitution on the church was presented to the bishops who gathered for the First Vatican Council on January 21, 1870. Its first chapter bore the title "The Church is the Mystical Body of Christ." This draft was never officially discussed by the bishops at Vatican I, as many expressed serious reservations regarding the attempt to speak about the church as the "Mystical Body of Christ." They considered such an approach too vague and preferred to define the church on the basis of its concrete structure. A subsequent draft returned to the preferred image, derived from Bellarmine, of the church as a perfect society, more focused on her visible and institutional form. It was only in 1943, in the teaching of Pope Pius XII's encyclical letter *Mystici Corporis*, that a more incarnational ecclesiology would be received into official Catholic teaching. Pius XII sought to marry the predominant notion of the church as a visible society with the more biblically oriented notion of the church as the Mystical Body of Christ. At Vatican II, we see an effort to build on the teaching of Pius XII and to integrate even more fully the insights of the biblical and patristic traditions. The council's use of an incarnational approach is most apparent in the first chapter of *Lumen Gentium*:

> But, the society equipped with hierarchical structures and the mystical body of Christ, the visible society and the spiritual community, the earthly church and the church endowed with heavenly riches, are not to be thought of as two realities. On the contrary, they form one complex reality comprising a human and a divine element. For this reason the church is compared, in no mean analogy, to the mystery of the incarnate Word. As the assumed nature, inseparably united to him, serves the divine Word as a living instrument of salvation, so, in somewhat similar fashion, does the social structure of the church serve the Spirit of Christ who vivifies it, in the building up of the body. (LG 8)

Note that the church is not identified directly with the incarnation in Christ. A critical distance is maintained between the human community gathered together in Christ's Body the church and Christ himself, the divine Word Incarnate. The church is compared with the incarnation of the divine Word of God in the human nature of Christ by way of *analogy*.

Analogy: A means of explaining something by comparing it with something else, recognizing some similarities or likenesses. In theological reasoning, one may draw an analogy or recognize some similarity between divine and human realities, while taking care to recognize the necessary differences between them.

The Teaching of the Council: The Church Is Like a Sacrament

In a reversal of the course of events witnessed during the First Vatican Council, the bishops of Vatican II severely criticized the first draft constitution on the church presented in 1962, which began from a consideration of the church "militant," that is to say, on the basis of its juridical and institutional form. Rather than repeat the teachings of Vatican I and Pius XII, the bishops at Vatican II favored the more biblical and patristic presentation of the church expressed in contemporary ecclesiology's notion of the church as a sacrament of salvation. A second, revised schema on the church, presented to the council in the fall of 1963, opened with a consideration of "The Mystery of the Church," where the idea of the church as sacrament figures prominently. To be sure, the term "sacrament" has a narrower, more specific meaning when it is applied to the seven liturgical actions of the church. The seven sacraments (baptism, confirmation, Eucharist, reconciliation, anointing of the sick, marriage, and holy orders) are understood to be actions instituted by Christ as visible and effective signs of God's grace that is brought about in the lives of those who are properly disposed to receive it. When *Lumen Gentium* applies the term "sacrament" to the church, it uses this term in a broader sense. To describe the church as a sacrament does not mean that it is a sacramental reality in the same intense manner as the seven sacraments.

It is sometimes forgotten that Pope Pius XII's teaching on the church as the Mystical Body of Christ was occasioned by a number of exaggerations in currents of romantic theology that interpreted the idea of the church as the ongoing incarnation of Christ in an overly literal manner. In at least one case, this led to thinking about the unity between the Mystical Body of Christ and the church as something comparable to the hypostatic union that exists between the divine and human natures in Christ. Others drew comparisons between the transubstantiated Body of Christ in the Eucharist and the presence of Christ in the church. A number of Protestant scholars complained that Catholic theology had fallen into a kind of "ecclesial Docetism," overly glorifying the church while ignoring the historical and human dimensions of the gathered people of God. This was the result of an overly literal or direct identification between Christ and the church. Critics feared that

> **Hypostatic Union:** From the Greek term "hypostasis," which refers to the underlying substance or personal subsistence of each of the three Divine Persons of the Trinity. The doctrine of the hypostatic union refers to the unity of the divine and human natures in the one person of Christ, who is truly divine and truly human.
>
> **Docetism:** Drawn from the Greek verb *dokein*, meaning "to appear or seem." Adherents held that Jesus only appeared to be human. This view was prominent among Gnostics and opposed
>
> *(sidebar cont'd)*

by Christians as heresy in the second century. The dualistic worldview of the Gnostics saw the spiritual dimension of life as good and devalued or considered evil all that was material and corporeal. They tended to deny the bodily realities of Christ's incarnation, suffering, death, and resurrection, effectively denying his human nature.

such an approach tended to obscure the primary role of Christ in the act of salvation. Pius XII, and so the bishops of Vatican II, hoped to present a properly balanced understanding of the human and spiritual, or the visible and invisible dimensions of the church, by appealing to the general framework of mystery or sacrament. They sought to apply this notion by way of analogy, drawing a parallel between the incarnation of the divine Word in the human nature of Christ and the work of God's Spirit in and through the human community of the church.

The Primacy of Christ

Returning to the opening words of *Lumen Gentium*, it is important to note the primacy of Christ: "Christ is the light of the nations." These words echo the language of Pope John XXIII when he explained his intentions for the council in a message delivered by radio just a month before it opened. This light of Christ, he said, must shine forth more brightly from the church. Christ, as we saw in our earlier reflection on the notion of *musterion* or sacrament, is the primary sacrament, the perfect sign and instrument of God's grace in human history. In John's gospel, Jesus proclaims, "I am the light of the world" (John 8:12; 9:5; see also 1:5, 9; 12:46). He reveals to us the love of the Father and is the source of God's redeeming grace. To the extent that the church is "in Christ," a reflection of that same light continues to shine forth for all humanity. In this analogous sense, Jesus could also say to his followers, "You are the light of the world" (Matt 5:14). The Constitution on the Sacred Liturgy points to the fact that the source of the church is in Christ, in whose passion it is born: "For it was from the side of Christ as he slept the sleep of death upon the cross that there came forth the wondrous sacrament of the whole church" (SC 5). The outpouring of blood and water from the side of Christ (John 19:33) symbolizes the sacraments of baptism and the Eucharist, from which the church is born. The church itself becomes a sacrament of Christ's self-emptying love whenever it follows his example of humble service. The human community gathered together by the grace of God in the church is called to be an instrument of Christ's saving action in the world. For this reason, St. Cyprian, the third-century bishop of Carthage, could refer to the church as the "sacrament of unity," an expression taken up first in the Constitution on the Sacred Liturgy (SC 26), and further developed in the Dogmatic Constitution on the Church (LG 9, 48, 59), in the Pastoral Constitution on the Church in the Modern World (GS 45), and in the Decree on the Church's Missionary Activity (AG 1). Before we consider these texts further, let us consider how Cyprian and the Second Vatican Council understand the nature of our salvation.

The Universal Sacrament of Salvation

Cyprian speaks of the church as a "sacrament of salvation" in his treatise *On the Unity of the Church* (no. 7). He compares the church to the seamless garment worn by Christ (John 19:23-24), and presents it as an image of how heaven and the earth have been inseparably woven together in the body of Christ. When the Constitution on the Sacred Liturgy wanted to insist on the corporate nature of Christian worship, it appealed to this same idea. Because the church is "the sacrament of unity," the action of the liturgy is understood as the work of "the whole body" and cannot be privatized (SC 26). The council's teaching on the "people of God" helps us to understand that we are not saved as individuals but as members of a "holy people." When we live in accord with the saving grace of God, our relationships are transformed. We are reconciled not only to God but also to one another, and are enabled to live in greater harmony with the world around us. The opening paragraph of *Lumen Gentium* conveys this same reality when it says the church is a sign "of communion with God and of the unity of the entire human race" (LG 1). In these few words it lays out the very high calling of the Christian community: we are called to be a living example of the unity God desires for the whole human community. Elsewhere, *Lumen Gentium* considers the church as "a chosen race, a royal priesthood, . . . God's own people" (1 Pet 2:9), established by the new covenant in Christ: "All those, who in faith look towards Jesus, the author of salvation and the source of unity and peace, God has gathered together and established as the church, that it may be for each and everyone the visible sacrament of this saving unity" (LG 9). It is in this sense that the council speaks of the church as a "*universal* sacrament of salvation" (LG 48; AG 1; GS 45; emphasis added). This means that in their daily living, the Christian community is to live a life that all people might aspire to: respecting the dignity of all persons, making sure that no one is in need, caring for the poor and vulnerable, working for a just sharing of the earth's resources and for just sustainable economic systems, challenging violence and injustice, and promoting peace. Just as Christ gave us a perfect example of what it means to be human, the church is to be a model for the whole human community. *Lumen Gentium* is unequivocal when it states, "Just as Christ carried out the work of redemption in poverty and oppression, so the church is called to follow the same path if it is to communicate the fruits of salvation to humanity" (LG 8).

For most of us, witnessing to the Good News of our salvation means living simple and authentic lives, serving others in the ordinary activities of work and family. We recognize the grace of God in the accumulation of faithful choices that shape our daily living. As an example, we might consider the Trappist monks of Tiberine, who eschewed enthusiastic evangelizing and lived a simple presence of prayer in North Africa. They were martyred when they refused to flee for their own safety but chose instead to remain in solidarity with their poor Muslim neighbors. Or again, we might ponder the example of the Amish community in Nickel Mines, Pennsylvania, that showed no hesitation in forgiving the young man who murdered their children in a violent rampage. This kind of solidarity and forgiveness surpasses a purely human capacity for loving; it is rooted in a profound and sustained experience of the love of God. When we live and act out of such an awareness, we ourselves become a reflection of the very love of God for others. At the same time, we must humbly admit that we remain subject to sin and failings, and are equally capable of becoming a counterwitness and an obstacle to God's love. The sad chapter of sexual abuse and exploitation by ministers of the church, and of the failures of some church leaders to protect real and potential victims of such abuse, is a warning that the Christian community is far from immune to dysfunction. Many rightly see in these failures a countersign that seriously undermines the credibility of the church's witness in the world. They reveal our continued need for grace, healing, and wholeness.

To overcome the danger noted earlier of emphasizing the divine life of the church to the exclusion of its very human character, *Lumen Gentium's* chapter on "The Mystery of the Church" is immediately followed by a chapter on the "People of God." In presenting this chapter of the revised draft to the bishops at the council the relator explained that the council's reflection on the church as a mystery of communion, begun in chapter 1, continues in this consideration of the church as the pilgrim community called together by God. The biblical image of the people of God has its roots in the Old Testament Scriptures where Israel is presented as the people called together and led to freedom by God. It plays an important role in the New Testament as well (1 Pet 2:9-10) and helps the Christian community see themselves against the long horizon of salvation history. The Greek term *ecclesia* or church echoes the Hebrew term *qahal*, used to refer to the people gathered together by God. The

> **Relator:** A relator was a member of a conciliar commission or subcommission charged with "relating" to the council members the reasons for changes that had been made in a text to be presented to the bishops.

image of the church as the pilgrim people of God helps us to understand the church in its human and historical dimension as a people "on the way." In fact, one of the earliest names given to the Christian community in the Scriptures is followers of "the Way" (Acts 9:2).

A proper understanding of the church's role as sacrament or instrument of salvation in the world entails an adequate appreciation of the eschatological nature of the church. *Lumen Gentium* reflects on the vocation of the church as the universal sacrament of salvation in human history within the context of its reflection on the eschatological or provisional nature of the church, mindful that it will only come to perfection in the consummation of God's plan at the end of time. We live "in between times," in a period of history when God's plan to reconcile us in Christ has already begun but is not yet fully realized.

It is in our striving, in our fidelity to the Gospel, that we proclaim and point toward Christ and, indeed, toward the goal of all creation. The nature of the church is to be the unity and the communion that it signifies. This is not a reality that is contained exclusively within the institutional boundaries of the church, but is a universal reality to be communicated to all humankind. The church "universal" or "catholic" is that community in which all peoples find a home. The message of reconciliation that it proclaims is "good news" for all peoples. Thus, the Decree on the Church's Missionary Activity builds on the understanding of the church as the universal sacrament of salvation. It considers the church, not as a reality distinct from the world or from the wider human community, but as the "salt of the earth and the light of the world" (Matt 5:13, 14), as an agent *in* the world, called upon to work "so that all things might be restored in Christ, and so that in him men and women might form one family and one people of God" (AG 1). The mission of the church is a continuation of Christ's reconciling mission in the world.

In its life and witness, the church is to be a reflection of Christ himself, witnessing to his love for the poor, to his mercy and forgiveness in the face of violence and injustice, to his desire that all might enjoy the fullness of life. We carry out this healing and reconciling mission when we care for the poor, the sick, and the vulnerable in our families and communities. We contribute to the building of a more human community when we work for greater justice in our workplace, city, and country. It would not be possible to continue Christ's mission without the presence and action of God's Spirit in our lives. Christ has sent his Spirit to dwell in us as a counselor (John 14:16-17) and guide so that we might discern how to live out the Gospel in our day. As we shall see in chapter 7, the council sought to recover a fuller appreciation of our reliance on the Holy Spirit in the life of the church.

Notes

[1] See especially *Symbolism: Exposition of the Doctrinal Differences Between Catholics and Protestants as Evidenced in their Symbolical Writings*, trans. James Burton Robertson (New York: Crossroad, 1997 [original German version, 1832]).

[2] Edward P. Hahnenberg, "The Mystical Body of Christ and Communion Ecclesiology: Historical Parallels," *Irish Theological Quarterly* 70 (2005): 3–30, at 7.

[3] Matthias Joseph Scheeben, *The Mysteries of Christianity*, trans. Cyril Vollert (St. Louis and London: B. Herder Book Co., 1946), especially pp. 539–92. (Original German version first published in 1865, revised in 1898, 1912, and 1941. This translation is based on the 1941 edition.)

Chapter Seven

The Holy Spirit in the Church

(*Lumen Gentium* 4)

> *The Spirit dwells in the church and in the hearts of the faithful, as in a temple (see 1 Cor 3:16; 6:19), prays and bears witness in them that they are his adopted children (see Gal 4:6; Rom 8:15-16 and 26). He guides the church in the way of all truth (see Jn 16:13) and, uniting it in fellowship and ministry, bestows upon it different hierarchic and charismatic gifts, and in this way directs it and adorns it with his fruits (see Eph 4:11-12; 1 Cor 12:4; Gal 5:22). By the power of the Gospel he rejuvenates the church, constantly renewing it and leading it to perfect union with its spouse.*

Background

The Holy Spirit is often referred to as the forgotten Person of the Trinity. Over the past thousand years Catholic ecclesiology has focused on the church's relationship to Christ. Consideration of the Holy Spirit was generally limited to guaranteeing the efficacy of the sacraments and the reliability of church teaching. Pneumatology received very little consideration in theological reflection on the church.

In the decades prior to Vatican II, the eminent Dominican theologian Yves Congar criticized this limited ecclesiology.[1] Congar, among other theologians, called for a recovery of the role of the Holy Spirit in the life of the church. His studies revealed a time in the early church when the Holy Spirit had much greater prominence. Early Christian writers like St. Augustine saw the Holy Spirit as the soul of the body of Christ. A late medieval reluctance to incorporate the Holy Spirit into a theology of the church may have been due in part to the frequent appeal to the Holy Spirit by heretical sects who tended to oppose the charismatic work of the Spirit to the institutions of the church. Moreover, since the Protestant Reformation, Christianity had suffered through an ongoing

> Pneumatology: A term drawn from the Greek word *pneuma*, which means "spirit" or "breath." Thus pneumatology refers to the field of theology dedicated to the study of the Holy Spirit.

polemic between Protestant and Catholic scholars over whether the early church was founded primarily on stable church offices (the hierarchical structure of the church) or on charisms given to all believers. From the Catholic side, any reference to a decisive role for the Holy Spirit risked sounding too "Protestant." The important nineteenth-century treatments of the Holy Spirit by Johann Adam Möhler and Matthias Scheeben were the exceptions that proved the rule.

In the early twentieth century Catholic ecclesiology recovered the ancient image of the church as the Mystical Body of Christ. The theme was picked up by Pope Pius XII in his encyclical *Mystici Corporis*. Although the pope did acknowledge the role of the Holy Spirit in the church, the focus of the encyclical was not on the work of the Holy Spirit but on the institutional elements of the church.

One of the most important and frequently overlooked contributions of the Second Vatican Council lay in the decisive steps the council took toward recovering the role of the Holy Spirit in the life of the church. Even the preparatory draft on the church that the bishops received during the first session of the council, in spite of its many shortcomings, included numerous references to the Holy Spirit and recovered the Augustinian view of the Holy Spirit as the soul of the church. Where St. Paul described the body of each believer as a temple of the Holy Spirit (1 Cor 3:16; 6:19), the bishops applied this image to the entire church.

The Holy Spirit in Council Teaching

The council's recovery of the place of the Holy Spirit in the church is evident in the very first chapter of *Lumen Gentium*, where we find a rich treatment of the church's trinitarian foundations. At Pentecost the Spirit was sent "to sanctify the church continually . . . so that believers might have access to the Father through Christ in the one Spirit" (LG 4). The council conjoined the church as Body of Christ with the image of the church as temple of the Holy Spirit (LG 17). This renewed emphasis on the Holy Spirit is further developed and amplified in the Decree on the Church's Missionary Activity, which asserts that the church is constituted by the trinitarian missions of Word and Spirit (AG 2). In chapter 5 we already considered the council's application of pneumatology to its understanding of the sense of the faithful (*sensus fidei*). In this chapter we will concentrate on three other applications of pneumatology to a theology of the church: (1) the Spirit's role in sustaining the communion of the church, (2) the council's theology of charism, and (3) recovering the charismatic character of consecrated religious life.

The Spirit and *Koinonia*

One of the great twentieth-century contributions to ecclesiology is the recovery of the biblical notion of *koinonia*. The term first appears in St. Paul's theology where it is often translated variously as "communion," "fellowship," "participation in," or "sharing in." If one includes all related forms of the noun *koinonia*, it appears in the New Testament thirty-six times, most frequently in the Pauline writings. Etymologically, its meaning is grounded in the Greek root *koinōn*, meaning "common." *Koinonia* refers to a spiritual sharing in some common reality.

In 1 Corinthians 1:9 Paul expresses gratitude for the Corinthians having been called by God into "fellowship" (*koinonia*) with Christ. A parallel usage is found in Paul's benediction to the Corinthians at the conclusion of the second epistle: "The grace of the Lord Jesus Christ, the love of God, and the communion [*koinonia*] of the Holy Spirit be with all of you" (2 Cor 13:13). This last passage affirms that this *koinonia* is a gift *from* the Spirit, suggesting that it is the Spirit who brings about a shared relationship among believers. Paul's understanding of *koinonia* is reflected in 1 Corinthians 10:16-17:

> The cup of blessing that we bless, is it not a sharing [*koinonia*] in the blood of Christ? The bread that we break, is it not a sharing [*koinonia*] in the body of Christ? Because there is one bread, we who are many are one body, for we all partake of the one bread.

We might speak of dual dimensions to Paul's usage of *koinonia*—the first is a vertical dimension, if you will, that stresses fellowship with God in Christ and the Spirit. The second, a more horizontal dimension, is oriented toward fellowship with other believers. These dual dimensions are also evident in the Johannine literature:

> This life was revealed, and we have seen it and testify to it, and declare to you the eternal life that was with the Father and was revealed to us—we declare to you what we have seen and heard so that you also may have fellowship with us; and truly our fellowship is with the Father and with his Son Jesus Christ. (1 John 1:2-3)

This passage highlights the simultaneity of the shared life among believers (horizontal dimension) and their shared life with God, that is, "with the Father and with his Son" (vertical dimension). The biblical author's intention apparently was to forestall any idea that fellowship with God provided a freedom to do as one wishes in the sphere of human relationships. The author of 1 John insists that true fellowship with God bears within it an ethical and even ontological imperative; one cannot separate fellowship with God from fellowship with fellow believers. Finally, we see evidence of the communal aspect of *koinonia* in Acts 2:42 in which the *koinonia* among the disciples is evident in their sharing all things in common.

In the decades prior to the council, a number of Catholic theologians drew on the biblical and ecumenical studies of *koinonia*, which was generally translated into Latin as *communio*, or "communion." They appreciated the ways in which these studies placed in the foreground of reflections on the church the sense of being-in-relationship. The Holy Spirit draws believers into a spiritual communion, a twofold "abiding" in fellowship with God in Christ and fellowship with other believers in the life of the church. The term *koinonia* expressed the fundamental connection between participation in the life of God and participation in Christian community.

The Second Vatican Council incorporated this theological line of thought, an approach that would eventually be referred to as *communio-ecclesiology*. Pope John Paul II, in his apostolic exhortation on the laity (*Christifideles Laici*), affirmed the judgment of the 1985 extraordinary synod that the notion of communion was the central and fundamental idea of Vatican II. Indeed the concept of *koinonia-communio* lies at the heart of this chapter's key text. At the beginning of the passage we are told that the Holy Spirit affirms our spiritual communion with God as children by adoption. Here we find an acknowledgment of the vertical dimension of *koinonia* that makes possible our spiritual intimacy with God. The church exists to draw us into life-giving relationship with God in Christ by the power of the Holy Spirit.

The second sentence focuses on the horizontal aspect of communion that is the work of the Holy Spirit to unite the church, establishing it as Christ's Body. We are reminded that to be baptized is to be baptized in Christ. Baptism establishes our Christian identity by initiating us into the life of the church. The council will return again and again to describe the church as a spiritual communion as in *Lumen Gentium* 9, which refers to the church as a "communion of life, love and truth." As we will see in the next chapter, this ecclesiology of communion is further developed by the council in relation to the Eucharist.

Few ecclesiological insights have been more fruitful for theological reflection in the decades since the council. Theologians have seen this emphasis on the church as communion as an antidote to an excessive preoccupation with rank, power, jurisdiction, and clerical privilege in the church. If the church is a communion maintained as such by the power of the Holy Spirit, then terms like power and rank have to be thoroughly reimagined as realities that have legitimacy only insofar as they serve the various relationships among believers that comprise the life of the church. Power and rank can have no autonomous value in a communion of believers.

The Council's Theology of Charism

We mentioned earlier the centuries-long impasse between Protestantism and Catholicism over the role of charisms in the life of the church. The council made several important, if only preliminary, steps toward addressing this disputed question.

There is no disputing the importance of the notion of charism in the writings of St. Paul. Paul insisted that the Holy Spirit con-

> Charism: A term taken from the Greek word *charis*, meaning "gift."

ferred on all of the baptized charisms, or gifts of the Spirit, offered for the building up of the church. These charisms or gifts come in a variety of forms, some more stable than others. In the long-standing Protestant-Catholic polemic, some Protestant theologians like Rudolph Söhm placed Paul's "charismatic" vision of the church in stark opposition to the institutional structures of Catholicism. Catholic polemicists, in turn, saw these charisms as important gifts given exclusively to the early apostolic community. Such gifts were gradually phased out of church life in favor of the essential place of stable church offices.

The Second Vatican Council sought to move beyond this polemic. Where St. Paul described the body of each believer as a temple of the Holy Spirit (1 Cor 3:16; 6:19), the bishops applied this image to the entire church. In this chapter's key text, "hierarchic gifts" refers to stable church office and "charismatic gifts" refers to those many charisms that the Spirit distributes among all the faithful. Charism and office are not opposed to one another since both have the Spirit as their origin. The council acknowledged that church office could not exist unless it was animated by the Holy Spirit and charisms could not survive unless they submitted to an ordering that sought the good of the whole church.

By appealing to the biblical concept of charism, the council was able to affirm the indispensable role of all the faithful in building up the church and assisting in the fulfillment of the church's mission in the world. The bishops wrote, "it is not only through the sacraments and the ministries that the holy Spirit makes the people holy, leads them and enriches them with his virtues. Allotting his gifts 'at will to each individual' . . . , he also distributes special graces among the faithful of every rank" (LG 12). Although few, if any, at the council could have anticipated the flourishing of lay ministries that would occur in the ensuing decades, it is this emphasis on the charisms of all the baptized that provided a helpful theological framework for interpreting that later postconciliar development of lay ministry.

One of the ways in which the council was able to get beyond the charisms vs. office binary was to stress the reciprocal relationship that obtains between the two terms. In several passages the council suggested a possible theology of ordained pastoral leadership within a community animated by many charisms. The pastoral leadership of the ordained need not compete with the exercise of the many gifts of the faithful. Each requires the other. According to conciliar teaching, those ordained to pastoral leadership were not to absorb into their own ministry all the tasks proper to building up the church. Rather the church's pastors were exhorted to recognize, empower, and affirm the gifts of all God's people. In the Decree on the Apostolate of Lay People (*Apostolicam Actuositatem*) the council held that, having received charisms from the Spirit through baptism,

> there follow for all christian believers the right and duty to use them
> in the church and in the world for the good of humanity and the
> development of the church, to use them in the freedom of the holy
> Spirit who "chooses where to blow" . . . , and at the same time
> in communion with the sisters and brothers in Christ, and with
> the pastors especially. It is for the pastors to pass judgment on the
> authenticity and good use of these gifts, not certainly with a view to
> quenching the Spirit but to testing everything and keeping what is
> good. (AA 3)

The Decree on the Ministry and Life of Priests (*Presbyterorum Ordinis*) likewise asserted the responsibility of the priest to affirm and nurture the gifts of the faithful: "While testing the spirits to discover if they be of God, they must discover with faith, recognize with joy, and foster diligently the many and varied charismatic gifts of the laity, whether these be of a humble or more exalted kind" (PO 9). These passages situated ordained pastoral ministry not above but within the Christian community. The ordained minister is responsible for the discernment and coordination of the charisms and ministries of all the baptized.

Recovering the Charisms of Consecrated Religious Life

Among the many topics that the bishops believed required their attention at the council, we must include consecrated religious life. Unfortunately there was, at least initially, little agreement regarding the vision of religious life that ought to be encouraged. On the one hand, many bishops advocated a primarily monastic vision of professed religious who dedicated their lives to prayerful contemplation in enclosures far removed from worldly concerns. Those who emphasized this perspective saw the apostolic work of noncontemplative or semicontemplative communities as an anomaly at best and a threat to the very integrity of religious life at worst. On the other hand, others had come to accept the dramatic emergence of apostolic religious communities from the sixteenth to the early twentieth centuries as a great gift to the church. Consequently, on the eve of the council, while there was a widespread agreement regarding the need for the renewal of religious life, there was a deep division regarding what that renewal was to look like.

The preliminary drafts of the Decree on the Up-to-Date Renewal of Religious Life (*Perfectae Caritatis*) maintained an essentially conservative vision of religious life. This draft was considerably improved, nevertheless, by a number of important amendments. The final text of the decree begins by presenting religious communities as unique gifts offered by the Spirit for the building up of the church:

> Thus, in keeping with the divine purpose, a wonderful variety of religious communities came into existence. This has helped considerably to equip the church for every good work . . . and for ministry aimed at building up the body of Christ. . . . It has also enabled it to display the assorted gifts of its sons and daughters, like a bride adorned for her husband . . . , and to manifest in itself the manifold wisdom of God. (PC 1)

Consecrated religious life is presented as one of the many ways in which the Holy Spirit provides for the building up of the church and the furtherance of its mission. The council strongly encouraged religious communities to explore the visions of their founders and to rediscover the unique charisms of their communities (PC 2). This theology of charism would eventually provide the basis for a new understanding of apostolic religious communities. Professed religious life ought not to be viewed as an auxiliary to hierarchical office; rather religious communities participate in a charismatic ecclesial mode of being. The council continued to affirm contemplative communities while also celebrating the important contributions of religious communities engaged in apostolic work. These apostolic communities were encouraged to revise their "observances and customs" to better meet the needs of their apostolic work (PC 8).

In spite of these important contributions, *Perfectae Caritatis* was limited by the fact that, after the first two sessions, there were enormous pressures to abbreviate the remaining drafts in order to facilitate a quicker process of approval. Consequently, a full appreciation of the council's teaching on consecrated religious life cannot be drawn from *Perfectae Caritatis* alone; the decree must be read in the context of chapters 5 and 6 of *Lumen Gentium*.

The preparatory draft of the constitution on the church was a far cry from the document that we now refer to as *Lumen Gentium*. The preparatory draft consisted of eleven chapters that often were content with rehearsing standard neoscholastic treatments of the church. The fifth chapter on the "States of Evangelical Perfection" asserted that perfection in holiness was achieved preeminently by those who pursued the evangelical counsels of poverty, chastity, and obedience. The implications were clear: those not called to ordination or consecrated religious life were capable of only a lesser path to holiness.

Fortunately, in the reworking of this schema, the "states of perfection" language disappeared. In its place we find a robust theology of vocation grounded in baptism. What appears in chapter 5 of *Lumen Gentium*, now titled "The Universal Call to Holiness," is a much more biblical theology, one that recalls that Jesus "preached holiness of life . . . to each and every one of his disciples *no matter what their condition of life*" (LG 40; emphasis added). The bishops wrote that "all Christians in whatever state or walk in life are called to the fullness of christian life and to the perfection of charity" (LG 40). Indeed, they went on to insist that "[a]ll, however, according to their own gifts and duties must steadfastly advance along the way of a living faith, which arouses hope and works through love" (LG 41).

Initially the council was content to treat the particular calling of professed religious within this chapter on the universal call to holiness. However, a group of religious superiors and religious bishops objected that since there was a separate chapter on the hierarchy and a separate chapter on the laity, there ought to be a separate chapter on consecrated religious life as well. This decision was unfortunate, for it undermined the important teaching of the council that religious life "is not to be seen as a middle way between the clerical and lay states of life" (LG 43). Nevertheless, the material relegated to the newly created chapter 6 was important as it broke down any opposition between monastic and apostolic forms of religious life; both were central to the life of the church and both provided the opportunity to intensify the professed religious' communion with Christ. The evangelical counsels were no longer presented as a superior path to holiness available only to religious; they were counsels to which all Christian are called. Professed religious, by virtue of their public ecclesial commitment, were to be public signs of that evangelical way of life to which *all* were called.

The late Yves Congar considered the council's treatment of charisms as its most important contribution to the recovery of a genuine theology of the Holy Spirit in the church.[2] This teaching retained the Catholic conviction that Christ had established stable church offices for the proper ordering of the church. At the same time, it dismantled a pyramidal conception of the church in favor of a vision that saw the Spirit building up the church in service of its mission through baptismal charisms, the unique contributions of consecrated religious life, and ordained ministries.

Together with the council's teaching on the church as a communion sustained by the work of the Spirit, its theology of charisms helped to correct a centuries-old tendency to overlook the Holy Spirit in the life of the church. It is a theology that looks with confidence for signs of the Spirit at work in the church and in the world to bring to light God's saving Word and to empower all peoples in service of the coming reign of God.

Notes

[1] Yves Congar, "Pneumatologie ou 'Christomonisme' dans la traditione latine," in *Ecclesia a Spiritu Sancto edocta*, Festschrift for Gérard Philips (Louvain: Duculot, 1970), 41–63.

[2] Yves Congar, *I Believe in the Holy Spirit* (New York: Crossroad, 1983), 1:170.

Chapter Eight

Eucharistic Ecclesiology

(Lumen Gentium 7)

> *For by communicating his Spirit, Christ mystically constitutes as his body his brothers and sisters who are called together from every nation.*
>
> *In this body the life of Christ is communicated to those who believe and who, through the sacraments, are united in a hidden and real way to Christ in his passion and glorification. . . . Really sharing in the body of the Lord in the breaking of the Eucharistic bread, we are taken up into communion with him and with one another. "Because the bread is one, we, though many, are one body, all of us who partake of the one bread" (1 Cor 10:17). In this way all of us are made members of his body (see 1 Cor 12:27), "individually members one of another."*

Background

As we saw in chapter 6, the bishops gathered at Vatican II found that it was no longer adequate to speak of the church solely in terms of its institutional and juridical structures by applying the notion of the "church militant" or Robert Bellarmine's model of a "perfect society." To better express the vocation of the church in both its divine/spiritual and human/institutional dimensions, they opted for a more sacramental approach. This is reflected in *Lumen Gentium*'s concept of the church as the sacrament of the unity or communion intended by God for all humanity (LG 1). The church as *koinonia*-communion is further presented as a pilgrim people gathered together and led by God on its way through history toward the full realization of its calling. The concept of the church as sacrament is informed by an incarnational theology centered on an understanding of how the love of God is revealed to us in and through the humanity of Jesus of Nazareth. In saying that the church is like a sacrament, *Lumen Gentium* affirms that Christ continues to work in the world in and through this very human community. We saw in chapter 7 that the Holy Spirit brings about our fellowship or *koinonia* with Christ and with one another, enabling the church to be this sign and agent of communion in the world. Vatican II's understanding of the church as a communion is further developed in the council's reflections on the interconnection between the Eucharist and the life of the church. A return to the teaching of the New Testament and the fathers of the church was decisive for Catholic theology's rediscovery of a eucharistic ecclesiology.

Sharing (*Koinonia*) in the Body of Christ

The New Testament writings of St. Paul consistently hold in balance our personal relationship of communion with Christ and our communion with all the baptized faithful signified simultaneously in the Eucharist. For St. Paul, the bond of unity that we celebrate in the Lord's Supper cannot be reduced to a bond between the individual believer and Christ. As we saw in chapter 7, the communion into which we are incorporated through the gift of the Spirit has both a vertical and a horizontal dimension. Our relationship with Christ is inseparable from, and introduces us into, a whole new set of relationships with all those who belong to his Body and are the firstfruits of a new humanity transformed in his image. When there is division in the community at Corinth at the table of the Lord, Paul is unwavering in his criticism of their failure to discern the presence of his Body—not only in the bread and wine but also in their relationships with one another. When they fail to show reverence for others or treat them unjustly, Paul regards their partaking in the Eucharist as a form of "idolatry" or false worship. In this context he reminds them of the *koinonia* that they all share (1 Cor 10:16-17). Paul's teaching is an exhortation to an ethical consistency in communal action; their actions must be consistent with the reality they celebrate in the Eucharist.

This eucharistic ecclesiology is developed in the writings of St. Augustine, who explains that each time we receive the Eucharist, the reality that we receive through the sacramental signs of bread and wine is at one and the same time the Body and Blood of Christ *and* the unity of the church. Commenting on Paul's letter to the Colossians, he states, "You become the bread, that is, the body of Christ."[1] Augustine carries forward the Pauline line of thought that holds together the eucharistic Body and the ecclesial Body. They are two indivisible aspects of one and the same reality. We become more deeply incorporated into Christ through the eucharistic memorial. For the central meaning of the Eucharist is love, the love of Christ poured out for us in the paschal mystery, the same love in which we share each time we set aside our own self-interest and reach out in concern for others. This is why Augustine contended that the Eucharist was a pedagogy in Christian living where we learn that love of God and love of neighbor are not separate realities. The experience of God's love widens our capacity to love others.

Members of One Another

Saint Paul refers to the church as the "body of Christ" in the New Testament and draws upon the image of the body to describe the relationship of the members of the ecclesial Body to one another as well as their collective relationship to Christ. In baptism we are incorporated into Christ and into his Body, the church. In the Eucharist this communion is nourished and deepened. By evoking the image of the body, Paul was appealing to an idea that circulated widely in his time. Menenius Agrippa, an official in the Roman Republic in the fifth century BCE, had employed the image of the body in a fable to help all members of society to understand their need for and dependence upon one another, whatever their rank or class. Paul made use of this familiar metaphor to convey the profound solidarity that should exist among the members of the church, in all of their diversity.

Perhaps the most familiar of these texts is found in the first letter to the Corinthians, where we find Paul's discourse on the variety of spiritual gifts or charisms given by the Spirit to the members of the church: "For just as the body is one and has many members, and all the members of the body, though many, are one body, so it is with Christ. For in the one Spirit we were all baptized into one body" (1 Cor 12:12-13). He describes how the many different parts of the body are necessary to the functioning of the whole. The body cannot do without a foot, or an ear, or a nose. Each member carries out an essential role in service to the whole body. So it is within Christ's ecclesial Body. All the members must care for one another. In fact, we are so closely bound together by the Spirit that "if one member suffers, all suffer together with it; if one member is honored, all rejoice together with it" (1 Cor 12:26).

This same idea is stated more directly in Paul's letter to the Romans: "For as in one body we have many members, and not all the members have the same function, so we, who are many, are one body in Christ, and individually we are members one of another" (Rom 12:4-5). Paul's teaching helps us to appreciate the common dignity that is shared by all the members of the ecclesial Body, whatever their charism. The whole Body needs the gifts of each one: prophets, ministers, teachers, exhorters, generous givers, leaders, the compassionate and the cheerful (Rom 12:8).

Paul's whole ecclesiology presupposed a fundamentally organic view of the church that suggested not just complementarity and diversity within the church but *coexistence*.[2] For Paul, life in Christ meant life in the Body of Christ, the church. The church was no mere aggregate of individuals. Rather, by baptism into the Christian community one participates in a new reality; one is a new creation. Individual believers do not *make* a church; initiation into the church through faith and baptism *makes* the believer—it introduces one into a new mode of existence.

Christ Is Head of His Body, the Church

The letter to the Colossians contains a christological hymn drawn from the prayer of the earliest Christians. Here Christ is presented within the broad scope of salvation history as the preexistent Son of God who reigns over all of creation. The church, of which he is the head, is placed within the context of God's plan for all of creation:

> He is the image of the invisible God, the firstborn of all creation; for in him all things in heaven and on earth were created, things visible and invisible, whether thrones or dominions or rulers or powers—all things have been created through him and for him. He himself is before all things, and in him all things hold together. He is the head of the body, the church; he is the beginning, the firstborn from the dead, so that he might come to have first place in everything. For in him all the fullness of God was pleased to dwell, and through him God was pleased to reconcile to himself all things, whether on earth or in heaven, by making peace through the blood of his cross. (Col 1:15-20)

Seen from this cosmic perspective, Christ's ecclesial Body, the church, appears to have a decisive role to play in God's plan. The members of his Body are among the firstfruits of those who have been reconciled to God through his death and resurrection.

Paul (or a disciple of his) writes to the Ephesians that God has given Christ as the head of the church, "which is his body, the fullness of him who fills all in all" (Eph 1:22-23). The Greek term for "fullness" used in this text is written in a passive form, to indicate that it is Christ himself who pours out the riches of his grace on the community of those who believe, and suggesting that Christ's own work is in a sense "completed" in the church. Christ's saving work begun in us is yet to be completed; we continue in the struggle to allow his grace to transform our lives, and to learn to live our lives more fully in his image.

In proposing that Christ is the "head" of his Body, the church, the Colossian hymn paints an image of the utter dependence of the church upon its founder. What would a body be without a head? The head directs all the functions of the body, both voluntary and involuntary movements. We know, for example, that anyone who receives a brain injury is likely to have their health seriously compromised—not only in their intellectual functioning but also in the many vital functions of their limbs and organs that depend upon the impulses of the central nervous system. The place of Christ is primary in this image, and the Christian community is organically linked to him for every aspect of its life.

Saint Augustine would later articulate the interdependence of Christ and the church in the expression *totus Christus*; for him, Christ the head together with his Body the church go together to make up the "whole Christ." The church can only be understood as the "fullness" of Christ in that everything that is accomplished in and through its agency in the world is an effect of his grace at work in us.

The Church and the Mystical Body

Sadly, in the Middle Ages this rich eucharistic ecclesiology began to recede into the background, replaced by a more juridical understanding of the church. There were always voices like St. Thomas Aquinas who kept the profound connections between the Eucharist and the church in the foreground, but they would be the exception rather than the rule. It was only in the nineteenth and early twentieth centuries that efforts were made to retrieve elements of this ancient eucharistic understanding of the church. The historical shift that transpired in the Middle Ages was masterfully explored a few decades prior to the council by the Jesuit theologian Henri de Lubac, in a work titled *Corpus Mysticum*.[3]

According to de Lubac, prior to the late Middle Ages, the term "Mystical Body" had referred principally to the eucharistic Body of Christ. However, as controversy emerged regarding how to account for the realism of Christ's presence in the Eucharist, medieval theologians began to distinguish between the "natural" or "true" body of Christ born of the Virgin Mary and now present in the bread and wine of the sacrament, and the "mystical" character of the ecclesial Body of Christ. As theological attention focused primarily on the realism of Christ's presence in the sacrament, the ancient convictions regarding Christ's presence and action in and through the ecclesial Body receded into the background. The effect of this was an unfortunate breakdown of the important link between the Eucharist and the church, and between the church and Christ its head, whom we encounter in the sacrament.

When it was first applied to the church, the term Mystical Body referred to the heavenly church, the communion of saints at the end of time. Following the Protestant Reformation in the sixteenth century, the Jesuit Counter-Reformer Robert Bellarmine systematically applied the idea of the Mystical Body of Christ to the pilgrim community of the church on earth. He sought to refute the Protestant juxtaposition made between the visible institution of the church on earth and the invisible spiritual reality of the true church.

In the nineteenth century, some theologians, like Johann Adam Möhler and, later, Matthias Scheeben, would begin to explore the power of the Pauline "body" image for understanding the church. This work would be continued in the twentieth century in the monumental study of Emile Mersch. Pope Pius XII would further this recovery in his encyclical *Mystici Corporis* even as he maintained his debt to Bellarmine's emphasis on the visible, institutional church. De Lubac, the Dominican theologian Yves Congar, and others would argue for the need to return to the eucharistic ecclesiology of Paul, Augustine, and the patristic tradition.

Vatican II: Ecclesial Communion and the Eucharistic Assembly

The arduous debates regarding the nature and mission of the church that transpired over the course of the council drew considerably on the work that had been done in the decades prior to the council to recover the ancient biblical and patristic connections between the Eucharist and the church. Yet it is noteworthy that *Lumen Gentium* stopped short of adopting the idea of the Mystical Body as an overarching image of the church. The council was careful to limit its affirmations to the meaning of "mystery" that is attested in the Scriptures and in the great tradition of the church, reaching back to the earliest witnesses. As we saw in chapter 6, the notion of the church as a mystery or a sacramental sign of communion serves as one of the principal categories for understanding the vocation of the church in the council's teaching. In its reflection on the church as the Body of Christ, *Lumen Gentium* makes a carefully nuanced affirmation concerning the ecclesial body: "For by communicating his Spirit, Christ mystically constitutes as his body his brothers and sisters who are called together from every nation" (LG 7). The mysterious or mystical aspect of the church derives from the risen Christ and his Spirit. Redeemed humanity is united to Christ in a mysterious yet real way in the church. It is not our doing and does not belong to the members of the church properly speaking, but to Christ whose grace is at work in us. This grace is nothing other than the love we receive when we encounter Christ and are nourished in the mystery of his eucharistic Body.

Vatican II's understanding of the church as the ecclesial Body of Christ is grounded in the mystical bond of communion with Christ that unites all those who partake in the sacrament of the Eucharist. The notion of *koinonia-communio* is central to the council's understanding of what it is we are called to be. This intimate communion with God and the unity we share with one another is realized most intensely each time we gather to celebrate the Eucharist: the sacrament of the Body and Blood of Christ transforms us into the living Body of the church, the Body of the risen Christ in the world.

Whenever we participate fully and consciously in the liturgical action, we are transformed more fully into the likeness of Christ. Our offering of thanks and praise to God is a measure of the offering of ourselves to others in friendship and love. We learn from Christ each day how to love more, and grow in love for him and for one another. So central is the sacramental realization of the church in the liturgy that *Lumen Gentium* refers to the celebration of the Eucharist as the "source and summit of the christian life" (LG 11). The priestly people of God offer this sacrifice together with Christ. "Then, strengthened by the body of Christ in the Eucharistic communion, they manifest in a concrete way that unity of the people of God which this most holy sacrament aptly signifies and admirably realizes" (ibid.). In and through their common liturgical action, the community of faith is brought into loving communion with Christ and with one another. Their vocation is to be agents of this same communion in the world.

The grace we receive in baptism and that is renewed each time we celebrate the paschal mystery in the Eucharist enables us to grow in the image and likeness of Christ. Paul writes to the Ephesians that the many gifts of the Spirit are given to the members of the church "for building up the body of Christ, until all of us come to the unity of the faith and of the knowledge of the Son of God, to maturity, to the measure of the full stature of Christ" (Eph 4:12-13). With a sense of eschatological humility, *Lumen Gentium* acknowledges that all the members of Christ's body "must be formed in his likeness" and recognizes that in this earthly life, we remain "pilgrims in a strange land, following in trial and in oppression the paths he trod" (LG 7). Some may be asked to endure real misunderstanding, persecution, suffering, and death as they witness to his love. Yet for most of us, the call to reproduce the sacrifice of Christ comes to us through our encounter with others in our families, workplace, and community. The ups and downs of daily living are the path we must travel as we grow to full stature in Christ and reproduce the pattern of his dying and rising. All of life's experiences are occasions for us to learn the measure of God's forgiveness and love for us, and for all persons. We grow to the full stature of Christ not only as individual Christians but as a whole body. The organic connection between the head and the body ensures that it will "grow with a growth that is from God" (Col 2:19). Continuing the work he has begun in us, Christ continues to "fill the whole body with the riches of his glory" (LG 7).

The Constitution on the Sacred Liturgy, the publication of which preceded the final elaboration of the council's reflection on the church in *Lumen Gentium*, pointed toward the importance of a eucharistic ecclesiology for the church's self-understanding early in the council's deliberation. We touched upon this idea when we considered how participation is a key to the liturgical reform undertaken by the council, but it is well worth repeating here: "They must be convinced that *the principal manifestation of the church* consists in the full, active participation of all God's holy people in the same liturgical celebrations, especially in the same Eucharist, in one prayer, at one altar, at which the bishop presides, surrounded by his college of priests and by his ministers" (SC 41; emphasis added). The "principal manifestation of the church" is the local church, understood as a eucharistic assembly. We experience what it means to be church, and we see that each local community has everything it takes to be a church (the preaching of the Gospel, the celebration of the sacraments, and the good ordering of many charisms and ministries in the service of all), when all are gathered together in prayer. This is especially so when we share in the church's great prayer of thanksgiving, where we renew our participation in the paschal mystery, and from which we are sent forth as witnesses into the world.

Yet no local church is self-sufficient or complete without the others. Each local church is conscious of its bond with every other local Christian community both synchronically (in the present context) and diachronically (with communities of believers throughout history). According to the council, the universal church is a communion of eucharistic communities or local churches, bound together by God's Spirit (LG 23). *Lumen Gentium* affirms that the church of Christ is present each time the people of God gather together in the local church to hear the Gospel of Christ and share in the mystery of the Lord's Supper. However small and poor they may be, Christ is active in each local church to ensure that the one, holy, catholic, and apostolic church is realized in each place (LG 26). In the Eucharist, we are built up into Christ's Body, the church.

Receive What You Are

The eucharistic ecclesiology of the Second Vatican Council returns to the roots of the Christian tradition to ground our understanding of the dynamic interdependence between the church and the Eucharist. As we saw, the writings of St. Paul in the New Testament emphasize the inseparable connection between the communion that we celebrate in the Eucharist and the unity of the church. De Lubac helped us to see that for the entire first millennium Christian theology was marked by the idea that the Eucharist makes the church, whereas in the second millennium, more emphasis was placed on how the church makes the Eucharist. The teaching of Vatican II reflects a profound appreciation for the Eucharist as the wellspring of the life, prayer, and mission of the church.

The church is fully realized each time it gathers to celebrate the memorial of Christ's dying and rising. The council must be credited with recovering those ancient convictions regarding the profound relationship between the Eucharist and the church that were affirmed so forcefully by St. Augustine. These are summed up well in his reflections with the newly baptized members of his church on the meaning of their participation in the Lord's Supper:

> So if it's you that are the body of Christ and its members, it's the mystery meaning you that has been placed on the Lord's table; what you receive is the mystery that is you. It is to what you are that you reply Amen, and by so replying you express your assent. What you hear, you see, is the body of Christ, and you answer, Amen. So be a member of the body of Christ in order to make that Amen true . . . Be what you can see, and receive what you are.[4]

To make true our "Amen" to the mystery of Christ in the Eucharist, our lives must become a reflection of his self-giving love. This is what it really means to be a member of the Body. In the celebration of Christ's paschal mystery God's holy people are led from the slavery of sin and death to new life and resurrection. God's outpouring of love in Christ is the basis of a new humanity marked by a new way of living together. As *Lumen Gentium* affirms, "the sharing in the body and blood of Christ has no other effect than to accomplish our transformation into that which we receive" (LG 26). We are sent out from the Eucharist, where we encounter and receive the healing and reconciling love of God, to be bread broken and wine poured out for others.

Notes

[1] St. Augustine, *Sermon* 227.

[2] Jerome Murphy-O'Connor, "Eucharist and Community in 1 Corinthians," in *Living Bread, Saving Cup*, ed. Kevin Seasoltz (Collegeville, MN: Liturgical Press, 1982), 4.

[3] Henri de Lubac, *Corpus Mysticum: The Eucharist and the Church in the Middle Ages: A Survey*, trans. Gemma Simonds with Richard Price and Christopher Stephens, ed. Laurence Paul Hemming and Susan Frank Parsons (Notre Dame: University of Notre Dame Press, 2007). The original French version was published in 1944, and revised in 1949.

[4] St. Augustine, *Sermon* 272.

Chapter Nine

The Baptismal and Ministerial Priesthood

(Lumen Gentium 10)

Christ the Lord, high priest taken from the midst of humanity (see Heb 5:1-5), made the new people "a kingdom of priests to his God and Father" (Apoc 1:6; see 5:9-10). The baptized, by regeneration and the anointing of the holy Spirit, are consecrated as a spiritual house and a holy priesthood, that through all their christian activities they may offer spiritual sacrifices and proclaim the marvels of him who has called them out of darkness into his wonderful light (see 1 Pet 2:4-10). Therefore, all the disciples of Christ, persevering in prayer and praising God (see Acts 2:42-47), should present themselves as a sacrifice, living, holy and pleasing to God (see Rom 12:1). They should everywhere on earth bear witness to Christ and give an answer to everyone who asks a reason for their hope of eternal life (see 1 Pet 3:15).

Though they differ essentially and not only in degree, the common priesthood of the faithful and the ministerial or hierarchical priesthood are none the less interrelated: each in its own way shares in the one priesthood of Christ. The ministerial priest, by the sacred power that he has, forms and governs the priestly people; in the person of Christ he brings about the Eucharistic sacrifice and offers it to God in the name of all the people. The faithful indeed, by virtue of their royal priesthood, share in the offering of the Eucharist. They exercise that priesthood, too, by the reception of the sacraments, by prayer and thanksgiving, by the witness of a holy life, self-denial and active charity.

Background

Acts of the Apostles reports that it was in Antioch that the original followers of Jesus were first called "Christians." These early followers of Jesus often referred to themselves as "disciples" (Acts 6:1; 9:1) or simply "the saints" (Rom 1:7; 1 Cor 1:2).[1] Some form of the word "disciple" appears in the New Testament over two hundred times. These names reflected the deep solidarity that early Christians shared with one another. Their attitude was reflected in the words of St. Paul: "There is no longer Jew or Greek, there is no longer slave or free, there is no longer male and female; for all of you are one in Christ Jesus" (Gal 3:28). Class distinctions among the first generation of believers had no formal place in the life of the church. When early divisions did emerge, they were roundly condemned. For example, Paul admonished the community at Corinth because of signs of social stratification evident in the way they celebrated the Eucharist. Neither did the New Testament churches know any formal distinction between church leadership and the rest of the community; there was no distinct class of persons referred to as clergy or laity. *Kleros* and terms that build on its root (e.g., *kleronomia, kleronomai*) referred to the instrument for casting lots, and as applied in the New Testament suggested the "lot" or "inheritance" that all believers received as God's people. Moreover, the Greek word for priest, *hiereus*, was never applied to a set of ministers within the whole community; it was applied either to Christ himself (Heb 2:17; 3:1; 4:14-15) or to the whole people of God as in 1 Peter: "you are a chosen race, a royal priesthood, a holy nation, God's own people, in order that you may proclaim the mighty acts of him who called you out of darkness into his marvelous light. Once you were not a people, but now you are God's people; once you had not received mercy, but now you have received mercy" (1 Pet 2:9-10).

The entire Christian community was "priestly" in character inasmuch as its communal life was to be a share in the one "priestly work" of Christ. A similar conviction was expressed in Romans 12: "I appeal to you therefore, brothers and sisters, by the mercies of God, to present your bodies as a living sacrifice, holy and acceptable to God, which is your spiritual worship" (v. 1). Paul believed that the most basic spiritual act of a Christian was not something that happened in a church; it was something that engaged their daily lives. Theirs was to be a living sacrifice drawn from the transformative power of the one sacrifice of Christ.

As the church grew and developed in the early centuries, the priestly consciousness of the whole church continued, even as the distinction between those called to public ministry (the clergy) and the rest of the Christian community became more pronounced. By the third century it became more common to distinguish between the ordained (the clergy) and the nonordained (the laity), yet the priority of their baptism remained.

However, by the end of the first millennium, the distinction between the clergy and the laity had gradually become more rigid. The influential twelfth-century canonist Gratian puts the matter quite straightforwardly: "There are two kinds of Christians, clerics and lay people."[2] This idea of classes would remain an essential element of Catholic ecclesiology; it could still be found in the 1917 Code of Canon Law. It is during this period that the liturgy becomes almost exclusively a clerical affair. The laity were reduced to spectators and increasingly did not receive Communion at all. At the same time, the emergence of monasticism led to a second distinction, that between the layperson and the monk who was called to a higher form of sanctity. As Edward Hahnenberg puts it, "if the laity were seen in contrast to the clergy on the level of leadership and activity, now they were seen in contrast to the monk on the level of holiness."[3]

The biblical teaching regarding the priesthood of all believers would fall into disuse only to be revived by Martin Luther in the sixteenth century. Unfortunately, Luther's recovery of the ancient belief that all Christians were priests by their baptism led him to repudiate the legitimacy of the church's ministerial (ordained) priesthood. The result was four centuries of Protestant/Catholic polemic in which Protestantism would emphasize the priesthood of all believers while Catholicism would vigorously defend the legitimacy of the ministerial priesthood. Serious attention to the priesthood of all believers in Catholic teaching would not come until the Second Vatican Council.

The Baptismal and Ministerial Priesthood in Council Teaching

When the council bishops received the preparatory draft on the church during their first session, they were disappointed with its overall quality. An important exception was the chapter on the laity. It offered a quite positive reflection on the role of the laity in the church and in the world. The chapter began with a reflection on the universal priesthood in which all believers participate by virtue of their baptism. The drafters invoked the experience of the Catholic Action movement over the previous several decades and affirmed the rights and the responsibilities of the laity. They also asserted that the laity were called not only to a more active involvement in the secular realm

Catholic Action: This was a spiritual renewal movement that began in Italy and was dedicated to fostering lay participation in the church's mission through their apostolic activity in the world. In 1930 Pope Pius XI formally approved Catholic Action as an umbrella movement of the laity. By 1938 it had grown to have 500,000 members throughout Europe.

but to a fuller participation in the life of the church as well. This material would be retained and further developed in later drafts of the document.

The preparatory draft of the constitution was substantially reworked in between the first and second sessions of the council. It now was comprised of four chapters. The first was titled "Mystery of the Church" and incorporated a much more biblical and trinitarian view of the church than had been found in the preparatory schema. The second chapter was on the hierarchy and the third was titled "The People of God and the Laity in Particular." The last chapter was on the universal call to holiness. A further change to this new schema would be proposed during the intersession. Cardinal Leo Suenens of Belgium suggested that the third chapter, "The People of God and the Laity," be split and that the material on the people of God be formed into a separate chapter and placed immediately after the opening chapter and *before* the chapter on the hierarchy. This new chapter would offer one of the council's most profound descriptions of the church:

> That messianic people has as its head Christ, "who was delivered up for our sins and rose again for our justification" . . . , and now, having acquired the name which is above all names, reigns gloriously in heaven. This people possesses the dignity and freedom of the daughters and sons of God, in whose hearts the holy Spirit dwells as in a temple. Its law is the new commandment to love as Christ loved us. . . . Its destiny is the kingdom of God which has been begun by God himself on earth and which must be further extended until it is brought to perfection by him at the end of time when Christ our life . . . will appear and "creation itself also will be delivered from its slavery to corruption into the freedom of the glory of the sons and daughters of God" . . . . Consequently, this messianic people, although it does not, in fact, include everybody, and at times may seem to be a little flock, is, however, a most certain seed of unity, hope and salvation for the whole human race. Established by Christ as a communion of life, love and truth, it is taken up by him also as the instrument for the salvation of all; as the light of the world and the salt of the earth . . . it is sent forth into the whole world. (LG 9)

There is perhaps no passage in the council documents that so poetically summarizes the distinctive themes employed by the council in its reflections on the church. In this beautiful passage we find the council's determination to retrieve a more biblical language for reflecting on the church. Here we see as well both the rich christological foundation and the new appreciation of the role of the Holy Spirit. This text presents the church as a people sent into the world in mission to serve the coming reign of God.

Finally, this text reflects the council's more eschatological orientation as it emphasizes a church that looks to the future with humility and hope.

What is said above pertains to *all* God's people. The chapter offers faith, baptism, and discipleship as foundational realities in the church. Its placement before the chapter on the hierarchy suggested a recovery of the convictions of the early church that the ministry of the hierarchy must be seen within the context of the common dignity of all the baptized.

It is in this chapter on the people of God that we find our chapter's key text, a passage exploring both the ministerial priesthood and the priest-hood of all believers. All Christians, by virtue of their baptism, share in the priesthood of Christ and all are called to render their entire lives "a sacrifice, living, holy and pleasing to God" (LG 10). This common priest-hood, the council taught, differs "essentially and not only in degree" from the ministerial priesthood, yet both share equally in the one priesthood of Christ. This conciliar recovery of the ancient theology of the priesthood of the baptized is all the more remarkable since it was a theme that for centuries had been so strongly identified with the theology of Luther and other Reformers.

This passage has been frequently cited but less frequently understood. For example, there is a tendency to equate "the common priesthood of believers" with a priesthood of the laity. This reading assumes the council was positing two different groups of priests within the church, one lay and one clerical. This is a dangerously flawed reading of the council's teaching. In fact, the council was describing two interrelated priestly realities. The priesthood of all the faithful was a synonym for Christian discipleship; all Christians, lay *and* clergy, participate in this common priesthood by virtue of their baptism. All are called to make of their lives "a sacrifice, living, holy and pleasing to God." The ministerial priesthood was then placed in relation to the priesthood of the faithful. This suggests that priestly identity cannot be discovered by way of contrast and separation; it can be discovered only when we ask the more basic question: What does it mean to live out the common priesthood of the faithful? What are the demands of authentic Christian discipleship? Only when we have some sense of the answers to these questions can we then consider how the ministerial priesthood is to be understood.

Reflections on the Baptismal Priesthood

In its most basic sense, a priest is one who offers sacrifice. In some sense, both terms, "priest" and "sacrifice," can be problematic today. There is widespread discomfort in Western society with the notion of sacrifice. Ian Bradley suggests that notions of sacrifice do not sit well in a culture focused on self-fulfillment, instant gratification, conspicuous consumption, and vacuous self-absorption.[4] Many today balk at the notion of religious sacrifice because of its associations with ritual slaughter and other acts of violence intended to pacify God. This association with violence is largely shaped by sacrifice as it functioned in ancient religions outside the Judeo-Christian tradition. In these ancient religions sacrifice could take many forms, but it usually involved the ritual killing of an animal in order to appease or restore communion with a god. Within this ancient religious paradigm, the priest is simply the one who formally offers the sacrifice to God or the gods.

The existence of this understanding of sacrifice and priesthood in other ancient religious traditions can create a problem for Christians for whom the notions of priesthood and sacrifice must be understood in a dramatically different way. For example, even in the Old Testament, while there are many different forms of ritual sacrifice, none was actually offered in order to appease an angry God.[5] In fact, as ancient Hebrew conceptions of sacrifice developed, the atoning blood sacrifice came to be understood less as a human action bent on restoring relationship with God and more as a divine action intended to restore God's relationship with humanity.[6] And in the prophetic biblical tradition we see a shift away from cultic sacrifice altogether and toward sacrificial living and the work of justice.

In the New Testament one of the most dominant Christian conceptions of sacrifice is rooted in Paul's theology of *kenosis*. Saint Paul's famous Philippians hymn speaks of Christ's *kenosis*, his emptying of himself of all divine prerogatives in a radical gift of self to the world. There is an important theological principle at work here. Sacrificial action never begins with humanity offering a sacrifice to God. Rather, it is God who, in a descending movement, initiates the work of reconciliation, coming to us in vulnerable, self-giving love.[7] Nor is the Christian understanding of Christ's atoning death, at least in the writing of Paul, technically a "substitutionary" atonement, since for Paul "the paschal mystery is not an event that merely happens on our behalf; it is rather something in which we are intimately involved; the theme of life through death and resurrection is meant to be realized throughout our own lives."[8]

The deepest intuition of our Christian tradition is that Jesus was not offered as *victim* by another in order to appease or pacify God. Rather, Jesus is the one who freely offers himself as the innocent victim of a violent action that is not perpetrated on him by God but by a sinful humanity.

This is why the radical shape of the one sacrifice of Christ is absolutely incomprehensible apart from the resurrection. It is cross and resurrection together, the paschal mystery as a whole, that reveals to the world that the deep grammar of the cosmos, in the divine intention, is not violent sacrifice but vulnerable, self-giving love. In Christ's life, death, and resurrection we encounter a love that overcomes all boundaries, a love that excludes only those who exclude themselves. It is this love, and this love alone, that merits the term Christian sacrifice.

This reflection on Christ's priestly action in offering himself as sacrificial gift for the world, a theological approach witnessed to so profoundly in the Letter to the Hebrews, governs the way we must think about the priestly living of all the baptized. The priestly life of ordinary Christians draws sustenance from the priestly action and sacrificial love of Christ. His self-giving love, manifested in the cross and resurrection, becomes the source of our own capacity to love. It is only out of a living dependence on Christ that we can make the paschal grammar of self-giving the deep grammar of our lives.

James Alison offers a wonderful image to communicate what it is to live out our baptismal priesthood. Imagine, Alison suggests, that you are an Albanian living in 1989 and you have just heard over the airwaves that the Berlin Wall has fallen. The evil power that is the Communist regime has been defeated. Now, the Communists may still be in power in Albania, but it doesn't matter because you know, and they know you know, that it is all over. You begin to celebrate because you know that the days of "the beast" are numbered. Now, that does not mean that the state police and party apparatchiks will cease to act as oppressive thugs. On the outside everything in Albania may seem as if nothing has changed when, in fact, everything has changed and you know now that it is only a matter of time before the effects of the fall of the Berlin Wall reach the streets of Albania. And so you begin to celebrate now, and perhaps, by celebrating now, your celebration will even hasten the spread of this decisive defeat to your own land.

So it is in the Christian life. Something decisive for the world happened in the Christ event. And by our baptism we are to live out of the liberating reality of the "something" that happened in Christ. We are to live out of that reality even if, at the level of superficial appearances, nothing appears to have changed. The lives of ordinary Christians are priestly to the extent that we surrender to the power of self-giving love embodied in the salvific self-gift of Jesus. As Alison provocatively puts it, to live out our baptismal priesthood means being implicated in "the beginning of the celebration of a new regime even while the old regime hasn't yet grasped the news of its own fall."⁹

Reflections on the Ministerial Priesthood

Against this broader background we can now consider the ministerial priesthood. The ordained priest's ministry can only be understood as a particular ministerial calling to be in service of the priesthood of all the baptized. This relationship is affirmed in the *Catechism of the Catholic Church*: "While the common priesthood of the faithful is exercised by the unfolding of baptismal grace—a life of faith, hope, and charity, a life according to the Spirit—the ministerial priesthood is at the service of the common priesthood. It is directed at the unfolding of the baptismal grace of all Christians" (CCC 1547). It is the priesthood of the baptized that determines the shape of the ministerial priesthood and not the other way around. *Lumen Gentium* 10 established the necessary link between the baptismal priesthood and the ministerial priesthood. This relationship would be elaborated on in other conciliar texts.

In its Decree on the Ministry and Life of Priests (*Presbyterorum Ordinis*) the council conceives the ministerial priesthood as a service to the priesthood of the baptized. It does so first through its emphasis on the priest's ministry of the Word (PO 4). The priest is called to preach the good news of Jesus Christ in word and deed. If we Christians are to make our ordinary lives a living sacrifice to Christ, we need to be nourished and inspired by the word of God. The priest must be one so grasped by the love of Christ that this love infuses his preaching, allowing him to bear the mystery of Christ's love to others. At the same time he must be an astute observer of the human condition, able to name the hidden grace of God often already at work in the lives of the people he serves. The council writes, "Moreover, the priest's preaching, often very difficult in present-day conditions, if it is to become more effective in moving the minds of his hearers, must expound the word of God not merely in a general and abstract way but by an application of the eternal truth of the Gospel to the concrete circumstances of life" (PO 4). Effective preaching requires both a deep commitment to the evangelical power of the Gospel and a deep understanding of the complexities of modern life.

The priest will also serve the baptismal priesthood through the exercise of his sacramental ministry within and not above the Christian community, especially in his liturgical presidency over the Eucharist (PO 5). The priest gathers to worship the people of God within his care. He presides over the liturgy, drawing together the prayers of the people, receiving their gifts and offering them to the Father in the person of Christ and in union with the entire eucharistic assembly. In the celebration of the Eucharist the profound connection between the ministerial priesthood and the baptismal priesthood is fully displayed. This is because the sacrificial nature of the Eucharist works in two directions. Recall what was said earlier. In the Christian economy, sacrifice always begins with God's action, not our own. The first movement in the Eucharist is the self-gift of God in Jesus Christ offered for our salvation in the power of the Holy Spirit. We acknowledge this in the Liturgy of the Word's recollection of the saving deeds of God and in the eucharistic prayer recited by the priest.

It is only in grateful response to God's self-gift in Christ that our own eucharistic offering makes any sense. We bring our own humble gifts to the altar, symbols of our lives, in the belief that these simple gifts will be drawn into the eternal dynamism of Christ's self-offering. In *Deus Caritas Est*, Pope Benedict XVI wrote that in the celebration of the Eucharist "we enter into the very dynamic of his [Christ's] self-giving" (13). Both St. Irenaeus and St. Augustine described the Eucharist as a kind of divine pedagogy wherein we are "schooled" in the paschal pattern, the priestly shape, of Christian love. It should not surprise us that the early church fathers would so frequently describe the Eucharist as a twofold transformation: the transformation of the eucharistic elements and the transformation of the gathered community. So it is under the eucharistic presidency of the priest that the baptized are schooled in the priestly and paschal grammar of Christian love and sent in mission into the world. The sacerdotal ministry of the priest is most profoundly realized in his presidency over the Eucharist and his distinct role in offering the eucharistic sacrifice on behalf of the people but it is not limited to the realm of the liturgy. All of the priest's sacramental ministry, and indeed his entire ministry, should be seen as a way of inviting men and women into the transformative power of Christ's sacrificial love.

Finally, *Presbyterorum Ordinis* notes the priest's pastoral ministry as pastoral leader of the people (PO 6). Here too the priest serves the baptismal priesthood. He does so through pastoral leadership, through the empowerment of the people of God, and through the ordering of the many gifts of the baptized so that those gifts may build up the church in service of its mission in the world.

We see in the treatment of the ministerial priesthood the employment of a common conciliar framework: the threefold office of Christ as priest, prophet, and king. For centuries this threefold office had been applied to the ministry of the ordained as it is on the decree on the priesthood. However, for the first time, the council would teach that all the baptized participate in this threefold office. Indeed, our earlier consideration of *Lumen Gentium* 10's development of the baptismal priesthood was part of a larger treatment of the sharing of all the baptized in the office of Christ as priest, prophet, and king. We must not overlook the significance of this development. By employing the *tria munera* the council grounded the entire church, and not just the clergy, in the missions of Christ and the Holy Spirit. It is the Holy Spirit who empowers all the baptized to participate in the work of Christ as priest, prophet, and king. Again, this applies to *all* the faithful. All Christians are called into the priestly work of offering their lives as a spiritual sacrifice, all are called to be hearers and proclaimers of the Word, and all are called to work for the coming of God's reign. This theological development provided yet one more way in which the council was able to transcend the tendencies toward a two-tiered church and move us toward a church grounded in the unity of faith, baptism, and Christian mission. Indeed, the priestly work of God's people leads to a share in the church's mission in the world, the topic of our next chapter.

> The "threefold office of Christ" is often referred to in Latin as either the *triplex munus* or the *tria munera*. This theological formulation was first developed by the great Reformer John Calvin, and was later brought into Catholic theology by canon lawyers. The Latin term *munus* is difficult to translate into English, though it is generally rendered as "office." Though the term has conventionally been used in Catholic canon law and theology in reference to positions of leadership, the Second Vatican Council seemed to invite a broader meaning by applying it to all the baptized. In this regard, the council was following the pioneering work of Yves Congar, who developed a theology of the laity built on this broader application.[10]

Notes

[1] Alexandre Faivre, *The Emergence of the Laity in the Early Church* (New York: Paulist, 1990), 5. This treatment of the emergence of the lay/clergy distinction draws primarily from this study.

[2] *Concordia discordantium canonum*, causa 12, q.1 c.7.

[3] Edward P. Hahnenberg, *Awakening Vocation: A Theology of Christian Call* (Collegeville, MN: Liturgical Press, 2010), 7.

[4] Ian Bradley, *The Power of Sacrifice* (London: Darton, Longman and Todd, 1995), 4.

[5] Kevin Seasoltz, *God's Gift-Giving: In Christ and Through the Spirit* (New York: Continuum, 2007), 52.

[6] Ibid., 54.

[7] Paul J. Philibert, *The Priesthood of the Faithful: Key to a Living Church* (Collegeville, MN: Liturgical Press, 2005), 69.

[8] Seasoltz, *God's Gift-Giving*, 59–60.

[9] James Alison, *Undergoing God: Dispatches from the Scene of a Break In* (New York: Continuum, 2006), 41.

[10] Yves Congar, *Lay People in the Church*, rev. ed. (London: Geoffrey Chapman, 1985).

Chapter Ten

The Church's Mission in the World

(*Gaudium et Spes* 40)

> *Thus the church, at once "a visible organization and a spiritual
> community," travels the same journey as all of humanity and shares
> the same earthly lot with the world: it is to be a leaven and, as it
> were, the soul of human society in its renewal by Christ and trans-
> formation into the family of God.*

Background

In a basic sense, it is impossible to make any theological claim about
the church without at the same time presupposing some fundamental
attitude toward the world. The church does not exist in a vacuum; it has
always understood itself as standing in some basic relationship toward the
world. Yet Christians have often adopted quite different understandings
of "the world."

If we look to the Scriptures, we find in the beginning of the book of
Genesis a world created by God as fundamentally good. It was human
sinfulness, the biblical narratives suggest, that transformed our relationship to the world. Consequently, in the New Testament we find passages
that associate the world with human sinfulness (Rom 5:12) and the place
where evil rules (John 12:31). At the same time, that broken and sinful
world is the object of God's redeeming love ("For God so loved the world
. . . ," John 3:16).

Christianity, in the first centuries of its existence, maintained a tensive,
complex understanding of the world as both good insofar as it was created
by God and wounded by sin and therefore in need of redemption. Those
early centuries were a time in which Christians underwent periodic persecution; there was an inclination to associate the world with those forces of
persecution. Some hermits and monks encouraged a flight from the world
(*fuga mundi*), yet Christians also battled against an extreme dualism that
saw the material order as fundamentally evil. In the view of many early
Christians, the world may have been a mess. It may have been tragically
fractured by human sinfulness. But it was also the arena for God's coming
among us in the person of Jesus of Nazareth.

After the Edict of Constantine (313 CE) made the practice of Christianity legal, a more cautious yet constructive attitude toward the world began to develop. Christians were called to live in the world and yet always to be aware of its ongoing need for redemption. An uneasy tension was maintained between a Christian realism that called the church to deal pragmatically with the world as it was, and an eschatological vision that always remembered that this world must ultimately pass away in the consummation of all history. This uneasy tension ultimately gave way to a new vision of human community often referred to as "Christendom." Christendom constituted a partnership of sorts between the church and civil society that produced magnificent artistic wonders and scientific achievements, all under the patronage of the church. It also created an environment that allowed many church leaders to abandon their ministerial vocation in favor of worldly success, often compromising, if not abandoning altogether, essential Gospel values.

Christendom was always more an ideal than a reality and in any event, it could not survive in the face of new developments in modern science that appeared at odds with religious authorities. The rise of the nation-state, the Enlightenment emphasis on the autonomy of reason, and the repudiation of church authority all created an ecclesial atmosphere of fearful and defensive hostility toward the world. This siege mentality would only be strengthened by the French Revolution. As T. Howland Sanks observed, "if the Age of Reason had threatened the authority of the church in various intellectual spheres, the Age of Revolution threatened its very existence."[1] In the middle of the nineteenth century the papacy attacked what was often referred to as "liberalism" in a series of encyclicals by Pope Gregory XVI and Pope Pius IX.

Catholic social teaching: This refers to the entire history of the church's teaching on social life. More narrowly, it refers to a body of teaching first developed in the late nineteenth century that seeks to address the social, economic, and political issues of the modern world in light of the Gospel of Jesus Christ as it has developed in the living tradition of the church. Key principles include the dignity of the human person, the rights and responsibilities of all humanity that flow

(sidebar cont'd)

At the end of the nineteenth century Pope Leo XIII promulgated his groundbreaking encyclical *Rerum Novarum*, a document that offered an extended analysis of the social ills of the modern world in a more positive, if still quite cautious, engagement with the issues of the larger world. The promulgation of this document is often viewed as the beginning of modern Catholic social teaching. This attitude of suspicion toward the world was exacerbated in the twentieth century by the rise of modern Fascist and Communist states. Centuries-long attacks on the authority and integrity of the church created a fortress mentality within Catholicism. Pope Benedict XV and Popes Pius XI and XII each saw himself engaged in the world as forces for diplomacy and peace, but it was an engagement characterized by caution and an inability to acknowledge the possibility of God's grace active outside the walls of the church.

The groundbreaking social encyclicals of Pope John XXIII, *Mater et Magistra* and *Pacem in Terris*, helped transform in new ways the church's manner of relating to the world. This new attitude toward the world was characterized by a desire for positive engagement. Pope John

from that human dignity, an emphasis on community and the common good, a preferential option for the poor and vulnerable, the dignity of human labor and the rights of all workers, stewardship of creation, solidarity with all humankind, the positive role of government, the principle of subsidiarity, and the promotion of peace. In addition to Vatican II's Pastoral Constitution on the Church in the Modern World (*Gaudium et Spes*), this social teaching was developed in key papal documents, including Pope Leo XIII's *Rerum Novarum* (1891); Pope Pius XI's *Quadragesimo Anno* (1931); Pope John XXIII's *Mater et Magistra* (1961) and *Pacem in Terris* (1963); Pope Paul VI's *Popolorum Progressio* (1967) and *Octogesima Adveniens* (1971); Pope John Paul II's *Laborem Exercens* (1981), *Solicitudo Rei Socialis* (1988), and *Centesimus Annus* (1991); and Pope Benedict XVI's *Caritas in Veritate* (2009).

addressed not just Catholics but all men and women of goodwill, and he invited a common commitment to promote the protection of human rights and the furtherance of peace in our time. Pope John died after the first session of the council, but the first encyclical of his successor, Pope Paul VI, continued this new mode of engagement with the world. In *Ecclesiam Suam* Paul VI used, for the first time, the language of "dialogue" to consider Christians' dominant mode of relating both to one another and to the world. This dialogical framework would be embraced by the council and it helped to create a new genre of ecclesiastical literature, the *pastoral* constitution.

Vatican II's Pastoral Constitution on the Church in the Modern World (*Gaudium et Spes*)

At the beginning of the council the plan was for the bishops to issue one major constitution on the church. However, on December 4, 1963,

Cardinal Leo Suenens gave a momentous speech to the council bishops in which he distinguished between the church *ad intra* (that is, a consideration of the basic nature and structure of the church) and the church *ad extra* (that is, the church understood from the perspective of its mission to the world). He believed that the council needed to address the church in both of these dimensions. What eventually resulted was a second document on the church devoted to the church's relationship to the world. This document had a long and tortuous history. It would first be known simply as Schema 17 (as it was last on the list of texts to be considered) and eventually as Schema 13 (after July 1964, when the order of the texts was rearranged). The project was given special encouragement by several bishops from developing countries, in particular, Archbishop Dom Helder Camara of Brazil. At one point he asked in exasperation, "are we to spend our whole time discussing internal church problems while two-thirds of humankind is dying of hunger?" Helder Camara joined forces with Cardinal Suenens and, in spite of quite different backgrounds, together they provided much of the impetus for the new constitution.

An important question early in the genesis of the document concerned the question of style. In April of 1963 Pope John XXIII's encyclical *Pacem in Terris* was released. It aroused a great deal of interest, even beyond the borders of Catholicism. Many attributed this to the pope's foregoing technical theological language in favor of a more pragmatic consideration of the pressing questions of the time. It seemed important to many that Schema 13 follow suit. As one draft followed another, what gradually emerged was a text comprised of two parts. Part 1 established the theological framework for the church's engagement with the world. One of the most novel elements of this first section was the development of a theological anthropology grounded in the biblical notion of the human person created in the image and likeness of God.

Part 2 was even more controversial than part 1, dealing as it did with practical questions of moral application and addressing such topics as marriage and family, economic and social life, and the fostering of peace and international relations. Up to the very end, there was a resigned assumption by many at the council that these particular questions would have to be addressed in a series of appendixes with significantly lessened authority. Indeed, so controversial was this unprecedented document that, were it not for Pope Paul VI's steadfast support of the entire schema, it is doubtful that it would have been promulgated at all.

Many of the bishops at the council agreed that a new form of engagement with the world was required. However, there were significant disagreements regarding the theological framework for that engagement.[2] Some bishops and *periti* were influenced by a more Augustinian theology of the world that emphasized the basic brokenness of the human condition and the need for the grace of Christ mediated by the church as the sole source and agent of the world's redemption. Others were more influenced by a Thomistic perspective that recognized the place of sin and evil in the world and the need for the healing grace

Periti (*peritus* in the singular) refers to theologians who were appointed as consultants to assist in the work of the council or who served as theological consultants for individual bishops.

of Christ, but that nevertheless granted the limited but still positive natural potentialities of the human person and human society. Both theological traditions can be found in the constitution, though most commentators feel that the more optimistic, Thomistic perspective dominates.

The formulation of the document's title is significant. An early version of the title read, "On the Church *and* the Modern World." However, the use of the conjunction here might suggest that the church was a self-contained entity radically distinct from the world and perhaps even opposed to it. Consequently, the title was changed to read, "On the Church *in* the Modern World Today." The constitution begins with a remarkable statement about the church's solidarity with all of humankind:

> The joys and hopes, the grief and anguish of the people of our time, especially of those who are poor or afflicted, are the joys and hopes, the grief and anguish of the followers of Christ as well. Nothing that is genuinely human fails to find an echo in their hearts. For theirs is a community of people united in Christ and guided by the holy Spirit in their pilgrimage towards the Father's kingdom, bearers of a message of salvation for all of humanity. That is why they cherish a feeling of deep solidarity with the human race and its history. (GS 1)

Following the lead of Pope John XXIII, the council fathers realized that if the church was not to be reduced to some irrelevant museum piece, it must take more seriously the particular challenges of the modern world. In this spirit the council wrote,

> In every age, the church carries the responsibility of reading the signs of the times and of interpreting them in the light of the Gospel, if it is to carry out its task. In language intelligible to every generation, it should be able to answer the ever recurring questions which people

ask about the meaning of this present life and of the life to come, and
how one is related to the other. We must be aware of and understand
the aspirations, the yearnings, and the often dramatic features of the
world in which we live. (GS 4)

Throughout the constitution one detects the overriding spirit of respect-
ful dialogue. On the one hand, the church has much to learn from the world:
"the church is not unaware how much it has profited from the history and
development of humankind. It profits from the experience of past ages, from
the progress of the sciences, and from the riches hidden in various cultures,
through which greater light is thrown on human nature and new avenues to
truth are opened up" (GS 44). On the other hand, the church offers to the
world the good news of Jesus Christ. This Gospel should not appear foreign
to the world, for Christ is not some superhuman avatar. Rather, "Christ the
new Adam, in the very revelation of the mystery of the Father and of his
love, fully reveals humanity to itself and brings to light its very high calling" (GS 22). The church, then, offers to the world the revelation of God's
saving offer: "The church is the guardian of the deposit of God's word and
draws religious and moral principles from it, but it does not always have
a ready answer to every question. Still, it is eager to associate the light of
revelation with the experience of humanity in trying to clarify the course
upon which it has recently entered" (GS 33). Here we have a vision of the
church unapologetic in its conviction that it had much to offer the world,
yet presenting itself with humility as open to be taught by persons, communities, and movements outside the boundaries of the church.

The Church as "Leaven"

Even in the preparatory draft on the church, which was largely rejected
by the council bishops, one finds a chapter on the laity that went beyond
more passive, preconciliar conceptions of the laity as little more than doc-
ile sheep bound to follow the directives of the clergy. The council moved
forward, however tentatively, to sketch out a more positive theology of
the laity, one that emphasized their responsibility to bring the good news
of Jesus Christ to the world.

In several council texts the role of the laity in the world was described
using the metaphor of "leaven." In *Lumen Gentium* 31, the Decree on the
Apostolate of Lay People (*Apostolicam Actuositatem*) 3, and the Decree on
the Church's Missionary Activity (*Ad Gentes*) 15, it is the laity who are
to be a "leaven" in the world. The Declaration on Christian Education

(*Gravissimum Educationis*) 8 refers to the students of Catholic schools as those prepared to be a "saving leaven in the community" and *Perfectae Caritatis* 11 refers to members of secular institutes similarly as a "leaven in the world." Significantly, it is only *Gaudium et Spes* that teaches it is the church itself, that is, all the Christian faithful, which is called to live out the church's mission in the world as "leaven." Later in that same article the council members wrote of the mission of the church to heal and elevate the dignity of the human person, to strengthen human society, and to help humanity discover the deeper meaning of their daily lives. "The church, then, believes that *through each of its members and its community as a whole it can help to make the human family and its history still more human*" (GS 40; emphasis added).

Imagining the church as "leaven" in the world suggests that the attitudes and actions of all members of the church, including the clergy and consecrated religious, have social and political import. The groundbreaking work done by pioneers in the liturgical movement, like Dom Virgil Michel on the profound connections between the celebration of the liturgy and the Christian vocation to work for justice, challenged any notion of the clergy as belonging to some self-enclosed ecclesiastical/spiritual sphere. Nor does it seem possible to imagine the proclamation of the Gospel having any purchase on the lives of believers if it is not rooted in the "worldly" concerns of daily living. And how are we to conceive the evangelical counsels of the consecrated religious as "evangelical" unless we are witnesses to the values of the kingdom directed to the world from within the world? It may be true that this bracing vision of the pastoral constitution will require some corrective in changing circumstances.[3] Nevertheless, in its basic contours the pastoral constitution's teaching remains relevant to the situation of the church today as it resists the suggestion that only some segments of the church are to be concerned with the problems and challenges of our age.

The "leaven" metaphor was chosen expressly to indicate that the church was sent into the world to transform it *from within*. The council was

> Dom Virgil Michel (1890–1938): A Benedictine monk of Saint John's Abbey in Collegeville, Minnesota. In the early twentieth century he was a disciple and friend of Dom Lambert Beauduin, and was one of the most influential figures in the liturgical renewal movement that paved the way for many of the liturgical reforms of the council. He founded the liturgical journal *Orate Fratres* (which would become *Worship*) and was noted for his emphasis on the intrinsic connections between the liturgy and work for justice.

repudiating any attempt to define the church over against the world as if it were some autonomous entity, a "perfect society" (*societas perfecta*) un-affected by the issues and concerns of humankind. Rather, as the Decree on the Church's Missionary Activity reminded us, "the church on earth is by its very nature missionary" (AG 2). As Stephen Bevans and Roger Schroeder write, "One of the most important things Christians need to know about the church is that the *church* is not of ultimate importance."[4] The church exists as a universal sacrament of salvation (AG 1, 5) and as such is defined by its orientation toward the world. If Christians are to be faithful to the church's mission, they must resist the temptation to stand on the sidelines of the worldly arena. If they are to be leaven, Christians must be willing to "get their hands dirty," to work side by side with other men and women of goodwill for the improvement of the human condition and the work for justice. Christians will do so with a particular set of convictions and motivations, of course, for they will see their work as a cooperation with the grace of God. They will see their work as a modest preparation for the coming of God's reign, for the coming of a time when

> he shall judge between many peoples,
>   and shall arbitrate between strong nations far away;
> they shall beat their swords into plowshares,
>   and their spears into pruning hooks;
> nation shall not lift up sword against nation,
>   neither shall they learn war any more. (Micah 4:3)

Notes

[1] T. Howland Sanks, *Salt, Leaven & Light: The Community Called Church* (New York: Crossroad, 1992), 99.

[2] For an excellent summary of these different approaches, see Joseph Komonchak, "Vatican II and the Encounter between Catholicism and Liberalism," in *Catholicism and Liberalism: Contributions to American Public Philosophy*, ed. Bruce Douglass and David Hollenbach (Cambridge: Cambridge University Press, 1994), 76–99.

[3] For example, in the final document of the 1985 extraordinary synod of bishops, the synod affirmed the teaching of *Gaudium et Spes* but also noted that "the signs of our time are in part different from those of the time of the council, with greater problems and anguish. Today in fact, everywhere in the world we witness an increase in hunger, oppression, injustice and war, sufferings, terrorism, and other forms of violence of every sort. This requires a new and more profound theological reflection in order to interpret these signs in the light of the Gospel." "The Final Report," *Origins* 15 (December 19, 1985): 449.

[4] Stephen B. Bevans and Roger P. Schroeder, *Constants in Context: A Theology of Mission for Today* (Maryknoll, NY: Orbis Books, 2004), 7.

Chapter Eleven

The Role of the Laity in the World

(*Gaudium et Spes* 43)

One of the gravest errors of our time is the dichotomy between the faith which many profess and their day-to-day conduct. As far back as the Old Testament the prophets vehemently denounced this scandal, and in the New Testament Christ himself even more forcibly threatened it with severe punishment. Let there, then, be no pernicious opposition between professional and social activity on the one hand and religious life on the other. Christians who shirk their temporal duties shirk their duties towards [their] neighbor, neglect God himself, and endanger their eternal salvation. Let Christians follow the example of Christ who worked as a craftsman; let them be proud of the opportunity to carry out their earthly activity in such a way as to integrate human, domestic, professional, scientific and technical enterprises with religious values, under whose supreme direction all things are ordered to the glory of God.

It is to the laity, though not exclusively to them, that secular duties and activity properly belong. When therefore, as citizens of the world, they are engaged in any activity either individually or collectively, they will not be satisfied with meeting the minimum legal requirements but will strive to become truly proficient in that sphere. . . . let them not hesitate to take the initiative at the opportune moment and put their findings into effect. . . . For guidance and spiritual strength let them turn to the clergy; but let them realize that their pastors will not always be so expert as to have a ready answer to every problem, even every grave problem, that arises; this is not the role of the clergy: it is rather the task of lay people to shoulder their responsibilities under the guidance of Christian wisdom and with careful attention to the teaching authority of the church.

Very often their christian vision will suggest a certain solution in some given situation. Yet it happens rather frequently, and legitimately so, that some of the faithful, with no less sincerity, will see the problem quite differently. Now if one or other of the proposed solutions is readily perceived by many to be closely connected with the message of the Gospel, they ought to remember that in those cases no one is permitted to identify the authority of the church exclusively with his or her own opinion. Let them, then, try to guide each other by sincere dialogue in a spirit of mutual charity and with a genuine concern for the common good above all.

Background

We have already discussed in previous chapters the ancient priority of Christian baptism over all other subsequent distinctions within the Body of Christ. The demands of baptism impelled Christians to bring their faith and values to bear on their daily lives. With the medieval emergence of Christendom, this imperative was weakened somewhat as most assumed that the world in which they lived had already been christianized. In the nineteenth century the church's reawakened social consciousness was reflected in the papal encyclicals that developed Catholic social teaching of the time. However, this tradition reflected a more deductive approach to Catholic moral teaching in which the magisterium moved from universal moral principles to concrete judgments with very little consideration of the particular contexts of these judgments. The sole task of the laity was simply to align their attitudes and actions with these judgments.

In the early twentieth century a number of interrelated movements emerged that sought to emphasize a more constructive role for the laity in the mission of the church. We have already spoken of Catholic Action but we must consider the particular contributions of a Belgian priest, Joseph Cardijn, who helped found the Young Christian Workers movement. This movement emphasized the workplace as the proper arena for Christians to realize their baptismal vocation, infusing Gospel values into the world. Characteristic of this movement was a three-step process of communal reflection: see, judge, act. Members were encouraged to be attentive to the social, economic, and political contexts of their lives (see), evaluate those contexts in the light of their Christian faith (judge), and develop a plan of action based on that analysis (act). Begun in Belgium, the movement received the official support of Pope Pius XI in 1925. Cardijn's contributions would influence the council; he was made cardinal in 1965. The methodology would be employed by other Catholic movements like the Christian Family movement. As the council opened, the influence of these practical lay movements, accompanied by the theologies of the laity being developed by such noted theologians as Yves Congar and Marie-Dominique

Chenu, ensured that the council would place the laity in the forefront of their deliberations.

Vatican II and the Participation of the Laity in the Mission of the Church

In search of a more positive and constructive theology of the laity, the council focused on the secular character of the laity, that is, their complete immersion in the world by way of work, family, and citizenship. In *Lumen Gentium* the council wrote,

> *To be secular is the special characteristic of the laity*. Although people in holy Orders may sometimes be engaged in secular activities, or even practice a secular profession, yet by reason of their particular vocation they are principally and expressly ordained to the sacred ministry, while religious bear outstanding and striking witness that the world cannot be transfigured and offered to God without the spirit of the beatitudes. *It is the special vocation of the laity to seek the kingdom of God by engaging in temporal affairs* and directing them according to God's will. They live in the world, in each and every one of the world's occupations and callings and in the ordinary circumstances of social and family life which, as it were, form the context of their existence. (LG 31; emphasis added)

This secular vocation is similarly explored in the Decree on the Apostolate of Lay People (see AA 2, 7). The idea, however, was not to assert some strict definition of the laity that distinguished them from the clergy or professed religious, but rather to describe the typical situation of the layperson and then explore the theological significance of that situation. Neither did this represent an effort to exclude the laity from participation in church activity and ministry. Elsewhere the council affirmed the right and obligation of Christians to exercise their gifts both in the church and in the world (AA 3; LG 37). However, it is in *Gaudium et Spes* 43 that we find the council's most mature reflection on the laity's Christian obligations in virtue of their immersion in the world of ordinary human activity.

The council documents are surprisingly free of the kind of sweeping condemnations that many leading Catholic conservatives had desired. It is all the more striking to discover in *Gaudium et Spes* 43 the following condemnation: "One of the gravest errors of our time is the dichotomy between the faith which many profess and their day-to-day conduct." Here we find a frank recognition that one of the great Christian scandals of the modern world is that so many Christians could profess their faith while participating in manifest injustice. The council was, after all, only a few decades removed from the Second World War in which so-called "Christian nations" had perpetrated gross injustices on whole populations.

The council exhorted all Christians to integrate their faith into their daily lives. In service of this cause, it invoked a traditional theme of Catholic spirituality, the imitation of Christ. But this theme was given a very different interpretation as Christians were told to imitate Christ, "the craftsman." Catholics were thereby reminded that Jesus spent the vast majority of his adult life, not teaching or performing miracles, but simply practicing a trade. The implication was that disciples of Jesus should expect to see opportunities for applying their Christian faith in their workplace. "[L]et them be proud of the opportunity to carry out their earthly activity in such a way as to integrate human, domestic, professional, scientific and technical enterprises with religious values, under whose supreme direction all things are ordered to the glory of God" (GS 43). This text anticipates by several decades Pope John Paul II's profound theological reflections on the intrinsic dignity and even sanctity of human labor in *Laborem Exercens*. In the workplace, in the household, in neighborhoods, and in the political realm, it was the laity who were to take the initiative in making Christian values concrete. With this new emphasis, church leadership was, for the first time in centuries, moving away from a paternalism in which Catholics were to do no more than docilely follow the directives of the hierarchy.

To appreciate this new vision, we need only to recall the teaching of Pope Pius X, who wrote in 1906,

> It follows that the Church is essentially an *unequal* society, that is, a society comprising two categories of persons, the Pastors and the flock, those who occupy a rank in the different degrees of the hierarchy and the multitude of the faithful. So distinct are these categories that with the pastoral body only rests the necessary right and authority for promoting the end of the society and directing all its members towards that end; *the one duty of the multitude is to allow themselves to be led, and, like a docile flock, to follow the Pastors.* (*Vehementer Nos* 8; emphasis added)

In dramatic contrast, the council fathers were calling for a more adult form of participation in the life of the church. It was the laity who were to take the lead in applying the Gospel to the pressing concerns of the modern age.

Earlier in *Gaudium et Spes* the council offered a nuanced presentation of the unique contributions the church could make to the world: "The church is guardian of the deposit of God's word and draws religious and moral principles from it, but it does not always have a ready answer to every question. Still, it is eager to associate the light of revelation with the experience of humanity in trying to clarify the course upon which it has recently entered" (GS 33). Here was a vision of the church cooperating with all humankind in confronting the most important challenges of the age. This cooperation was the responsibility of all Christians who were charged with proclaiming the reign of God in word and deed. In this passage we see the surprising realism and modesty of the council in its assessment of the contribution that divine revelation makes. Without shying away from the belief in the truth of Christ, the council recognized that divine revelation needed to be integrated into a more complex form of human reflection and that this could not follow the deductive methodology that had dominated Catholic teaching for the previous century. What was needed was a more inductive approach in which church teaching would have to be applied by those most familiar with the patterns and contours of modern life, the laity. The integration of Christian values in the familial, social, political, cultural, and economic spheres would happen not by ecclesiastical decree but by ordinary Christians who would make use of their own expertise.

But what, then, was to be the role of the traditional teachers of the faith, the pope and bishops? The council wrote, "For guidance and spiritual strength let them turn to the clergy; but let them realize that their pastors will not always be so expert as to have a ready answer to every problem, even every grave problem, that arises; this is not the role of the clergy" (GS 43). The council saw the task of the clergy, from the normative teaching of pope and bishops to the catechetical activities and preaching of priests and deacons, as that of proclaiming the moral vision of the Gospel as it has been perpetuated in the living tradition of the church. It was the particular duty of all the baptized to take this moral vision and integrate it into their daily lives and apply it to the complex issues of the age. This process of integration and application went beyond the province of the clergy; this was the realm of concrete prudential judgment.

Thomas Aquinas emphasized the importance of the virtue of prudence in the moral life. Following Aristotle, he held that prudence was an exercise of practical reason and was oriented toward the search for the good to be found in any circumstance.[1] Put simply, prudence is that virtue that leads one to move from moral principle to concrete action while taking into account all relevant circumstances. The exercise of prudence requires that one have a solid knowledge of the pertinent moral principles, but it also requires that one attend to the concrete particulars of each situation.

These particulars, unlike the principles themselves, are fluid and changing, and one's grasp of them is necessarily more tentative than one's knowledge of a principle. This means that one's certitude about the rightness or wrongness of one's judgments diminishes the more the judgments depend on contingent empirical data. To the extent that contingency limits our certitude, there should be a greater willingness to tolerate disagreement.

The council bishops were surprisingly realistic about the complexity of the prudential realm and recognized that "[v]ery often their christian vision will suggest a certain solution in some given situation. Yet it happens rather frequently, and legitimately so, that some of the faithful, with no less sincerity, will see the problem quite differently." How is this disagreement to be adjudicated? "Let them, then, try to guide each other by sincere dialogue in a spirit of mutual charity and with a genuine concern for the common good above all" (GS 43). This passage reflects a sophisticated grasp of both the necessity and the complexity of Christian participation in the public realm.

Not everyone has appreciated the practical significance of the council's acknowledgment of the place of prudential judgment. Implicit in the council's teaching is the acknowledgment that Catholics who embrace the full range of church moral teaching may legitimately disagree with one another regarding the concrete implementation of these teachings in society. For example, church social teaching calls Catholics to a preferential option for the poor, a special concern for those who are poor and powerless in the world. No conscientious Catholic is free to dismiss the plight of the poor as somebody else's problem. Yet, even as two Catholics may agree that they have a religious and moral obligation toward the poor, they may legitimately disagree on the particular policy initiatives that will best alleviate poverty. In like manner, two Catholics might disagree regarding whether the application of Catholic moral teaching requires a legal remedy.

Finally we should note the council's injunction to dialogue in cases of disagreement. We live in a time in which civil discourse is fast being replaced by the politics of demonization. Cable television and talk radio is populated by "talking heads" whose primary rhetorical strategy is to impute ill will to those with whom they disagree. The motivation is simple. If you disagree with me and I can turn you into an evil or ignorant person, I no longer have to take your views seriously. This uncharitable rhetorical strategy is, sadly, often being replicated in the church. Consequently, it is worth recalling the council's sage advice that in the face of disagreement Christians should commit themselves to humble dialogue and a determination to place the common good above their own private interests. Later in the pastoral constitution the council writes, "Such a mission requires us first of all to create in the church itself mutual esteem, reverence and harmony, and to acknowledge all legitimate diversity; in this way all who constitute the one people of God will be able to engage in ever more fruitful dialogue, whether they are pastors or other members of the faithful" (GS 92).

Although the council was unable to offer a fully developed and completely consistent theology of the laity, its contributions nevertheless lay the foundation for a new age of the church. No more were the laity to be relegated to servile obedience to clerical mandates. Now the laity were to engage the world with initiative, courage, and conviction. In the postconciliar era we have witnessed a renewed emphasis on the priority of Christian baptism and the demands of Christian mission calling every baptized follower of Jesus to be a servant of God's reign.

Notes

[1] *Summa Theologiae* II-II, q. 47, a. 2. For a detailed study of the virtue of prudence in Thomistic ethics, see Daniel Mark Nelson, *The Priority of Prudence* (University Park: University of Pennsylvania Press, 1991).

Chapter Twelve

Christian Marriage and Family

(*Gaudium et Spes* 48)

> *The intimate partnership of life and the love which constitutes the married state has been established by the creator and endowed by him with its own proper laws; it is rooted in the [covenant] of its partners, that is, in their irrevocable personal consent. It is an institution confirmed by divine law and receiving its stability, in the eyes of society also, from the human act by which the partners mutually surrender themselves to each other; for the good of the partners, of the children, and of society this sacred bond no longer depends on human decision alone. . . . By its very nature the institution of marriage and married love are ordered to the procreation and education of the offspring and it is in them that it finds its crowning glory. Thus the man and woman, who "are no longer two but one" (Mt 19:6), help and serve each other by their marriage partnership; they become conscious of their unity and experience it more deeply from day to day. The intimate union of marriage, as a mutual giving of two persons, and the good of the children demand total fidelity from the spouses and require an unbreakable unity between them. . . . Authentic married love is caught up into divine love and is directed and enriched by the redemptive power of Christ and the salvific action of the church, with the result that the spouses are effectively led to God and are helped and strengthened in their lofty role as fathers and mothers.*

Background

For the vast majority of Christians, marriage will be the central vocational context in which they will live out the life of discipleship. In spite of this fact, we have to admit that the Christian tradition's treatment of marriage has been uneven. Consider the Bible's treatment of marriage. On the one hand, there are numerous texts that offer a positive vision of marriage in the plan of God. The book of Genesis speaks of God creating humanity as male and female in the divine image. The text suggests that human sexuality in some way participates in the divine image (Gen 1:26-27). In Genesis, chapter 2, the union of man and woman and the fecundity of their relationship are also presented as manifestations of God's desire and will. Later the prophetic literature will use marriage as an image of God's covenantal love for Israel (Hos 3). In the New Testament, Jesus condemns divorce, affirming God's will that in marriage "the two become one." Many scholars believe that Jesus' repudiation of divorce is in effect a repudiation of the treatment of the wife as chattel. Saint Paul affirms what appears to be a sexual egalitarianism ("There is no longer Jew or Greek, there is no longer slave or free, there is no longer male and female; for all of you are one in Christ Jesus" [Gal 3:28]). Later either Paul or a disciple of his will use marriage to explore the profound bond between Christ and his church (Eph 5:21-32).

On the other hand, it is difficult to avoid the patriarchal character of the understanding of marriage and family in the Old Testament. In the Mosaic Law husbands can divorce their wives but wives cannot divorce their husbands. Women are often treated as the property of either their fathers or their husbands. Their worth is measured by their ability to bear children.[1] In the New Testament Jesus relativizes the significance of a family constituted by blood relations, stressing instead the priority of a new family established by discipleship (Mark 3:31-35; 10:29-30). Paul, assuming that Christ would be returning within his lifetime, suggests that celibacy may be preferable to marriage (1 Cor 7) Finally, either Paul or a disciple of his appears to advocate the wife's subordination to her husband in Ephesians 5.

> **Patriarchy** refers to a society that is structured around the authority of the male/father (*pater* in Latin), often reflected in laws and practices that confirm the second-class status of women.

This ambiguity continues in the postbiblical tradition. Against heretical movements like the Encratists, Christianity consistently affirmed the goodness of the institution of marriage. Opposing social customs that viewed marriage as a legal contract among families, St. John Chrysostom insisted that "marriage is not a business venture, but a fellowship for life."[2] Chrysostom saw marriage and

> **Encratism:** An early Gnostic movement that employed Christian themes and images in varying degrees but embraced a largely dualistic view of the world in which the material order (including the body and sexual relations) was evil. The Encratists, in particular, formally renounced marriage. Theories of salvation generally involved a spiritual escape from the material order.

family as the spiritual glue that held society together. At the same time, he did see the need for a proper authoritative ordering in the family with the father serving as the *paterfamilias*. He insisted that "where there is equal authority, there never is peace. A household cannot be a democracy, ruled by everyone; the authority must necessarily rest in one person."[3]

In the late fourth century Augustine identified three goods of marriage: (1) childbearing and rearing, (2) mutual fidelity, and (3) the sacramental symbolism of marriage. Of these three goods, Augustine generally privileged the first, procreation. If Augustine joined most early church writers in insisting on the goodness of marriage, he also joined most others in affirming the general goodness of sexuality and sexual intercourse. However, in the concrete, his assessment of sexual pleasure in marital intercourse was much less positive. Augustine contended that sex in marriage was permitted for the sake of procreation but to the extent that a couple experienced sexual pleasure, the sex act was at least minimally sinful.

There can be no question that some of the patriarchal traces found in the Bible continued in the Christian tradition, but neither should we overlook the often positive changes that Christianity introduced to a Greco-Roman culture. That culture had long functioned on a shame-honor code that "celebrated male dominance and courage but also insisted on female submission and the circumscription of their daily activities."[4] Yet early Christianity subverted this code by calling married couples, and especially men, to an ethic of mutuality and self-giving love. Rodney Stark contends that this shift contributed to Christianity's rapid early growth in the first three centuries. According to Stark, in 40 CE there may have been as few as 1,000 Christians, yet by the beginning of the fourth century that number appears to have risen to approximately 33,000,000 or 56 percent of the population of the Roman Empire.[5] One factor appears to have been Christianity's attractiveness to women who were drawn to Christianity because it rejected the Greco-Roman double standard regarding sexual behavior and the male's right to divorce his wife. Christianity also prohibited both infanticide (where female infants were often targeted) and abortion, which was employed when a family felt it had a sufficient number of sons. Christians also simply out-procreated their non-Christian neighbors. The result was an essentially pro-family and pro-marriage ethic that dramatically furthered Christianity's growth.

There was not a great deal in the early church written on marriage, in part because, unlike other sacraments, there was no ritual to be administered by a church official. Divorce was generally frowned upon but not absolutely prohibited. Some bishops, particularly in the East, would allow divorce in cases of adultery. The question of divorce was often viewed more as a legal question and a concern of the state rather than the church.

By the eleventh century marriage was recognized as one of the seven sacraments of the church and from the eleventh to the thirteenth centuries a coherent theology of marriage began to develop, along with an accompanying legal structure. It is during this period that we have the first systematic reflection on marriage as a sacrament. The marriage relationship was considered a visible sign of Christ's love for his church, employing biblical imagery taken from the Letter to the Ephesians.

Much of Catholic teaching on marriage was formalized at the sixteenth-century Council of Trent. The council addressed a controversy that had lingered on in the church during the Middle Ages, namely, what constitutes a marriage, consent or sexual consummation? The council's response was to speak of consent as establishing an "initiated marriage" (*matrimonium initiatum*) and sexual consummation as establishing a "completed marriage" (*matrimonium ratum et consummatum*). During the period between the exchange of consent and consummation, a marriage was legitimate but not indissoluble; only after sexual consummation was it viewed as indissoluble. Trent also stipulated that this consent must be exchanged before a priest and two witnesses. Only at this point do wedding ceremonies become strictly mandatory in the church. Given this emphasis on mutual consent, marriage came to be viewed as a binding contract between two consenting Christians. Finally, Trent repudiated the position of Martin Luther that marriage was a spiritual state superior to that of consecrated celibacy.

> The Council of Trent: An ecumenical council convened in response to the Protestant Reformation. It met over several sessions and was presided over by multiple popes from its first convocation in 1545 to its close in 1563. In addition to offering a direct response to many of the attacks of the Reformers, it also inaugurated a number of reforms in sacramental theology and practice.

In the late nineteenth century, Cardinal Pietro Gasparri wrote an influential text on marriage titled *Tractatus Canonicus de Matrimonio*. His work emphasized three themes. First, he defined marriage primarily as a contract; second, he stressed that this contract conferred the permanent and exclusive right of each spouse to each other's body for the purpose of sexual intercourse. Third, procreation was seen as the primary end of marriage. In 1917 the Roman Catholic Code of Canon Law followed Gasparri in teaching that marriage was to be understood primarily as a contract. The principal end of marriage is listed as the procreation and education of children while the secondary end is mutual support. In the early twentieth century Pope Pius XI's encyclical *Casti Connubii* (1930) taught that along with the contractual foundation, marriage must be built on mutual love as well. Still, the pope maintained the distinction between the primary end of marriage (procreation) and the secondary end of mutual support.

What had developed over the course of a century was an excessively legalistic conception of marriage strongly skewed toward the purpose of procreation and child rearing. However, in the decades immediately preceding the council, growing numbers of theologians had begun to question the adequacy of this legal framework. Some, like Dietrich von Hildebrand, drew on personalist philosophy to develop a theology of marriage attentive to the loving communion between husband and wife.

Vatican II on Marriage and Family

As the council worked its way along the tortuous path to the final promulgation of *Gaudium et Spes*, some bishops called for a more robust assertion of dogmatic teaching on marriage and family while other bishops insisted that what was needed was a more pastoral treatment of the topic, one that reflected the changing context of marriage and family in the modern world. At one point, when there was a proposal to simply drop the material on marriage and family altogether, it was the lay auditors who advocated most forcefully for the need to address the topic. The result was the lead chapter, "The Dignity of Marriage and the Family," in part 2 of the pastoral constitution.

Auditor: A guest invited to witness the council deliberations without actually participating as a voting member. Auditors included laypersons, women religious, and Protestant, Orthodox, and even Jewish observers. These auditors were sometimes invited to provide written input on certain texts under conciliar consideration.

This chapter's key text is taken from article 48 and it describes the marriage relationship as an "intimate partnership of life and love." It is a partnership "rooted in the [covenant] of its partners, that is, in their irrevocable personal consent." This language represents a dramatic move away from the earlier, more juridical language of marriage as an exchange of sexual rights. Here we find instead an emphasis on covenant, partnership, and personal relationship. Marriage was more than the exchange of conjugal rights in the context of a valid marriage contract; it was the mutual self-gift between husband and wife, a concrete expression of love offered and accepted, of a love that unites and is productive of new life, a love that is, in short, nothing less than the love of God. The council bishops presented marriage as a unique sacrament that signifies the union of love of God and love of neighbor. The love between two spouses is both the response to and the expression of the love of God.

To appreciate the full import of the language employed here, it is worth recalling that the council's Theological Commission entertained 190 different *modi*, which in varying degrees objected to the characterization of marriage as a community grounded in covenantal love. Many bishops preferred more contractual language because they feared that the indissolubility of marriage would be relativized. That is, when the couple felt they had "fallen out of love," they would see that as the dissolution of their marital bond and feel free to seek divorce. To these objections the commission remarked that covenantal love was not to be equated with emotional love but with an act of the will involved in an irrevocable consent, a consent of persons. Indeed, many theologians forcefully argued that it is precisely the language of contract, with its implicit understanding that a contract can be revoked by mutual consent, that is presupposed in divorce legislation. The language of covenant also served to strengthen the third of Augustine's three goods of marriage, namely, the sacramental sign value of marriage. If the marriage of husband and wife is to reflect Christ's love for his church, the language of contract is clearly inadequate.

> *Modus* (pl. *modi*): An amendment proposed by an individual bishop or group of bishops to a draft text being considered by the council.

The language of covenant was also crucial for a reconsideration of marital sexual relations. For much of the previous century, the theological justification for marital sexual relations had been oriented toward procreation. The pastoral constitution, by contrast, considers the conjugal act as an expression and even perfection of the couple's irrevocable, mutual self-giving (GS 49). The council avoided giving priority to procreation over the unitive dimension of marital lovemaking. Of course, the council had no intention of severing the relationship between procreation and marriage. Its intention, rather, was to ground the procreative dimension of marital sexuality in the expansive communion of marital love. Childbearing and child rearing are the *fruit* of the intimate sharing of life and love. The fecundity of marriage is aptly expressed in procreation but it also has a generative dimension that cannot be reduced to procreation.

Over the course of the council, there were many bishops who felt that the time had come to reconsider the vexing issue concerning the appropriate means for exercising "responsible parenthood" and morally regulating births. The issue became more pressing with the advent of the birth control pill. Pope Paul VI, however, asked the council to forego an in-depth debate on the topic, promising to create a separate pontifical commission to explore the issue. The council more or less obliged, limiting itself to some general observations, but that did not prevent some prelates from frankly speaking out. For example, the senior Melkite patriarch Maximos IV Saigh offered the following forthright intervention:

> It is an urgent problem because it lies at the root of a great crisis of the Catholic conscience. There is a question here of a break between official doctrine of the Church and the contrary practice of the immense majority of Christian couples. The authority of the Church has been called into question on a vast scale. The faithful find themselves forced to live in conflict with the law of the Church, far from the sacraments, in constant anguish, unable to find a viable solution between two contradictory imperatives: conscience and normal married life . . . Frankly, can the official positions of the Church in this matter not be reviewed in the light of modern theological, medical, psychological and sociological science? In marriage, the development of personality and its integration into the creative plan of God are all one. Thus, the end of marriage should not be divided into "primary" and "secondary." This consideration opens new perspectives concerning the morality of conjugal behavior considered as a whole. And are we not entitled to ask if certain positions are not the outcome of outmoded ideas and, perhaps, a bachelor psychosis on the part of those unacquainted with this sector of life? Are we not unwillingly setting up a Manichaean conception of man and the world, in which the work of the flesh, vitiated in itself, is tolerated only in view of children? Is the external biological rectitude of an act the only criterion of morality, independent of family life, of its moral conjugal and family climate, and of the grave imperatives of prudence which must be the basic rule of all our human activity?[6]

In the final version of *Gaudium et Spes*, article 51 reaffirms a condemnation of forms of birth regulation prohibited by the magisterium, but carefully avoids specifying which forms were prohibited. It recognizes that there are often sound reasons leading couples to limit the number of children they will have, at least temporarily.

Finally, we must note other conciliar texts that address marriage and family. Of particular significance is the council's revival of an ancient image of the family as a "domestic church." The council viewed marriage and the Christian family as more than mere recipients of the sacraments. Christian marriage was itself a manifestation of the church. In other words, marriage was not ecclesial in an only indirect sense dependent on the actions of the church's ministers; marriage was itself now a participation in the church's own reality as an effective sign of God's grace in the world. The eminent German theologian and council *peritus* Karl Rahner wrote, the love that unites marital spouses "is just as much formative of the Church as sustained by the Church." [7] This intimate connection between marriage and the church is what made it possible for the council to recover and reflect on the ancient image of marriage and family as a *domestic* church.

In *Lumen Gentium* 11 the council recognizes the unique gifts that married couples bring to the life of the church. Indeed the bishops stressed the evangelical dimension to Christian family life: "In what might be regarded as the domestic church, the parents are to be the first preachers of the faith for their children by word and example." We can read this text as yet another example of Vatican II's consistent emphasis on the role of the laity in the fulfillment of the mission of the church. The council will again consider the family in the context of the church's mission in the Decree on the Apostolate of Lay People:

> The mission of being the primary vital cell of society has been given to the family by God. This mission will be accomplished if the family, by the mutual affection of its members and by family prayer, presents itself as a domestic sanctuary of the church; if the whole family takes its part in the church's liturgical worship; if, finally, it offers active hospitality, and practices justice and other good works for the benefit of all its sisters and brothers who suffer from want. Among the various works of the family apostolate the following may be listed: adopting abandoned children, showing a loving welcome to strangers, helping with the running of schools, supporting adolescents with advice and help, assisting engaged couples to make a better preparation for marriage, taking part in catechism-teaching, supporting married people and families in a material or moral crisis, and, in the case of the aged, providing them not only with what is indispensable but also procuring for them a fair share of the fruits of economic progress. . . . christian families bear a very valuable witness to Christ before the world when all their life they remain attached to the Gospel and give clear examples of christian marriage. . . . To attain the ends of their apostolate more easily it can be of advantage for families to organize themselves into groups. (AA 11)

This rich conciliar text develops a central theme of the council: the family household, as a true ecclesial community, cannot be isolated from the larger fabric of human society.

The council's many insights would provide the foundation for a new generation of theological reflection on marriage and family. These new reflections would be found in the papal encyclicals and apostolic exhortations of Popes Paul VI and John Paul II but also in the unique contributions of a growing number of lay theologians who would bring to the topic the fruit of their own Christian experience.

Notes

[1] For more on biblical patriarchy, see Anne Clifford, *Introducing Feminist Theology* (Maryknoll, NY: Orbis, 2001), 66–72; and Phyllis Trible, *Texts of Terror: Literary Feminist Readings of Biblical Narratives* (Philadelphia: Fortress, 1984).

[2] St. John Chrysostom, "How to Choose a Wife," in *St. John Chrysostom on Marriage and Family Life* (Crestwood: St. Vladimir's Press, 1986), 89–114, at 97.

[3] St. John Chrysostom, "Homily 20 on Ephesians 5," in *St. John Chrysostom on Marriage and Family Life*, 53.

[4] Don Browning, *Marriage and Modernization* (Grand Rapids: Eerdmans, 2003), 60.

[5] Rodney Stark, *The Rise of Christianity* (San Francisco: HarperCollins, 1996), 12.

[6] Acta *Synodalia* III/6, 59–62.

[7] Karl Rahner, "Marriage as a Sacrament," in *Theological Investigations*, vol. 10 (New York: Seabury Press, 1977), 212. For a profound theological exploration of this notion, see Florence Caffrey Bourg, *Where Two or Three are Gathered: Christian Families as Domestic Churches* (Notre Dame: University of Notre Dame Press, 2004).

Chapter Thirteen

The Ministry of the Bishop

(*Christus Dominus* 11)

> *A diocese is a [portion] of God's people entrusted to a bishop to be guided by him with the [cooperation of his priests] so that, loyal to its pastor and formed by him into one community in the holy Spirit through the Gospel and the Eucharist, it constitutes one particular church in which the one, holy, catholic and apostolic church of Christ is truly present and active.*
>
> *Individual bishops to whose charge particular dioceses are committed, under the authority of the supreme pontiff, care for their flocks in the name of God, as their proper, ordinary and immediate pastors, teaching, sanctifying and governing them.*

Background

At the same time that Pope John XXIII announced his intention to call an ecumenical council, he made known his plans to revise and update the Code of Canon Law, and to convoke a synod in the local church of Rome. In doing so, he indicated that this ecumenical council would not simply examine the teaching, structures, and policies of the universal church, but that it would be intimately linked to the renewal of the local churches. He was deeply aware of his ministry not only as the pastor of the universal Catholic church but also as the bishop of a local church, the church of the Diocese of Rome. The papal office belongs to whoever is the bishop of the local church of Rome, the church where the apostles Peter and Paul were martyred. Catholic tradition has consistently recognized the bishop of this local church as succeeding to the office of the apostle Peter.

> Canon law: From the ancient term "canon," which designated a unit of measure, a basic rule, or a principle of law. Canon law is a body of ecclesiastical laws that govern the good ordering of the life of the church so that its structures and practices protect the rights and serve the pastoral needs of all the faithful.

The pope's role as bishop of a local church had been somewhat obscured by the development of the papacy during the nineteenth century, which culminated in the solemn definition of the conditions for an infallible exercise of the papal teaching office by the First Vatican Council in 1870. This teaching focused the attention of believers almost exclusively on the pope's role as supreme pontiff and pastor of the universal church, eclipsing his role as the pastor of the local church at Rome. The teaching of Vatican I on the papacy is found in that council's Dogmatic Constitution on the Church of Christ (*Pastor Aeternus*), a document left incomplete when the council was interrupted by the Franco-Prussian War. This constitution was dedicated to expounding the church teaching on papal infallibility and papal primacy. The council taught that the pope's jurisdiction over the entire church was both ordinary and immediate. Its four chapters, which center almost entirely on the primacy of Peter and his successor, the Bishop of Rome, leave us with a very truncated image of the church. Those who hoped that Vatican I would say much more regarding the life and ministry of all the bishops and the vocation of all the faithful were disappointed when the council was cut short before these topics could be fully considered.

Following Vatican I, many assumed that since the church had so exalted the authority of the pope, recognizing his direct jurisdiction over all the local churches, the bishops were left with no real authority and functioned only as officials to carry out the bidding of the pope. These ideas were spread in Germany by Bismarck, the German chancellor, who issued a letter describing the Catholic bishops as mere officials or agents of the pope. However, the German bishops issued a rebuttal in 1875, declaring, "it is a complete misunderstanding of the Vatican decrees to believe that because of them 'episcopal jurisdiction has been absorbed into the papal,' that the Pope has 'in principle taken the place of each individual bishop,' that the bishops are now 'no more than tools of the Pope, his officials, without responsibility of their own.'"[1] Citing the teaching of *Pastor Aeternus*, the German bishops insisted that "under appointment of the Holy Spirit, they succeed in the place of the apostles, and feed and rule individually, as true shepherds, the particular flock assigned to them" (PA 3). The bishops further insisted that the source of the pope's authority was the same as their own, namely, in the episcopal office, and that not even the pope could alter the rights and duties that belong to their episcopal ministry by divine right. Vatican I had, in fact, described the jurisdictional power of the pope as "episcopal." Pope Pius IX strongly defended the declaration of the German bishops as an accurate reflection of "the genuine Catholic doctrine, which is also that of the holy Council and of this holy see," and insisted that the teaching of the First Vatican Council did not change in any way the genuine authority of the bishops as pastors of their dioceses.[2]

The Teaching of Vatican II

Despite these efforts to correct an exaggerated emphasis on the papal office, some of these ideas still persist today among many who regard the pope as a kind of "CEO" of a large multinational corporation, and the bishops as managers of the branch offices. This kind of thinking has been reinforced in recent times by a cult of personality that has surrounded the holders of the papal office. In the words of the Dominican theologian Jean-Marie Tillard, for many, the pope had become "more than a pope."[3] For obvious reasons, many council fathers looked to the Second Vatican Council to redress this imbalance and complete some of the unfinished agenda of Vatican I by providing a more fulsome description of the ministry of bishops and by clarifying their relationship to the Bishop of Rome.

A Ministry of Unity

Vatican II's Decree on the Pastoral Office of Bishops in the Church (*Christus Dominus* [CD]) offered a description of the ministry of the bishop in his local diocese that developed the patristic image of the local church first described in the council's Constitution on the Sacred Liturgy. As we saw in chapter 8, the Constitution on the Liturgy describes the diocese or local church along the lines of the eucharistic assembly. That same text refers to the bishop, who presides over its life and prayer, as "the high priest of his flock from whom the life of his people in Christ is in some way derived and on whom it in some way depends" (SC 41). The ancient image of the bishop as the "high priest" and the council's teaching that episcopal consecration conveys the "fullness of the sacrament of orders" (LG 21) point to an ordering in the ministerial offices of the church. The three ordained ministries in the church are distinguished according to the orders of the diaconate, the presbyterate, and the episcopate. Bishops and priests share in the same priesthood, though in differing degrees (LG 28). The bishop is assisted in his ministry by presbyters and deacons, who are his collaborators in the service of the people of God.

This understanding of collaboration in ministry can be traced back to the very earliest days of the Christian church. From New Testament times until the fourth century, "churches" were very small communities that often met in households for the breaking of the bread. It is hard for those of us who live in large urban centers today to imagine that all the Christians in town could fit into the same place for each celebration of the Lord's Day. By the second century a ministerial structure emerged where one *episkopos* or overseer was ordained to serve as the leader of each community and

Episkopos: The Greek term that we find in the New Testament and early Christian writings to refer to those who served as leaders in the Christian church. Sometimes translated as "pastor" or "shepherd," it refers literally to one who has "oversight" or who "watches over" the community. It is the root for terms such as "episcopate," which we use to refer to the order of bishops, or "episcopal," an adjectival form that qualifies the ministry of those belonging to this order.

Basilica: A large rectangular building with a rounded wall at one end and a row of stone columns on each side to support the roof. Appearing in the Roman Empire centuries before the Christian era, these buildings served as legal courts, public buildings, or places of commerce. When Christianity became the accepted religion of the empire, they were adapted for the public worship of the church.

to preside over its life of prayer. He was assisted by presbyters or elders, and deacons. When Christianity became the official religion of the Roman Empire, all of this necessarily changed. Christian communities were now much larger and were organized on the scale of the territories of the empire: in dioceses, metropolitans, provinces. It was no longer possible for the *episkopos* or bishop to gather all the Christians of the local church under one roof for a single celebration, even in the local basilica—the largest public building available. Soon it was not even possible for him to travel to all the communities within his diocese. Instead, he delegated presbyters to celebrate the sacraments as his representatives in newly organized parishes. In the city of Rome the unity between the bishop and the people was symbolized sacramentally in the *fermentum*, a morsel of consecrated bread that was sent out from the altar of the bishop with each of his presbyters and mingled with the wine during the celebration of the Eucharist in the surrounding churches within the diocese of Rome.

The church is fully realized each time the people of God gathers together at the table of the Word and the Eucharist, the sacrament of Communion. One of the principal tasks of the bishop, symbolized through his presiding over the life and prayer of the eucharistic assembly, is to "form it into one community" (CD 11), to ensure that God's people are nourished by Word and sacrament and watch over its unity. The ministry of unity that belongs to every bishop entails a concern for the internal unity and cohesion of the local diocese, but also the unity of this local church with all of the other local churches. The communion of the local churches is symbolized sacramentally during the rite of ordination of the bishop when the bishops of the neighboring local churches lay hands on the *ordinand*.

By this gesture they confirm that the *ordinand* is a worthy candidate for the office of bishop, one who is a living witness to the faith of the church and will therefore faithfully oversee the handing on of that faith to others. While the Bishop of Rome has a particular care for the bonds of communion among all the local churches in the universal church, all the bishops are "bound to be solicitous for the entire church" (LG 23). As a sign of communion among the local churches and to assist the Bishop of Rome in his particular ministry of presiding over the unity of the universal church, each bishop travels to Rome once every five years for an *ad limina* visit, to report on the life of the local community.

Vicars of Christ

One of the questions that *Lumen Gentium* sought to address in its third chapter was the authority of the bishops and their jurisdiction over the life of a diocese. As we saw above, an ultramontane view had crept into large sectors of Catholic theology that claimed bishops were little more than priests who were given a special task by the pope for the administration of the diocese. The power or "faculties" needed to carry out this task were said to be "delegated" to them by the pope, who was viewed as the source and center of all power and authority in the church. Careful study

> Ultramontanism: This term literally means "beyond the mountains" and refers to the conviction that all church decisions should be deferred to the pope, who stood, in relation to most of Western Europe, "beyond the mountains," that is, the Alps. Any tendency to hold that all church authority resides in the pope can be called "ultramontane."

of the broader tradition of the church, however, revealed a very different understanding of the episcopal office, which the council sought to restore.

Since the time of Pope Innocent III in the Middle Ages, popes had reserved to themselves the title "Vicar of Christ." *Lumen Gentium* recovers the more ancient usage of this term, which could be attributed to any bishop. As "vicars and legates of Christ," *Lumen Gentium* insists, bishops are the true leaders of the local churches and are not "to be regarded as vicars of the Roman Pontiff" (LG 27). Each bishop serves as a representative of Christ in his ministry of service to the people of God in each place. Their authority has its source, not in the pope, but in Christ.

Lumen Gentium provides an important clarification when it takes up a more traditional understanding of the sacrament of orders. The council recalled that "the apostles were endowed by Christ with a special outpouring of the holy Spirit coming upon them" in order to pastor the churches entrusted to them (LG 21). The council taught that the apostles passed on this gift of the Spirit to their collaborators through the laying on of hands, a tradition that has continued in the sacrament of episcopal consecration. Further, it teaches that the sacramental consecration of the bishop confers "the fullness of the sacrament of Orders" (ibid.), implying that they receive everything needed to carry out their ministry through their consecration to the order of the episcopate. The authority of each bishop to preside over the life of his church as a representative of Christ is rooted in the grace of his ordination. By virtue of this same sacrament the bishop is authorized to ordain others to serve the local church in the orders of the presbyterate and diaconate; they collaborate with him to care for the pastoral life of the faithful.

The Authority of the Bishop in the Local Church

The council uses three canonical or technical terms to describe the authority of each bishop in his diocese: "proper, ordinary, and immediate" (CD 11; LG 27). To say that one's authority is "proper" implies that it belongs to him personally, that is to say, he is not acting on behalf of anyone else, as someone else's agent or delegate. The authority and power to carry out the responsibilities of proclaiming the word of God, celebrating the sacraments, and maintaining discipline and good governance in the diocese is not delegated to the bishop by anyone else, but is a spiritual grace entrusted to him through the sacramental ordination to the episcopate. The newly ordained bishop may not exercise this authority without the "canonical mandate" granted by the pope. This mandate is a confirmation that the local bishop is acting in communion with the Bishop of Rome, who presides over the communion of all the local churches. The term "ordinary" conveys the notion that the authority needed to carry out this ministry belongs to the bishop by virtue of his office. Finally, the term "immediate" is used to express the idea that the bishop has direct authority. He has full executive power in the governance and administration of the diocese and his decisions have direct effect and legal consequences.

Teaching, Sanctifying, Governing

The ministry of the bishop is described in the documents of Vatican II according to the threefold office of Christ as priest, prophet, and king. These three are correlated to the three principal concerns of the bishop in the life of the diocese, which are presented as responsibilities for teaching, sanctifying, and governing. The council gives pride of place to the bishop's participation in the prophetic office and his responsibility to ensure that the Gospel is proclaimed faithfully. Bishops are called "authentic teachers," "endowed with the authority of Christ" to be witnesses of the faith (LG 25). In practice, this means that it is their responsibility to ensure that through the proper formation of priests, deacons, and other ministers, the Gospel will be unfolded in well-prepared homilies, in first-rate catechesis and religious instruction that can assist the faithful to understand the demands of the Gospel and relate it to their daily living. The ministries of preaching and teaching are aimed at the formation of mature followers of Christ.

In his opening remarks to the bishops at Vatican II, Pope John XXIII indicated that while one of the bishops' primary tasks is to "guard the precious treasure" of the church's doctrine, a council would not be necessary were they to simply repeat the church's teaching in the formulas of the previous councils. He invited them to a "deeper penetration and formation of conscience" and to express the riches of the Gospel by using the best methods of research available and the "literary forms of modern thought" so that its message might be communicated more effectively to men and women of the day.[4] He understood that to succeed in handing on the tradition, it has to be made "actual" in each new context. This perennial task is echoed in the reflections of *Christus Dominus* on the teaching role of the bishop: "Bishops should present Christ's teaching in a manner relevant to the needs of the times, providing a response to those difficulties and problems which people find especially distressing and burdensome" (CD 13). Today, no less than at the time of Vatican II, bishops are to ensure that the best methods possible are employed in the preaching and educative activities of the church in order to form authentic witnesses of faith in the contemporary world.

The bishops' participation in the priestly office of Christ is accomplished in their role as "the principal [stewards] of the mysteries of God" who direct, "promote and protect the entire liturgical life of the church entrusted to them" (CD 15). The sanctifying mission of the bishop reflected in St. Ignatius of Antioch's image of the bishop as the principal presider over the prayer of the gathered people of God (SC 41) extends to the ordering of the life of prayer throughout the diocese. The bishop is responsible for the quality of the community's life of common prayer. The liturgy in his cathedral church should be a model for the whole diocese. It is his task to provide for the spiritual care of all the faithful, by ensuring that they receive the sacraments and preaching they need. Bishops "should therefore see to it that the faithful know and live the paschal mystery more deeply through the Eucharist, forming one closely-knit body, united by the charity of Christ; 'devoting themselves to prayer and the ministry of the word'" (CD 15).

The sanctifying function of the bishop includes oversight for the proper conferral of the sacraments. This includes ensuring that candidates for the sacraments of initiation (baptism, confirmation, and Eucharist) receive proper instruction and understand the commitment they are undertaking. Similarly he is to see that those preparing for marriage or holy orders enter freely into their new way of life and with as much understanding as possible of their vocation.

The bishop fulfills a legislative role in matters of church discipline and the administration of the church's resources within his diocese. The council presents the governing function of the bishop as a pastoral ministry that is always to be exercised with "love and solicitude" (CD 16). The bishops are characterized not as cool and distant administrators but as compassionate "fathers and pastors" who "should be with their people as those who serve" (ibid.). Their ministry involves not only the spiritual care of the Catholic faithful but also concern for the spiritual needs and social conditions of all who live in their diocesan territory, including immigrants, refugees, the poor, and the vulnerable. They are to reach out to those who for various reasons are no longer active in the life of the church, to encourage ecumenism and engage in dialogue with members of other Christian churches, as well as with members of other religions. The bishop is to witness to the charity of Christ before all.

As this brief description reveals, the council's description of the scope of the bishop's ministry is wide ranging and, with the large population or geographical expanse of some of our contemporary dioceses, even daunting. It cannot be carried out without the support of other competent persons, lay and ordained, who collaborate in the ministry of the church. The demands of modern administration and communication make it challenging at times for the bishop to be seen, heard, and experienced as a genuine shepherd and pastor of the people, yet this is the fundamental character of his ministry. He serves as brother to all the faithful in the local church, and is called upon to create the conditions where all members of the baptized faithful may exercise their right and responsibility to "disclose their needs and desires to the pastors with that liberty and confidence which befits children of God and brothers and sisters in Christ" (LG 37). The council cites St. Augustine as a model of the relationship that ought to exist between the bishop and the faithful in his diocese: "When I am frightened by what I am to you, then I am consoled by what I am with you. To you I am the bishop, with you I am a Christian. The first is an office, the second a grace; the first a danger, the second salvation" (LG 32).

Some commentators have remarked that Vatican II's teaching on the relationship of the bishop to the faithful in his diocese remains somewhat underdeveloped. This is perhaps understandable, when we consider that the principal concern of the council was to arrive at a better balance in the understanding of the role of all the bishops of the world in relationship to the ministry of the Bishop of Rome, in light of the lopsided teaching of the First Vatican Council and its reception, a question we considered at the outset of this chapter. The effort to arrive at a more just equilibrium between papal primacy and the authority of the whole college of bishops in the universal church would lead to one of the more contentious debates at the Second Vatican Council, as we will see in the next chapter.

Notes

[1] "Collective Declaration of the German Hierarchy (1875)," cited in *The Christian Faith: Doctrinal Documents of the Catholic Church*, 6th rev. and enl. ed., ed. Jacques Dupuis (New York: Alba House, 1996), no. 841, 298–99.

[2] Pius IX, "Apostolic Brief of March 6, 1875," cited in *The Christian Faith*, no. 840, 298. Cf. DS 3117.

[3] Jean-Marie Tillard, *The Bishop of Rome* (Wilmington: Michael Glazier, 1983), 18.

[4] John XXIII, "*Opening Address*," in The Documents of Vatican II, ed. W. Abbott and J. Gallagher (New York: Guild, 1966), 710–19.

Chapter Fourteen

Episcopal Collegiality

(*Lumen Gentium* 23)

Collegiate unity is also apparent in the mutual relations of indi-
vidual bishops to particular dioceses and to the universal church.
The Roman Pontiff, as the successor of Peter, is the perpetual and
visible source and foundation of the unity both of the bishops and of
the whole company of the faithful. Individual bishops are the visible
source and foundation of unity in their own particular churches,
which are modelled on the universal church; it is in and from these
that the one and unique catholic church exists. And for that reason
each bishop represents his own church, whereas all of them together
with the pope represent the whole church in a bond of peace, love
and unity.

Individual bishops . . . exercise their pastoral office over the por-
tion of the people of God assigned to them . . . But as members of
the episcopal college and legitimate successors of the apostles, by
Christ's arrangement and decree, each is bound to be solicitous for
the entire church . . . Individual bishops, therefore, provided it does
not impede the fulfilment of their own particular obligations, are
obliged to collaborate with one another and with Peter's successor, to
whom, in a special way, the noble task of propagating the christian
name was entrusted.

Background

We have already learned in the preceding chapter about the emerging
office of the bishop in the early church. We know that by the end of the
second century the practice of having a single bishop preside over each
local church was fairly well established. Since each local church believed
itself to be in communion with all other local churches, the bishops of
a particular region would often meet together to address pastoral and
doctrinal issues of common concern. The default assumption of early
Christianity was that most church issues were to be dealt with at the
local level and only when issues clearly had consequences for the broader

community were decisions made by representative gatherings of regional churches called synods. We have evidence of such regional synods meeting in North Africa, Rome, and elsewhere in the early centuries. The decisions made at these synods were considered binding for their member churches. Often these synods would also communicate to Rome their final decisions as an expression of their unity with the church of Rome.

In the fourth century, Emperor Constantine convoked another synod or council to be held in Nicaea in order to preserve the unity of the empire in the face of the growing divisions being caused over Arianism. Those bishops present at Nicaea (325 CE) were mostly from the East and, apart from the council having been convoked by the emperor, there was little to separate it from earlier regional synods. However, its teaching would soon have universal import, leading the church, in subsequent decades, to refer to it as an "ecumenical" council since its decrees were received by the entire "inhabited world" (*oikoumenē*). For much of the first millennium, the universal church sought to resolve its most pressing problems by way of such regional synods and ecumenical councils. As Christopher Bellitto puts it, "The councils are where the church does her thinking by providing a place and event where problem solving, often at work for decades or even centuries beforehand, can come together in a critical mass."[1]

> Synod: This term is taken from the Greek *synodos*, comprised of two roots, *syn* = "together," *hodos* = "way." Synods, then, are meetings in which bishops "walk together" toward common agreement. It is the term given to meetings of church leaders of one kind or another to reflect on the pastoral concerns of the church. In this chapter we will focus on synodal gatherings of bishops, but there are other kinds of synods in today's church, including diocesan synods that are meetings of representative members of a local diocese under the presidency of the local bishop to deliberate on matters of pastoral concern.

> Arianism: Refers to the views of Arius, a presbyter from Alexandria (ca. 250–336), who held that since God the Father alone is "unbegotten" the Son did not share eternity with the Father. Jesus was truly superior to all other humans and savior of the world but he did not share the same divine being as the Father. The Council of Nicaea condemned the views of Arius and taught that the Son was "one in being" (*homoousios*) with the Father.

Even as councils of bishops would continue to play an important role in the first millennium, the papacy grew in significance, originally as a court of final appeal and eventually as claimant to jurisdiction over the whole church. Although councils would continue throughout the second millennium and bishops would continue to find reason to gather in their own regions, canon law increasingly circumscribed their authority. The medieval papacy became suspicious that bishops of a given region would be unduly influenced by their own secular rulers and become a threat to papal authority.

In the late fourteenth and early fifteenth centuries, the Great Western Schism (1378–1417) was characterized by a lamentable state of church affairs in which there were first two and then three claimants to the papacy. The Council of Constance was convened in 1414 to resolve the crisis, dismissing two false claimants while allowing a third to "resign," thereby clearing the way for the election of a new pope in 1417. In doing so Constance asserted that a council received its authority directly from Christ and that, at least in some circumstances, it could exercise authority even over the pope. Some went beyond this limited claim to insist that councils were fundamentally superior to the pope, a position referred to as *conciliarism*. The extreme version of conciliarism would soon be repudiated by the Council of Florence. However, in the centuries that followed, any attempt on the part of bishops of a particular region or nation to assert limited autonomy for their national churches would be condemned as new forms of conciliarism. Hence we find condemnations of Gallicanism (France) in the late seventeenth century, Febronianism (Germany) and Josephinism (Austria) in the eighteenth century.

In the nineteenth century, the Italian unification movement challenged the right of the pope to act as a secular sovereign over the Papal States. The First Vatican Council (1869–70) responded to what it saw as unwarranted attacks on the papacy by reasserting both the universal primacy of the pope and papal infallibility. As we pointed out in the preceding chapter, in the ninety years that followed Vatican I, a one-sided ecclesiology dominated, one that emphasized the authority of the pope, often at the expense of the authority of the bishops. There were, of course, many exceptions to this papocentric tendency, but Catholic ecclesiology seemed to suffer, if not from any fundamen-

Papal States: The territory in what is now central Italy that since the eighth century had been under the temporal sovereignty of the pope. In 1861, all the lands, save for Rome itself, were annexed by the kingdom of Italy and in 1870 Rome was absorbed into the Italian kingdom against widespread Catholic protests. It was not until the Lateran Treaty of 1929 that territory that now comprises Vatican City was ceded to the Catholic Church and granted the status of an independent sovereign state.

tal defect, then from a certain imbalance. In the late nineteenth century John Henry Newman was remarkably prescient in his letter to a young Anglican clergyman regarding Vatican I's definition on papal infallibility:

> Another consideration has struck me forcibly, and that is, that, looking at early history, it would seem as if the Church moved on to the perfect truth by various successive declarations, alternately in contrary directions, and thus perfecting, completing, supplying each other. Let us have a little faith in her I say. Pius is not the last of the popes. The fourth Council modified the third, the fifth the fourth. . . . Let us be patient, let us have faith, and a new Pope, and a re-assembled Council may trim the boat.[2]

In 1958, the church had a new pope and in 1962, a new council.

Vatican II on Episcopal Collegiality

As preparations began for the council, many bishops and *periti* were convinced of the need to take up anew the question of the pope's relationship to the bishops. The council would reiterate Vatican I's teaching on papal primacy that "the Roman Pontiff, by reason of his office as Vicar of Christ and as pastor of the entire church, has full, supreme and universal power over the whole church, a power which he can always exercise freely" (LG 22). But it also taught that just as "St. Peter and the other apostles constitute one apostolic college, so in like fashion the Roman Pontiff, Peter's successor, and the bishops, the successors of the apostles, are joined together" (ibid.). The council asserted that the pope and bishops together formed a "college" and, as such, shared leadership over the entire church. This teaching repudiated the common Catholic assumption that the pope was effectively bishop of the whole church and that all the other bishops were mere delegates of the pope who served at his pleasure.

Collegiality and the Communion of Churches

The council's teaching on episcopal collegiality represented a true development of doctrine. However, because of the controversial nature of the subject matter, numerous compromises were made in the formulation of the key texts on collegiality. These compromises led to certain inconsistencies. For example, in some places the college of bishops was presented within a "universalist" framework that focused on the college's relationship to the universal church (see LG 20–22). From this perspective a bishop's primary relationship is to the college; his relationship to the local church is strictly secondary. However, there are other conciliar passages that offer a different starting point. These texts start with each bishop's relationship to his own local church. So in the key text for this chapter we find the following:

> Individual bishops are the visible source and foundation of unity in their own particular churches, which are modelled on the universal church; it is in and from these that the one and unique catholic church exists. And for that reason each bishop represents his own church, whereas all of them together with the pope represent the whole church in a bond of peace, love and unity. (LG 23)

Here the starting point is not the universal church per se, but rather the universal church conceived as a communion of local churches. It is "in and from these" local churches "that the one and unique catholic church exists." Just as the universal church is constituted by the communion of local churches, so too the college of bishops is constituted by the communion of the bishops of those local churches. In the view of many theologians, the advantage of this second approach is twofold: (1) it treats the universal church not as a monolithic pyramid of which each local church is merely a small subdivision, but rather as a communion of local churches in which each local church "is wholly church" but "not the whole Church";[3] (2) it more profoundly connects the college of bishops to the communion of churches. The college becomes less a "governing board" and more a formal expression of the *communio ecclesiarum*.

Papal Primacy and Episcopal Collegiality

The council recalled the bond of communion shared between the bishops and the Bishop of Rome that was attested to in the ancient tradition and reflected in the regular gathering of bishops at synods and councils over the centuries. The council taught that although the college of bishops has no authority on its own apart from communion with its head, the pope, nevertheless, the college shares with the Bishop of Rome, and never apart from him, "supreme and full authority over the universal church" (LG 22).

The essential core of the council's teaching on collegiality rests in the assertion of shared power and authority over the universal church. This teaching overcame a centuries-long tendency to pit the bishops against the pope in a kind of "zero-sum" relationship—to assert the authority of the bishops was to take away from the authority of the papacy, and vice versa—as was evident in the conciliarist controversy. The council moved beyond this opposition primarily by placing the pope *within* the college of bishops as its head. This approach made it possible, in the eyes of some commentators, to assert that even when the pope exercised his authority apart from the explicit cooperation of the bishops (as with a solemn papal definition), his actions must presuppose an enduring communion between the pope and the entire college within which the pope always stood as head.

Although this development of the teaching on episcopal collegiality was in many ways little more than a return to the practices and ecclesial self-understanding of the first millennium, a persistent minority among the council bishops worried that the teaching on collegiality would undermine Vatican I's assertions regarding papal authority. In order to quell these fears, the chapter on the hierarchy in *Lumen Gentium* was peppered with passages reasserting papal authority and a controversial "explanatory note" was appended to *Lumen Gentium* at the eleventh hour and without a council vote. This note appeared to minimize the ecclesiological significance of the council's teaching on collegiality.

In spite of certain inconsistencies, *Lumen Gentium* offered a framework for relating the ministry of the pope to that of the college of bishops that drew its inspiration from the church of the first millennium. Vatican II had no interest in dismantling the teaching of Vatican I; it did wish to recall a more ancient understanding of the ministry of the pope and his relationship with the other bishops. No longer was the pope to be conceived in the image of a secular monarch or emperor. The pope was pope only because he was a *bishop*, the bishop of the local church of Rome.

We must remember that papal election has never been considered a sacramental ordination. The papacy is not a fourth degree of the sacrament of orders. The sacramental foundation of the papacy lies in the episcopate. The pope is both a member of the episcopal college (because he is *Bishop* of Rome) and head of the college (because he is Bishop of *Rome*). Put differently, a pope is only pope because he is bishop of a local church, the church of Rome. Rome possessed a special prestige because, among other things, it was the church that had witnessed the martyrdom of Sts. Peter and Paul. Later the connection with St. Paul would recede into the background and the pope would be seen as the "successor of Peter." This gave the Bishop of Rome a special authority to preserve the unity of faith and communion in the universal church.

In the years since the council, Catholic ecclesiology has continued to expand and develop some of the nascent insights on collegiality proposed in the council's teaching. For example, contemporary ecclesiologists like Jean-Marie Tillard have insisted that once we recognize that the sacramental basis of the pope's primacy is rooted in his episcopal ministry as Bishop of Rome and not in papal election per se, then the relationship between papal primacy and episcopal collegiality becomes more apparent.[4] A pope is, above all, a bishop among bishops. It is *as* a member of the college of bishops that the pope is head of that college. *Every* exercise of papal primacy is at the same time an exercise of the pope's episcopal office as member and head of the college. If this is the case, then all exercises of papal primacy must be at least implicitly collegial. Papal acts must be seen as, in some sense, genuine collegial acts as well. As the church gradually embraces this vital ecclesiological insight we will expect a further strengthening of the relationship between the pope and the other bishops.

Institutional Expressions of Collegiality

If the council's teaching on collegiality was of historic importance, nevertheless, the council did not consider in any depth the detailed structures that would put collegiality into practice. The council did encourage the formation of regional associations of bishops, referred to as episcopal conferences, as limited exercises of episcopal collegiality. In the Decree on the Pastoral Office of Bishops in the Church the council acknowledged the pastoral importance of episcopal conferences. It noted that these conferences had their origins in the ancient tradition of regional bishops meeting in synods (CD 36). *Christus Dominus* avoided, by and large, the tricky question regarding the precise authority to be accorded to these episcopal conferences (CD 37–38).[5]

Episcopal conference: A permanent ecclesiastical institution comprised of all the bishops of a given geographic region. These regional conferences are established in order to encourage and assist in the shared exercise of the bishops' pastoral ministry over the local churches in their care.

Elsewhere the council affirmed the value of these episcopal conferences in the church's mission in the world. In the Decree on the Church's Missionary Activity, episcopal conferences were offered as a valuable instrument in service of the church's catholicity. In article 22 of that decree the council described the process of allowing the Gospel to take root in different cultures while drawing on the gifts and customs of the region. Episcopal conferences were well equipped, the council insisted, to oversee this process. In like manner, the council granted authority to episcopal conferences regarding certain liturgical questions, including the approval of vernacular translations of liturgical texts (SC 22, 36).

A second example of a specific implementation of the council's teaching on collegiality was the creation of a synod of bishops. Even before the council began, Cardinal Bernard Alfrink of Utrecht had called for the creation of a permanent body of bishops to assist the pope in the government of the universal church. He had in mind an institution modeled on the permanent synods of the Eastern churches. Various versions of this idea were proposed during council debates and many bishops made a formal request for the creation of a permanent body of bishops to collaborate with the pope in shared pastoral ministry over the whole church. A muted expression of this proposal is found in *Christus Dominus* 5. Even before the close of the council, Pope Paul VI responded to some of the requests from the council floor by establishing the world synod of bishops in his *motu proprio, Apostolica Sollicitudo*. However, what he proposed was not to be a standing synod with deliberative authority but an occasional gathering of representative bishops for a limited period of time with strictly consultative power. As the synod of bishops has developed over the intervening four decades, three different synodal forms have emerged: ordinary synods that meet every three or four years; extraordinary synods that are convened to address special topics, often at the behest of the pope; and special synods that address issues of concern to particular regional churches. None of these forms appears to approximate the structure that many of the council participants had sought.

In the decades since the council, episcopal collegiality has only grown in importance. As Catholicism has engaged in ecumenical dialogues with other Christian traditions, questions regarding the structures of church authority have naturally arisen. Other churches share a historical episcopate or are at least willing to acknowledge its value, but many continue to question how the Catholic Church's belief in the need for papal primacy can be reconciled with a genuinely collegial and collaborative model of exercising church authority. Moreover, as the global catholicity of the Catholic Church becomes ever more pronounced with the growth of Catholicism in the global south, the authentic exercise of church authority becomes crucial. When is it preferable to allow the episcopate of a particular region limited autonomy over the pastoral life of the church of their region, and when will it be necessary for the papacy to assert its own authority in service of the unity of faith and communion? Questions like these suggest that Vatican II's teaching on collegiality may still be at an early stage of doctrinal development.

Notes

[1] Christopher M. Bellitto, *The General Councils: A History of the Twenty-One Church Councils from Nicaea to Vatican II* (New York: Paulist, 2002), 1.

[2] John Henry Newman, *The Letters and Diaries of John Henry Newman*, vol. 27, ed. Charles S. Dessain and Thomas Gornall (Oxford: Clarendon Press, 1973), 310.

[3] Jean Jacques von Allmen, "L'Église locale parmi les autres églises locales," *Irénikon* 43 (1970): 512.

[4] Jean-Marie Tillard, *The Bishop of Rome* (Wilmington: Michael Glazier, 1983).

[5] This question would be a matter of considerable debate in the decades after the council. The authoritative status of episcopal conferences was clarified in Pope John Paul II's apostolic letter *Apostolos Suos* (1997).

Chapter Fifteen

The Global Catholicity of the Church

(*Lumen Gentium* 13)

In virtue of this catholicity, each part contributes its own gifts to other parts and to the entire church, so that the whole and each of the parts are strengthened by the common sharing of all things and by the common effort to achieve fullness in unity. Hence, it is that the people of God is not only an assembly of different peoples, but in itself is made up of various ranks. This diversity among its members is either by reason of their duties—some exercise the sacred ministry for the good of their brothers and sisters; or it is due to their condition and manner of life, since many enter the religious state and, in tending to sanctity by the narrower way, stimulate their brothers and sisters by their example. Again, there are, legitimately, in the ecclesial communion particular churches which retain their own traditions, without prejudice to the Chair of Peter which presides over the entire assembly of charity, and protects their legitimate variety while at the same time taking care that these differences do not diminish unity, but rather contribute to it.

Background

In the Nicene Creed that many Catholics recite at Mass every Sunday we profess belief in "one, holy, catholic and apostolic Church." These are often referred to as the four marks of the church. Of these four marks, the church's catholicity may be the most misunderstood. Many Catholics grew up being taught that "catholic" simply means "universal." Although this is not wrong, neither does it capture the full richness of the term. *Katholikos* is derived from the Greek root *kat'holou*, which might be translated as "pertaining to or oriented toward the whole." Whereas "universal" suggests "the same everywhere," true catholicity is more about a unity-in-difference.

Even though the term does not appear in the New Testament, the Acts of the Apostles amounts to a narrative exposition of the "catholic" nature and origin of the church. The narrative begins with the story of Pentecost. In this story human language becomes a metaphor for how the catholicity of the church unfolds in the church's mission:

> When the day of Pentecost had come, they were all together in one place. And suddenly from heaven there came a sound like the rush of a violent wind, and it filled the entire house where they were sitting. Divided tongues, as of fire, appeared among them, and a tongue rested on each of them. All of them were filled with the Holy Spirit and began to speak in other languages, as the Spirit gave them ability. Now there were devout Jews from every nation under heaven living in Jerusalem. And at this sound the crowd gathered and was bewildered, because each one heard them speaking in the native language of each. Amazed and astonished, they asked, "Are not all these who are speaking Galileans? And how is it that we hear, each of us, in our own native language? Parthians, Medes, Elamites, and residents of Mesopotamia, Judea and Cappadocia, Pontus and Asia, Phrygia and Pamphylia, Egypt and the parts of Libya belonging to Cyrene, and visitors from Rome, both Jews and proselytes, Cretans and Arabs—in our own languages we hear them speaking about God's deeds of power." (Acts 2:1-11)

After Christ's death and resurrection, the Holy Spirit came down upon the believers gathered in Jerusalem. As those who received the Holy Spirit gave testimony to God's deeds, Jewish foreigners from throughout the known world all heard and comprehended their testimonies. The differences of language were transcended by the Spirit, allowing each to understand the other. Yet note that those from other lands heard those giving witness *in their own languages.* Cultural difference was not destroyed but rather had become the means for realizing a more profound spiritual unity.

In the story of Pentecost we discover a basic ecclesiological principle: the Holy Spirit does not erase difference but renders difference nondivisive. The account suggests that the church, born of the Spirit, is from its beginning open to diverse languages and cultures. Those gathered in Jerusalem were still Jews, even if from the culturally diverse Jewish Diaspora. Acts of the Apostles tells the story of a new religious movement that began in Jerusalem and then moved outward, becoming progressively more inclusive in its reach.[1] Chapter 8 recounts the ministry of Philip who first preaches, quite successfully, to the despised Samaritans, and then to the Ethiopian eunuch. The former were considered, at best, half Jews, and the eunuch was likely a member of a group of people known as "God fearers" who were uncircumcised yet sympathetic to Judaism.

The next stage is reflected in Acts 10–11's narrative of "the conversion of Peter."[2] After receiving a disturbing vision in which he was instructed by God to eat unclean food, Peter was invited to the house of the Gentile centurion, Cornelius. There Peter perceived more fully the universal scope of the Christian mission: "I truly understand that God shows no partiality, but in every nation anyone who fears him and does what is right is acceptable to him" (Acts 10:34-35). This insight was confirmed when he witnessed the Holy Spirit descending upon all who heard him preach, Jew and Gentile (Acts 10:44-48), in an echo of Pentecost.

This expanding catholicity achieved a new phase in the momentous "council of Jerusalem" recounted in Acts 15. Paul and Barnabas had already been successfully preaching the Gospel to both Jews and Gentiles. Apparently this outreach to the Gentiles was not welcomed by all the followers in Antioch. Consequently, Paul and Barnabas were sent to Jerusalem to obtain the approval of the Jewish-Christian leadership there. After momentous debate, the missionaries received the approval of the Jerusalem leadership and with that Christianity underwent a shift that would have ramifications for centuries to come. There could no longer be a question of limiting the mission to share the Gospel of Jesus Christ: the good news of Christ was to be offered to all peoples and therein lies the heart of the church's catholicity.

Christianity is commonly viewed as a Western religion. This is doubtless because, throughout much of the past thousand years, Christianity flourished in Europe and North America. Moreover, it was largely from Europe that Christianity eventually spread, first to the Americas and later to Africa and Asia. However, more recent historiography has pointed out that for much of the church's *first* thousand years it was far more global in character than is often appreciated today. For example, early Christianity grew as fast or faster both east of Jerusalem and along the Nile southward toward Ethiopia.[3] Some of the most ancient Christian communities were established northeast of Palestine with the Gospel finding expression in the language of Syriac, a dialect closely related to Aramaic. Syriac Christianity retained a strongly Semitic character, particularly in its liturgy and theology. This presented a striking contrast to the more Hellenized forms of Christianity that would eventually flourish in Byzantium and the Western church. It is primarily in the language of Syriac that the Gospel would spread eastward through Mesopotamia and Persia, on to India, Tibet, Mongolia, and even to China.[4]

When we consider the global spread of Christianity, particular attention must be given to the remarkable missionary endeavors of two brothers, Constantine (later known by his monastic name, Cyril) and Methodius, who in the ninth century undertook a dramatic missionary endeavor to the Slavic nations that had begun to populate the Danube River basin. Traveling together to Moravia, the brothers created a Slavonic alphabet and translated the Scriptures and certain liturgical texts into the Slavic language. This endeavor was opposed by the neighboring Frankish bishops who were scandalized that the liturgy was being translated into a vernacular tongue.[5] At that time it was commonly held that only Hebrew, Greek, and Latin were suitable languages for Christian worship.

Philip Jenkins captures the main import of these new historiographic studies: "Founded in the Near East, Christianity for its first thousand years was stronger in Asia and North Africa than in Europe, and only after about 1400 did Europe (and Europeanized North America) decisively become the Christian heartland."[6]

Christianity spread rapidly in part because it was free to communicate not only the Scriptures but also the Christian message itself in the language and culture of various peoples. By the end of the first millennium Christianity had long been transposed from its original Hebrew cultural context into a surprising diversity of cultures: Hellenist, Coptic, Armenian, Persian, Syrian, Indian, Slavic, and even Chinese.

Unfortunately, it is also the case that by the end of the first millennium many of the Eastern Christian communities outside of Byzantium eventually dissolved into minority Christian enclaves in the face of the spread of the Islamic cultural revolution (consider, for example, the Coptic Church in Egypt). The Western church, in turn, increasingly aligned itself with Western political powers and retained very little contact with the diverse Christian forms that emerged out of quite different cultural contexts.

Put simply, the sense of the church's catholicity changed dramatically over the course of the second millennium. In general it must be said that Christian missionary endeavors lost the sense of bringing the Gospel to different peoples and cultures and allowing these communities to make the Christian faith their own. Between the sixteenth and the nineteenth centuries in particular, Christian missionary work often rode the wave of European colonialism. During that period the Roman Catholic Church often functioned, as Karl Rahner famously put it, as "an export firm which exported a European religion as a commodity it did not really want to change but sent throughout the world together with the rest of the culture and civilization it considered superior."[7]

Rahner wrote this in an essay on the contributions of the Second Vatican Council. At the heart of the renewal of Vatican II was a reaffirmation of the church's catholicity as something more than geographic expansion. Central to this was the growing recognition of the theological significance of diverse human cultures, a recognition that began, however haltingly, in the first half of the twentieth century.

In the early decades of the twentieth century we find several magisterial statements by Popes Benedict XV, Pius XI, and Pius XII that suggested a new openness to the value of local cultures in the missionary work of the church.[8] As the council began, gathering an unprecedented number of bishops from throughout the world and every continent, the time seemed ripe to reconsider the church's catholicity in a new context.

Vatican II on the Catholicity of the Church

In some sense, the seeds for a more profound grasp of the church's catholicity were sown in the concrete experiences of so many of the bishops at the council. Often it was something as practical as the seating assignments at the council sessions. Within St. Peter's Basilica, where the general sessions were held, the bishops were not seated by region but by their seniority as bishops. This created a situation where bishops were often sitting next to bishops from different parts of the world. The informal conversation that this seating arrangement encouraged may have nudged many bishops toward a greater appreciation of the tremendous diversity already present in the church. The result was a profound broadening of the council's understanding of the church's catholic character.

In *Lumen Gentium* the bishops developed the theological foundations for the catholicity of the church, grounding it in the unity-in-diversity of the triune God. As the key text for this chapter acknowledges, this catholicity is evident in the diversity of gifts and roles found among the whole people of God. In *Lumen Gentium* 13 the council describes the wide-ranging diversity reflected in the various charisms and ministries exercised by the baptized and the different paths to holiness (e.g., marriage, professed religious). Of particular significance was the council's mention of "particular churches which retain their own traditions," a clear reference to the Eastern Catholic churches.

Catholicity and the Eastern Catholic Churches

Many of the bishops who attended the council had had little, if any, practical contact with the Eastern churches and were largely unaware of their distinctive theological and liturgical heritage. Though numerically overwhelmed (there were only about 130 bishops at the council from the Eastern Catholic churches), the Eastern bishops were able to make their presence felt and helped redirect the course of the council in important ways. Often it was the practical interactions the Western bishops had with their

Eastern brothers that helped them recognize the diversity that had always been present in the church, however much it had been muted and even suppressed in the West. One should not underestimate the practical impact of the conciliar practice of celebrating the Eucharist daily during the council sessions, on a rotating basis in the different liturgical rites of the churches. For many of the bishops, this was their first exposure to the already existing diversity of liturgical rites in the Catholic communion of churches.

The Decree on the Catholic Eastern Churches (*Orientalium Ecclesiarum*) insisted on the need to preserve the distinctive heritage of these churches. The decree also called for a return "to their ancestral traditions" and a purging of Western practices that had obscured the distinctive contributions of the Eastern churches. The council was not content to affirm the legitimate diversity of various rites; it insisted on the diversity of the Eastern churches themselves. Consequently, the council taught that these churches had a right to their own hierarchy and their distinctive methods of governance:

> [T]he churches of the east like those of the west have the right and duty to govern themselves according to their own special disciplines. For these are guaranteed by ancient tradition, and seem to be better suited to the customs of their faithful and better fitted for bringing about the good of their souls. (OE 5)

This decree did not fully address the concerns of many of the Eastern bishops; it remained, in many ways, a Western document *about* the Eastern churches. Nevertheless, *Orientalium Ecclesiarum* brought new prominence to the place of the Eastern churches in the Roman Catholic communion and thereby enhanced the council's teaching on the catholicity of the church.

Catholicity and Inculturation

One of the most important developments in the council's treatment of catholicity lay in its recognition that a diversity of language and culture enriches the unity of the church. The council taught that the church "fosters and takes to itself, in so far as they are good, people's abilities, resources and customs" (LG 13).

In one of the council's earliest documents, this revitalized understanding of catholicity was applied to the liturgy itself:

> Even in the liturgy the church does not wish to impose a rigid uniformity in matters which do not affect the faith or the well-being of

the entire community. Rather does it cultivate and foster the qualities
and talents of the various races and nations. Anything in people's way
of life which is not indissolubly bound up with superstition and error
the church studies with sympathy, and, if possible, preserves intact.
It sometimes even admits such things into the liturgy itself, provided
they harmonize with its true and authentic spirit. (SC 37)

As important as this text was, it appeared in one of the council's earlier
documents and still reflected vestiges of a superficial understanding of
culture as something external, akin to "costume." The council could not
yet envision the creation of any new rites but merely the possibility of
"grafting" on to the Roman Rite certain local cultural customs.

However, over the course of the council one can trace a marked maturation in the bishops' understanding of the role of culture in the church. In
one of its more mature documents, *Gaudium et Spes*, the bishops wrote, "It
is a feature of the human person that it can achieve true and full humanity
only by means of culture, that is through the cultivation of the goods and
values of nature. Whenever, therefore, there is a question of human life,
nature and culture are intimately linked together" (GS 53). The council
went on to define what constitutes culture:

> The word "culture" in the general sense refers to all those things
> which go to the refining and developing of humanity's diverse mental
> and physical endowments. We strive to subdue the earth by our
> knowledge and labor; we humanize social life both in the family
> and in the whole civic community through the improvement of
> customs and institutions; we express through our works the great
> spiritual experiences and aspirations of humanity through the ages; we
> communicate and preserve them to be an inspiration for the progress
> of many people, even of all humanity.
> Hence it follows that culture necessarily has historical and social
> overtones, and the word "culture" often carries with it sociological
> and ethnological connotations; in this sense one can speak about a
> plurality of cultures (GS 53).

This passage offers a fuller recognition that a culture is much more than a
mere costume that one chooses to put on or take off at will; it pertains to
the very substance of human existence. It follows then that, far from being
a matter indifferent to the life of faith, the diverse human cultures enrich
the Christian life. As the church fulfills its mission in the proclamation of
the good news of Jesus Christ to all nations, it recognizes that this saving
Gospel, the foundation of our Christian unity, must find expression in

Inculturation: In theological usage, this refers to the ecclesial process of allowing the Christian faith to find its expression in a diversity of cultural forms. Although the theological sense of the term underlies much of the council's treatment on the catholicity of the church, the term itself was never employed in the council documents; instead we find reference to cultural "adaptation" and "accommodation." Pope John Paul II would develop the concept in his apostolic exhortation *Catechesi Tradendae*:

As I said recently to the members of the Biblical Commission: "The term 'acculturation' or 'inculturation' may be a neologism, but it expresses very well one factor of the great mystery of the Incarnation." We can say of catechesis, as well as of evangelization in general, that it is called to bring the power of the Gospel into the very heart of culture and cultures. For this purpose, catechesis will seek to know these cultures and their essential components; it will learn their most significant expressions; it will respect their particular values and riches. In this manner it will be able to offer these cultures the knowledge of the hidden mystery and help them to bring forth from their own living tradition original expressions of Christian life, celebration and thought. Two things must however be kept in mind.

On the one hand the Gospel message cannot be purely and simply isolated from the culture in which it was first inserted (the biblical world or, more concretely, the cultural milieu in which Jesus of Nazareth lived), nor, without serious loss, from the cultures in which it has already been expressed down the centuries; it does not spring spontaneously from any cultural soil; it has always been transmitted by means of an apostolic dialogue which inevitably becomes part of a certain dialogue of cultures. (CT 53)

and through human culture. Authentic Christian mission requires authentic inculturation.

Finally, we see the relationship of faith and culture developed along the analogy of the incarnation in the council's Decree on the Church's Missionary Activity:

The seed which is the word of God grows out of good soil watered by the divine dew, it absorbs moisture, transforms it, and makes it part of itself, so that eventually it bears much fruit. So too indeed, just as happened in the economy of the incarnation, the young churches, which are rooted in Christ and built on the foundations of the apostles, take over all the riches of the nations which have been given to Christ as an inheritance. . . . They borrow from the customs, traditions, wisdom, teaching, arts and sciences of their people everything which could be used to praise the glory of the Creator, manifest the grace of the saviour, or contribute to the right ordering of christian life. (AG 22)

Culture is the soil in which all life grows and so the faith of the church, if it is to grow and flourish, must draw from that soil.

In the four decades since the close of Vatican II, few topics have received as much theological development as the catholicity of the church. This new development is a by-product, in part, of the dramatic growth of Catholicism in the global South. Consider John Allen's summary description of these shifts:

> In 1900, there were 459 million Catholics in the world, 392 million of whom lived in Europe and North America. Christianity 100 years ago remained an overwhelmingly white, first world phenomenon. By 2000, there were 1.1 billion Catholics, with just 380 million in Europe and North America, and the rest, 720 million, in the global South. Africa alone went from 1.9 million Catholics in 1900 to 130 million in 2000, a growth rate of almost 7,000 percent. This is the most rapid and sweeping demographic transformation of Catholicism in its 2,000 year history.[9]

Clearly, the church of the third millennium must make the global character of our church more a focal point of theological and pastoral reflection.

Notes

[1] What follows draws considerably from Stephen B. Bevans and Roger P. Schroeder, *Constants in Context: A Theology of Mission for Today* (Maryknoll, NY: Orbis Books, 2004), 14–30.

[2] James D. G. Dunn, *Acts of the Apostles* (Peterborough, UK: The Epworth Press, 1996), 10.

[3] Bevans and Schroeder, *Constants in Context*, 75–98.

[4] Dale T. Irvin and Scott W. Sunquist, *History of the World Christian Movement*, vol. 1 (Maryknoll, NY: Orbis Books, 2001), 57.

[5] Ibid., 368.

[6] Philip Jenkins, *The Next Christendom: The Coming of Global Christianity* (New York: Oxford University Press, 2002), 15.

[7] Karl Rahner, "Basic Theological Interpretation of Vatican II," in *Theological Investigations*, vol. 20 (New York: Crossroad, 1981), 77–89, at 78.

[8] Many of these can be found in *Modern Missionary Documents and Africa*, ed. Raymond Hickey (Dublin: Dominican Publications, 1982).

[9] See "Ten Mega-Trends Shaping the Catholic Church," *All Things Catholic* (December 22, 2006), http://ncrcafe.org/node/782.

Chapter Sixteen

The Right to Religious Freedom

(*Dignitatis Humanae* 2)

> *The Vatican council declares that the human person has a right to religious freedom. Freedom of this kind means that everyone should be immune from coercion by individuals, social groups and every human power so that, within due limits, no men or women are forced to act against their convictions nor are any persons to be restrained from acting in accordance with their convictions in religious matters in private or in public, alone or in association with others. The council further declares that the right to religious freedom is based on the very dignity of the human person as known through the revealed word of God and by reason itself.*

Background

The Declaration on Religious Liberty (*Dignitatis Humanae*) affirms a principle that is largely taken for granted in Western society today but that generated some of the most heated debates during the council. To understand why, it is necessary to consider both the historical context for this teaching and its significance for the relationship of the Catholic Church to other Christian churches and other religions. Some authors see this teaching of the Second Vatican Council as a symbol of the end of the "Constantinian era" of the church.

Constantine was the Roman emperor from 306 to 337 CE. Unlike his predecessors, who led violent campaigns of persecution and martyrdom against Christians, the pagan Constantine was very tolerant of the church. Eusebius recounts that in 312, on the eve of a momentous battle over the city of Rome, Constantine saw the Christian cross in a dream bearing the message *in hoc signo vinces* ("in this sign you will conquer"). He sent his soldiers into battle the next day with the cross painted on their shields, and afterwards attributed his victory to the Christian God. In early 313 Constantine issued the Edict of Milan, which lifted all penalties against those who professed the Christian faith and allowed them the freedom to follow the faith of their choosing. His mother Helena embraced Christianity and became a great patron of the church, sponsoring the construction of major basilicas in Jerusalem and Rome. While scholars debate when or whether Constantine himself embraced the Christian faith, he nonetheless styled himself as a protector of the church, sponsoring battles against heretics who threatened the unity of his empire, and convoking the Council of Nicaea in 325. Following his reign, the state sponsorship of Christianity continued. By 380, Emperor Theodosius I declared that Christianity would henceforth be the only religion tolerated in the empire, and ended state support for traditional Roman religion. While in subsequent centuries there were long periods of relatively peaceful coexistence between Christians and Jews or Christians and Muslims, the notion of one religion in a single unified state remained a virtually unchallenged model of church-state relations in the West up until the sixteenth-century Protestant Reformation.

When it became clear that the followers of Martin Luther's movement for religious reform, supported by a good number of German princes, would not be reconciled with the Roman church, Holy Roman Emperor Charles V negotiated the Peace of Augsburg in 1555. This treaty established conditions for the coexistence of two religious groups within the empire according to the principle *cuius regio, eius religio* ("whose region, his religion"), which required that the people adopt the chosen faith of their princes. Each opted for either Catholicism or Lutheranism. Those not wishing to conform to the religious choice of their princes migrated to regions that followed their preferred expression of Christian faith. The experience of division in Western Christianity was exacerbated by periods of intolerance, violent conflict, and religious wars. In 1648 a series of treaties were signed, establishing the Peace of Westphalia and putting an end to thirty years of war in the Holy Roman Empire (1618–48) and eighty years of war between Spain and the Dutch Republic (1568–1648). These agreements extended the principles of the Augsburg Settlement to include the establishment of Catholic, Lutheran, or Calvinist (Reformed) religious denominations according to the determination of the princes. While each territory would follow one of these as the state religion, the Peace of Westphalia also provided for the toleration of the public practice of the other two denominations. These principles continue to influence the laws of European nations down to our own day.

A unique and tumultuous history of the idea of an established or state-supported religion played out in the modern-day United Kingdom. In 1534 King Henry VIII issued the Act of Supremacy, rejecting papal authority and declaring himself supreme head of the Church of England. The Church of England, which gave rise to contemporary Anglicanism, sought to maintain traditional Catholic practices, while accepting many principles of the continental Reformation. Violent conflict ensued in the seventeenth century between radical Puritans and Catholic sympathizers, leading to civil war and efforts to impose a form of Presbyterian state church. A more catholic expression of Christianity was reestablished as the state church following the Restoration of Charles II in 1660. Those not belonging to the Church of England, including Catholics and dissenting Protestants, were penalized by restrictions on public worship and the ownership of property, burdened with harsh taxes, and forbidden to hold public office or serve in the military.

Many "dissenting" or "nonconformist" groups, including Puritans, Presbyterians, and later Baptists and Methodists, fled to the colonies of New England in search of freedom from the imposition of a state church and in the hope of building a more tolerant society. It is perhaps not surprising that when the colonies won their independence from the British crown, the ratification of the American Constitution would hinge, in part, on the acceptance of the First Amendment (1791). It stated simply, "Congress shall make no law respecting an establishment of religion, or prohibiting the free exercise thereof." The First Amendment sought to exclude the possibility of government-sponsored churches or of granting any one religion preference over another, including preference of belief over nonbelief. The American experiment with religious freedom would be an important resource for the church as it sought to address this question in the twentieth century.

Back on the European continent, the idea of a separation between church and state was introduced with the violent overthrow of the monarchy and the aristocratic Catholic clergy during the French Revolution (1789). Church properties were confiscated, religious orders were suppressed, and tens of thousands of priests fled the country to escape prison or the guillotine. In the ultimate symbol of humiliation, French armies took over the Papal States, seized an elderly Pope Pius VI, and held him in exile until his death in 1799. The nineteenth century saw a series of revolutions and similar confrontations between European states and the church as the leaders of new nation-states sought to diminish the influence of ecclesial authorities in state affairs. In the face of such violence and aggression, it is hardly surprising that church leaders viewed new democratic ideas, including the separation of church and state and religious freedom, as dangerous and suspect. Unable to come to terms with the loss of temporal power and clinging to a monarchical understanding of church leadership, Pope Pius IX included the notion of religious freedom among the perils listed in his 1864 Syllabus of Errors. The principle of religious freedom, rooted in the rationalist philosophy of the Enlightenment and the ideals of secularism, was also among the errors of Modernism condemned by Pope Pius X in his 1907 encyclical, *Pascendi Domenici Gregis*.

The long shadow of the sixteenth-century Protestant Reformation and the wounds inflicted on the Catholic Church by the revolutions of the late eighteenth and nineteenth centuries stretched well into the twentieth. When authors such as the American Jesuit John Courtney Murray began to argue openly in favor of accepting religious freedom as a basic human right, they were accused of entertaining Modernist ideas and contradicting the teachings of the magisterium. On the eve of the Second Vatican Council many Catholics, particularly those in the Latin countries bordering on the Mediterranean and in Latin America, continued to exist as "Catholic" countries, with governments and laws that favored the Catholic Church and were largely intolerant of other religious groups. In Central and Eastern Europe, however, many Catholic communities lived under the harsh rule of atheistic communist regimes. Many were forcibly integrated into Eastern Orthodox churches and forbidden to worship publicly according to their convictions. Priests and bishops who opposed these measures were imprisoned. Indeed, some of those bishops remained in Soviet prisons when the council began its deliberations. While Spanish and Latin American bishops favored repeating the teachings of Popes Pius IX and X, bishops from the Eastern Catholic churches saw things differently and recognized the need to promote the principle of religious freedom for all peoples.

Defenders of the prior teaching argued that Catholics ought to enjoy an exclusive right to exist in areas where they were in a majority and supported state-backed intolerance of other Christian communities. Yet they also held that Catholic communities ought to be tolerated and protected wherever they existed in a minority. These attitudes had serious consequences for Protestant communities in Spain and Latin America in the first half of the twentieth century. Similar attitudes led many

> Proselytize: To engage in an effort to "convert" someone from one belief to another. In the New Testament, the term "proselyte" refers to a Gentile considering conversion to the Jewish faith. In ecumenical relations, it has a pejorative connotation and is understood to refer to any effort to induce another into accepting one's faith perspective by unfair means that do not respect the genuine freedom of others. It has been described as a corruption of witness through undue pressure and intimidation. The methods of proselytism may include a variety of behaviors ranging from physical coercion to social and moral constraint or psychological pressure.

to regard Eastern Catholic churches as a vehicle for proselytizing among Eastern and Oriental Orthodox Christians. Behind these attitudes was a common conviction that "error has no rights," and the judgment that those outside the Catholic Church were in error or lacking in good faith.

The Teaching of the Council

Those who argued in favor of religious freedom called on the church to step outside this circular logic and to consider both the breadth of the Christian tradition and the facts of history in perspective. In his opening speech, Pope John XXIII had invited the bishops gathered for the council to learn from the lessons of history, "the teacher of life," and to be attentive to the "new conditions of modern life."[1] The history of the council's Declaration on Religious Liberty (*Dignitatis Humanae*) is complex and cannot be fully developed here. During the preparatory period there was no plan to issue a separate decree on religious liberty. The topic was considered almost exclusively in the preparatory schema on the church, in a chapter on "Church-State Relations and Religious Tolerance." The Secretariat for Christian Unity had drafted a document on religious freedom during the preparatory phase of the council but it was rejected by the Central Preparatory Commission on the grounds that the Secretariat was not competent to draw up schemata to be proposed for discussion. With the full support of Pope Paul VI, a newly prepared draft document on ecumenism was presented for the consideration of the bishops in 1963. Appended as chapters to this text were drafts on religious freedom and on the Jews. These were later pared off in April 1964 to become separate decrees.

Much of the controversy associated with the document was due to the widely perceived view that the council was being asked to consider a genuine change in church doctrine. Indeed, John Courtney Murray, principal architect of the council's treatment of the topic, once noted that the question of the development of doctrine was "the issue under all issues" at the council.[2] At the very least the Declaration on Religious Liberty reflected the council's effort to interface the rich doctrinal heritage of the church with the realities of a very new world, where the Catholic Church was coming to a new consciousness of itself as a world church, and where the context for living the Gospel could no longer be conceived according to the old model of Christendom under the rule of a single unified empire.

Freedom to Seek the Truth

Dignitatis Humanae begins from the recognition of the increasing awareness of the dignity of the human person and the aspiration of people to "exercise fully their own judgment" in matters of faith, free of coercion and excessive restriction in their actions. The council set out to consider how these aspirations "are in accord with truth and justice" by turning to the tradition "from which it draws forth new insights in harmony with the old" (DH 1). Reaffirming its conviction that the "one true religion" resides in the Catholic Church, and that all are bound to seek and adhere to the truth, it also recognizes a very traditional principle that had, at moments of our history, been obscured from view, namely, that all persons are bound to follow the dictates of their conscience. A renewed understanding of the primacy of conscience, coupled with a deeper understanding of the commitment of faith as a free response to the gift of God's grace, would lead the council to affirm the right to religious freedom. This right is understood not only as a moral principle that can be known through human reason and ought to be protected in the constitutional ordering of society but is also seen as belonging to the truth about human dignity revealed by the word of God (DH 2). This twofold appreciation of the principle of religious freedom is reflected in the two-part structure of the declaration: the first treats the "general principle," and the second examines religious freedom "in light of revelation." The principle of religious freedom is not, therefore, simply a matter of the good ordering of human society but is "rooted in divine revelation" (DH 9) and born out of our understanding of the responsible freedom that belongs to each person created in the image and likeness of God. The growing recognition of the dignity of human persons is linked, in the council's teaching, to growth in understanding the Gospel: "Thus, the leaven of the Gospel has long been at work in people's minds and has contributed greatly to a wider recognition by them in the course of time of their dignity as persons" (DH 12).

> Conscience: A capacity for judgment that impels us to do good and avoid evil. While popular notions of conscience envision an inner dilemma between a right or wrong choice, Christian philosophy considers conscience as an inner voice directing us to do what we conclude is good or to make the best choice possible. We are created for the good; our deepest desire is for goodness and genuine happiness. This implies a responsibility to develop a properly informed conscience, capable of discerning what is truly good and contributes to authentic fulfillment.

Note that while the general principle of religious freedom, articulated in this chapter's key text, is expressed as immunity *from* coercion or restraint, to be fully understood, we must see it as a freedom *for*. According to the conviction of our faith, the end of our searching is a personal God who endows us with the gift of freedom to discover and grow in relationship with others, to mature in our relationship with God, and to assume our responsibilities as coparticipants in God's project for the world. The freedom that is envisioned here is not unlimited or a reckless disregard for others, but a responsible freedom to develop an informed conscience and live in accord with the image of God that is imprinted deep within us.

The search for the truth and the journey of faith engages the whole person. While we are influenced by the community around us, we must ultimately make our own choices if our adherence is to lead to an authentic orientation of who we are as persons. For this reason, *Dignitatis Humanae* recognizes that while all have a duty to seek the truth, "[t]he search for truth, however, must be carried out in a manner appropriate to the dignity and social nature of the human person" (DH 3). The role of conscience is key in this process, and in the council's teaching, it is intimately linked to the freedom of faith:

> [T]he individual must not be forced to act against conscience nor be prevented from acting according to conscience, especially in religious matters. The reason is because the practice of religion of its very nature consists primarily of those voluntary and free internal acts by which human beings direct themselves to God. Acts of this kind cannot be commanded or forbidden by any merely human authority. . . . Consequently, to deny the free exercise of religion in society, when the just requirements of public order are observed, is to do an injustice to the human person and to the very order established by God for human beings. (DH 3)

Further, the council declares that any state authority that presumes to control the religious behavior of its citizens "must be judged to have exceeded the limits of its power" (ibid.). These principles are applied not only to individuals but also to entire religious communities who have a right to worship in public, educate their adherents and ministers, establish places of worship, and generally live in accordance with their faith convictions.

Faith and Freedom

This understanding of the act of faith is further developed in the second part of the declaration, which observes that the word of God and the fathers of the church have "constantly" taught "that human beings should respond to the word of God freely, and that therefore nobody is to be forced to embrace the faith against their will. The act of faith of its very nature is a free act" (DH 10). This does not mean that the church is setting aside its commitment to proclaim the Gospel. Rather, it must seek methods of evangelization that are in accord with the way of teaching modeled by Christ:

> For Christ, who is our master and Lord and at the same time is meek and humble of heart, acted patiently in attracting and inviting his disciples. He supported and confirmed his preaching by miracles to invite the faith of his hearers and give them assurance, but not to coerce them. . . .
>
> He did not wish to be a political Messiah who would dominate by force but preferred to call himself the Son of Man who came to serve, and "to give his life as a ransom for many." (DH 11)

Christ and his followers taught by word and example, rather than by force. Their approach was not one of coercion or condemnation. The only force at their disposal was the persuasion of an authentic witness.

Thus, while the Catholic Church claims for itself the freedom to proclaim and to give witness to the Gospel, including freedom from the interference of civil authorities in church matters, it commits itself to carry on its evangelizing mission in a manner that shows the utmost respect for the freedom and the religious convictions of others. It seeks to proclaim Christ not "by applying coercion or with the use of techniques unworthy of the Gospel but, above all, by the power of the word of God" (DH 11). This teaching echoes the orientation given to the council fathers by Pope John XXIII when he said that in its teaching to contemporary men and women, the church "meets the needs of the present day by demonstrating the validity of her teaching rather than by condemnations."[3]

Although *Dignitatis Humanae* does not address the practice of proselytism directly, it insists that "in spreading religious belief and in introducing religious practices everybody must, at all times, avoid any action which seems to suggest coercion or dishonest or unworthy persuasion, especially when dealing with the uneducated or the poor. Such a manner of acting must be considered an abuse of one's own right and an infringement of the rights of others" (DH 4). This and other affirmations are indicative of a clear intention to set aside a style of evangelizing that so many Christians of other denominations and members of other religious traditions found offensive in the history of interchurch relations and Catholic missionary activity.

The History of Violence and the Gospel

Anyone who knows the history of Christianity cannot forget the many sad chapters where confessions of faith were extracted through violent means: Jews and Muslims were forcibly "converted" with the support of state powers; Christian missionaries enforced the suppression of traditional cultural and religious practices; and church leaders promoted the rounding up of Jews into ghettos and the elimination of whole communities. *Dignitatis Humanae* acknowledges frankly that "in the life of the people of God in its pilgrimage, through the vicissitudes of human history, there have at times appeared patterns of behavior which was [sic] not in keeping with the spirit of the Gospel and were even opposed to it" (DH 12). The Second Vatican Council gathered to reflect on the matter of religious freedom less than twenty years after the end of the Second World War, where government forces, often supported by Christian communities harboring anti-Jewish prejudice, carried out one of the most massive and systematically organized campaigns of genocide in human history, exterminating six million Jews for no other reason than their race and religious conviction.

The bishops of Vatican II were thus deeply aware of the grave consequences of failing to abide by the constant teaching of the church that "no one is to be coerced into believing" (DH 12). Pope John Paul II, who was himself a witness to the violent conflict of the mid-twentieth century and a bishop at Vatican II, marked the beginning of Lent in the holy year for the new millennium in 2000 by presiding over a liturgy of repentance, where he and other church leaders asked forgiveness for the times when violent means have been used in the name of the Gospel.

A Basis for Ecumenical and Interreligious Relations

In light of both the difficult and at times contentious history of the Catholic Church's relations with other Christian churches and the council's stated purpose to advance the cause of reconciliation and unity, the Declaration on Religious Liberty—a document that was produced through the efforts of the new Secretariat for Christian Unity established by John XXIII to ensure the achievement of this goal—is an important counterpart of the council's teaching on ecumenism. Albert C. Outler, the great Methodist scholar and an official observer at the council, writes that this text "had become the test of sincerity of the Council's profession of concern for open and honest dialogue with other Christians and with the rest of the world as well." He considered the vote in favor of the declaration "one of the great moments in modern Church history."[4]

During the preparatory period leading up to the council, the staff of the Vatican Secretariat for Christian Unity met with leaders of the World Council of Churches and the leaders of many world confessional families who indicated their great concern that this matter be addressed by the council, especially due to the experience of Protestants in the Latin countries. World Council leaders had been instrumental in the drafting of Article 18 of the United Nations' Universal Declaration of Human Rights in 1948, which affirms "the right to freedom of thought, conscience and religion" for all peoples. In that same year the World Council of Churches issued its own Declaration on Religious Liberty out of concern for the rights of Protestant and Eastern Orthodox minorities in Catholic countries.[5] It would not be an exaggeration to say that without the support of the affirmation of these most basic principles in *Dignitatis Humanae*, the Catholic commitment to dialogue with other Christians reflected in the council's Decree on Ecumenism (*Unitatis Redintegratio*), or with people of other faiths in the Declaration on the Relation of the Church to Non-Christian Religions (*Nostra Aetate*), would surely have lacked credibility and substance in the eyes of those partners in dialogue.

Notes

[1] John XXIII, "Opening Address," in *The Documents of Vatican II*, ed. W. Abbott and J. Gallagher (New York: Guild, 1966), 710–19.

[2] John Courtney Murray, "This Matter of Religious Freedom," *America* (Jan. 9, 1965): 43.

[3] John XXIII, "Opening Address," 716.

[4] Albert C. Outler, *Methodist Observer at Vatican II* (Westminster: Newman Press, 1967), 147 and 152.

[5] "*Declaration on Religious Liberty* (Amsterdam, 1948)," in A. F. Carillo de Albernoz, *The Basis of Religious Liberty* (London: SCM, 1963), 157–59.

Chapter Seventeen

Communion in Faith with Other Christians

(*Unitatis Redintegratio* 3)

> For those who believe in Christ and have been properly baptized
> are put in some, though imperfect, communion with the Catholic
> Church. Without doubt, the differences that exist within varying
> degrees between them and the Catholic Church—whether in doc-
> trine and sometimes in discipline, or concerning the structure of the
> church—do indeed create many obstacles, sometimes serious ones,
> to full ecclesiastical communion. The ecumenical movement is striv-
> ing to overcome these obstacles. But even in spite of them it remains
> true that all who have been justified by faith in baptism are incorpo-
> rated into Christ; they therefore have a right to be called Christians,
> and with good reason are accepted as sisters and brothers in the
> Lord by the children of the Catholic Church.

Background

By announcing the convocation of an ecumenical council during a
celebration of Evening Prayer on January 25, 1959, at the close of the
Week of Prayer for Christian Unity, Pope John XXIII signaled that one of
its primary aims was to be the restoration of unity among all Christians. In
his vision for the council, one shared by the wider ecumenical movement,
the renewal of the Catholic Church and of other Christian communities
would contribute to their rapprochement. To keep this ecumenical priority
at the forefront of the council's agenda, John XXIII established a new office
in the Roman Curia in September of 1960, the Secretariat for Promoting
Christian Unity, headed by Cardinal Augustine Bea.

The Secretariat for Unity had the important diplomatic task of securing
the participation of official ecumenical observers to represent other Christian churches and confessional families at the council. In addition, it was
to advise the pope and the various conciliar commissions to ensure that
matters of ecumenical concern were adequately addressed in the council's teaching. In October of 1962, during the first session of the council,

the pope widened the competencies of the Secretariat, enabling it to act as a conciliar commission and draft a number of documents in collaboration with other conciliar commissions. The council's Decree on Ecumenism (*Unitatis Redintegratio*), the Declaration on Religious Liberty (*Dignitatis Humanae*), and the Declaration on the Relation of the Church to Non-Christian Religions (*Nostra Aetate*) were all products, at least in part, of the Secretariat. The Secretariat for Christian Unity also played an important role in the drafting of the Dogmatic Constitution on Divine Revelation, *Dei Verbum*, as it touched upon the relationship between Scripture and tradition, a question of great significance for Catholic-Protestant understanding.

> Ecumenical: This term comes from the Greek word *oikumene*, which appears in the New Testament and refers to the whole inhabited world. Its root is in the term *oikos*, which means "household." The twentieth-century ecumenical movement for the visible unity of the churches was called "ecumenical" because it seeks the unity of Christians throughout the world, of the entire household of God. "Ecumenical" activity, which concerns relationships among the Christian churches, is to be distinguished from "interfaith" relationships among the different world religions.

The ecumenical movement was among the "signs of the times" to which Pope John XXIII drew the attention of the church in his official convocation of the council. An organized movement of churches began to develop early in the twentieth century in response to a new and deeper awareness that division among the churches is a counterwitness to the Gospel. The earliest leaders of the ecumenical movement were Protestant and Anglican missionaries who knew from experience how dissension and rivalry between churches undermined their ability to proclaim the Gospel message of reconciliation and love. Their conviction grew that unity was necessary not only for the purpose of collaboration in mission and common witness but also because the very nature of the church demanded it. On the European continent, churches began working together to care for the many refugees left destitute following the First World War. In the aftermath of war, the ecumenical patriarch of Constantinople, head of the Eastern Orthodox churches, addressed an encyclical letter calling all Christians to work for Christian unity and inviting them to consider the formation of a "league of churches" like the "league of nations"—the predecessor to the United Nations—that was then being established.

In 1927 an international meeting was organized in Lausanne, Switzerland, for theologians from the major Christian denominations to examine the doctrinal issues or matters of "Faith and Order" over which the churches were divided. Organizers hoped that Catholic representatives might attend. Their hopes were dashed by the cool response of Pope Pius XI, who wrote in his letter *Mortalium Animos* (1928): "The union of Christians cannot be fostered otherwise than by promoting the return of the dissidents to the one true Church of Christ, which in the past they so unfortunately abandoned; return we say, to the one true Church of Christ which is plainly visible to all." The Catholic Church regarded the early ecumenical movement with considerable suspicion. When the World Council of Churches was officially organized and held its first assembly in 1948, Catholic participation was again prohibited. Nonetheless, Pope Pius XII began to recognize the ecumenical movement as a positive development inspired by the Holy Spirit. In 1949 he authorized the participation of Catholics in ecumenical meetings with other Christians. Exchanges between Catholic representatives and the leaders and theologians of other Christian churches provided important opportunities for growth in mutual knowledge and trust, and led many to discover—after centuries of estrangement—how very much the churches share in common. They prepared the ground for the Second Vatican Council to lay a foundation for renewed relationships with other Christians and opened new paths for deepening ecclesial communion.

The Council's Teaching on Ecumenism

As we saw above, the Catholic Church was initially quite reluctant to embrace the modern ecumenical movement. Some of this reluctance and suspicion was in evidence in the early attempts to have the council say something positive about the ecumenical movement. Before the beginning of the council, the Secretariat for Christian Unity had already drafted its own document on Christian unity. But since it did not receive the approval of the Central Preparatory Commission, it was not distributed to the bishops for their consideration. In addition to the document of the Secretariat, the Commission on the Oriental Churches produced a draft titled "That They May Be One." Finally, the Theological Commission had included a chapter on ecumenism in its original schema *de Ecclesia.*

At the end of the first session, the bishops agreed that a new schema ought to be prepared that would combine the three separate drafts. This revised schema reached the floor during the final two weeks of the second session. The schema had been prepared by a joint commission. The new schema consisted of five chapters. Some of the more conservative bishops continued to object to the term "ecumenism." They contended that it was Protestantism that applied this term to the task of achieving unity. From the Roman Catholic perspective, this unity was already present in the church. In addition, chapter 4, which treated Judaism, and chapter 5, which concerned religious liberty, provoked their own controversies, often for quite different reasons. The last two chapters were subsequently split from the draft Decree on Ecumenism and became the basis of the Declaration on Non-Christian Religions, *Nostra Aetate*, and the Decree on Religious Liberty, *Dignitatis Humanae*. The remaining three chapters were forged into the Decree on Ecumenism, *Unitatis Redintegratio*.

In order for the Catholic Church to enter fully into the wider ecumenical movement, a commitment expressed by the Decree on Ecumenism, the council had to wrestle with three important issues. The first of these concerned the recognition of those Christians who were not in full communion with the Catholic Church. The second, closely related to the first, had to do with the self-understanding of the Catholic Church and its relationship to the one church of Christ. The third concerned the possibility that one might speak of different degrees of belonging to the one church of Christ. Unfortunately, each of these issues was shrouded in centuries of controversy and alienation.

The Positive Recognition of Other Christians

The roots of division among the churches can be traced to three important moments in history. The first of these followed the Council of Chalcedon, the fourth of the ecumenical councils, which met in 451 in an effort to resolve a dispute regarding the proper understanding of the divine and human natures of Christ. A number of churches—those known today as the Oriental Orthodox churches (Armenian, Ethiopian, Eritrean, Syrian, Coptic, Malankara)—did not receive the teachings of this council and thus separated from the churches of Constantinople and Rome. In 1054, after a long period of estrangement, the heads of the churches of Rome and Constantinople mutually excommunicated one another, initiating another schism and further dividing Christianity along the lines of the Eastern (Byzantine) and Western (Latin) empires, or Eastern Orthodox and Catholic churches. No one anticipated that this schism would last over nine hundred years! Throughout this prolonged period of schism and estrangement each of these communities continued to regard the

> Schism: From the Greek *schisma*. The division or rupture of church unity that involves an official dissociation or severing of ties.

other, for the most part, as churches. Two serious but unsuccessful efforts were made to reconcile at the Councils of Lyon in 1274 and Florence in 1439.

The Protestant Reformation of the sixteenth century began as an effort to reform and purify the Catholic Church from within. It did not have as a goal the creation of new churches. In the polemic that ensued between sometimes overzealous Reformers and Catholic leaders slow to comprehend both the need for reform and the scale of the crisis, entire communities separated from the Roman church to follow the teachings of Martin Luther, John Calvin, Ulrich Zwingli, and others. In the eighteenth, nineteenth, and twentieth centuries, a series of revivals within Anglicanism and Protestantism spawned new evangelical communities. The Catholic Church did not have a theological category for these Christians, and regarded them essentially as a collection of Catholics who had "fallen away" or lapsed. Such an attitude was still apparent in Pope Pius XI's initial assessment of the nascent ecumenical movement among "dissidents." They were not "schismatics" like the members of the Orthodox churches. Protestants were often considered simply as "heretics": not true Christians, but those who followed a false doctrine.

The fragmentation and splintering of the church brought about by the Reformation was without precedent. Catholic theology and teaching had a tradition of acknowledging that individuals outside the Catholic Church who lived lives of justice and charity might be saved by the grace of God. But it tended to consider other Christians in the same way that it thought of righteous non-Christians: such persons were considered to be baptized *in voto*, or by an implicit desire to participate in the communion of God's grace that gives birth to the church. Few Catholic theologians had reflected on how the faith and practice of their *communities* might serve as effective means for the communication of God's saving grace.

One Catholic theologian who began to treat this question in the early twentieth century was Yves Congar.[1] He saw in the rising ecumenical movement, which aimed at ecclesial reconciliation, a *votum ecclesiae*, or a desire for the church. This was not the attitude of heretics. Building on the thought of St. Augustine, he maintained that Christians belonging to the separated communities were participating in the life of grace *in* and *through* the very life of these *communities*, where many "elements of the Church" remained. Congar encouraged Catholic theology to develop a more positive assessment of the life of the separated Christian communities by considering these elements of the church as effective means or channels of God's saving grace.

The question of recognizing other churches arose when the newly founded World Council of Churches set out its requirements for membership. If all churches in the ecumenical movement considered each other to be churches in the full theological sense of the word, they would not be divided from one another. Yet, if they were unable to recognize one another as fellow Christians and their communities as "churchly," in some sense, how could they consider each other true partners in dialogue? Some such recognition, however limited, is a prerequisite to authentic dialogue and the grounds of genuine commitment to grow in unity.

In the polemic of the sixteenth century John Calvin had characterized the Roman church as something less than the church of Christ, a mere "vestige" or ruin of the church. The 1950 Basis for the World Council of Churches required that member churches recognize the presence of "vestiges" or "elements" of the church in other Christian communities as the foundation of their ecumenical engagement. In the end, most preferred Congar's more positive notion of "elements of the Church" to Calvin's more limiting "vestiges." This consensus was received in the teaching of the Second Vatican Council. From the very earliest drafts of the Dogmatic Constitution on the Church, the council affirmed the presence of "many elements of sanctification and truth" outside the visible boundaries of the Catholic Church. *Lumen Gentium* describes these elements as "gifts belonging to the church of Christ" that serve as "forces impelling towards catholic unity" (LG 8).

The Decree on Ecumenism develops a fuller understanding of the elements of the church. It explains that "some, even very many, of the most significant elements and endowments which together go to build up and give life to the church itself" are found outside the Catholic Church. Further, it insists, these gifts "come from Christ and lead back to Christ"; they "belong by right to the one Church of Christ" (UR 3). The presence of these elements of the church is an indication that other Christian churches and communities participate, in some measure, in the one church of Christ. They include not only the theological virtues of faith, hope, and charity but also the visible elements of the word of God and "liturgical actions [that] most certainly can truly engender a life of grace, and, one must say, are capable of giving access to that communion in which is salvation" (ibid.). This teaching is a clear answer to those who doubted whether those who confess their faith in Christ outside the Catholic Church are being saved. While it considers that the separated churches and communities "suffer from . . . defects," the council recognizes that "the Spirit of Christ has not refrained from using them as means of salvation" (ibid.).

The One Church of Christ and the Catholic Church

In the course of the Second Vatican Council, the doctrinal commission had to find a way to reconcile this new, more positive assessment of the separated churches with the teachings of the early twentieth-century popes. The result was a far more carefully differentiated understanding of the one church of Christ. As we saw above, Pope Pius XII did not hesitate to identify the Catholic Church with the "one true Church of Christ." In his 1943 encyclical letter *Mystici Corporis*, he identified the Mystical Body of Christ with the Roman Catholic Church. Early drafts of the Dogmatic Constitution on the Church repeated his teaching that "the Church of Christ is the Roman Catholic Church."

In the course of conciliar debate, however, two notable revisions were introduced. First, the doctrinal commission elected to speak simply of the "Catholic Church," dropping the adjective "Roman" in all council documents. This term reflects a fuller understanding of the Catholic communion of churches, a reality not limited to the Roman or Western church, whose liturgy, theology, and laws are derived from the Latin tradition. It includes twenty-two self-governing Eastern Catholic churches in full ecclesial communion with the Bishop of Rome whose roots are in the Byzantine, Syrian, Coptic, and other Eastern traditions. The "Catholic Church" is a communion of diverse churches, each with its own liturgical, theological, canonical, and spiritual heritage.

Second, instead of saying that the church of Christ *is* the Catholic Church, the doctrinal commission opted instead to say that the "unique church of Christ . . . *subsists in* the Catholic Church" (emphasis added). The commission explained that this statement is more in accord with the affirmation that immediately follows: "many elements of sanctification and of truth are found outside its visible confines" (LG 8). There has been much debate as to the precise interpretation of this expression in the decades since the council. The Vatican's Congregation for the Doctrine of the Faith has confirmed what the drafters of the text themselves had maintained, that "subsists in" should be understood to mean that the church of Christ "continues to exist in" the Catholic Church.[2] The roots of this teaching can be found in a desire to maintain, in the face of challenges from Protestant Reformers, that the one church of Christ has never ceased to exist, and cannot be reduced to an invisible reality known to God alone. The conviction of Catholic teaching is that, despite the weakness and infidelities of some of its members—from popes and bishops, to priests and laypersons, who throughout history have been less than exemplary models of Gospel living—this visible institution has continued to be an agent of God's saving presence and activity in the world. This belief is rooted in the confidence that God's fidelity to the church is unwavering.

The council makes a clear identification between the Catholic Church and the one church of Christ. Yet this is not a simple or exclusive equation of the two, given the council's recognition that God is present and active in other "churches and ecclesial communities" (UR 19; cf. LG 15). The recognition that the Spirit of God continues to work through the elements of the church that exist in other Christian communities entails an acknowledgment of their churchly or ecclesial character. "In these communities the one sole Church of Christ is present, albeit imperfectly," the doctrinal commission explained, "and by means of their ecclesiastical elements the Church of Christ is in some way operative in them."[3] The one church of Christ extends beyond the visible bounds of the Catholic Church.

Varying Degrees of Ecclesial Communion

In considering the relationship of the Catholic Church to other Christian communities, the council acknowledges the existence of differing degrees of communion. Its reflections on this matter are developed especially in the second chapter of *Lumen Gentium*, which presents an understanding of the church as the "people of God," and in the third chapter of the Decree on Ecumenism, which treats the churches and ecclesial communities separated from the Roman See. Baptism is the path to belonging in the universal people of God who are gathered together in the church. Those who belong to the Catholic Church and "accept its entire structure and all the means of salvation established within it," including its professions of faith, sacraments, and structures of ministry and governance under the college of bishops together with the Bishop of Rome, are said to be "fully incorporated" into the visible society of the church (LG 14). Many other Christians are joined to the church through the sacramental bond of baptism, even though they "do not possess the faith in its entirety or have not preserved unity of communion under the successor of Peter" (LG 15). They are in a real relationship of communion with Christ and with the Catholic Church, founded on the faith we profess in baptism (UR 3).

The recognition that the Catholic Church is joined to other Christian churches by varying degrees of communion is based on the fact that they have more or less in common with each other. This differentiated communion corresponds to varying degrees of incorporation into the new people of God or the one church of Christ. The council's teaching on these matters is carefully nuanced. Membership in the Catholic Church is no guarantee that any individual is fully incorporated into the church.

Lumen Gentium recalls the traditional doctrine that "[a] person who does not persevere in charity" or live by the grace of baptism "is not saved . . . Such people remain indeed in the bosom of the church, but only 'bodily' [and] not 'in their hearts'" (LG 14). In other words, they may belong to the church in name, or to its external reality, but their hearts remain closed, unconverted by God's offer of reconciling love, and they consequently fail to lead a life in harmony with God's grace. Living in a state of serious sin separates us from God and from that communion with one another of which the church is an expression.

The Catholic Church itself, although gifted with "the fullness of the means of salvation" (UR 3; LG 14), remains nonetheless a pilgrim church "still in its members liable to sin," still "growing in Christ" (UR 3) and thus always in need of purification, renewal, and reform (UR 6, LG 14). Though the Catholic Church is endowed, through its faith, sacraments, and ministries, with all the means Christ intended to ensure the path of salvation, "its members fail to live by them with all the fervor that they should" with the result that "the radiance of the church's face shines less brightly" (UR 4). The disunity of the churches is among the most serious impediments to the church's mission and witness, making it difficult to express the "full catholicity" of the church. For this reason all Catholics are exhorted to build upon the bond of communion already existing with other Christians and work for full Christian unity (UR 5).

Turning its attention to those churches and ecclesial communities not in full communion with the Catholic Church, the Decree on Ecumenism distinguishes between the Eastern churches (Oriental and Eastern Orthodox) and the "churches and ecclesial communities in the West." Among the latter, "the Anglican communion occupies a special place," given that "catholic traditions and institutions . . . continue to exist" there (UR 13). The relationship of the Orthodox churches with the Catholic Church is recognized as very close, like that which exists "between sisters" (UR 14). Because they have clearly maintained the apostolic succession in the episcopal structuring of their churches, Orthodox churches are said to "possess true sacraments." For this reason, where the discipline of each church and circumstances permit, sacramental sharing with Orthodox Christians is "encouraged" (UR 15).

Apostolic succession: The doctrine that the ministry of a continuous succession of faithful bishops ensures continuity in the teaching of the apostolic faith. The bishops are successors of the apostles and continue their ministry of witnessing to the faith.

The decree then considers the separated churches and ecclesial communities in the West,[4] noting that they are "bound to the Catholic Church by a specially close relationship" due to the common heritage they share from the many centuries prior to the Reformation, during which Christians in the West lived together in communion (UR 19). It regrets that "they lack the fullness of unity with us that flows from baptism" (UR 22). As many of these communities do not have a threefold structure of ministry, including the ministries of deacon, presbyter, and bishop, or in the case of the Anglican communion, where the sacramental orders of bishops has been judged invalid by Catholic authorities,[5] the council considers that "the sacrament of orders is lacking" (UR 22). Regrettably, some translations of this text speak of "the absence of the sacrament of orders." The original Latin text uses the term *defectum*, suggesting a deficiency or weakness, yet not a total absence of the sacrament. It is not so much the reality of God's grace as the ministerial structure of the church that is at issue, including the special role the bishops, as successors of the apostles, play in overseeing the bonds of communion in faith both within and among the local churches.

To the extent that this visible sign of ministerial communion is lacking, "we believe they have not preserved the proper reality of the eucharistic mystery in its fullness" (UR 22). The celebration of the Eucharist is the highest expression of our common faith in the paschal mystery and of our ecclesial communion. Because the full and mutual recognition of the sacrament of orders is lacking between the Catholic Church and the ecclesial communities of the Anglican communion and Protestantism, and they do not yet live in a state of full ecclesial communion, members of our communities do not generally receive the sacraments together (UR 8). Nonetheless, the council recommends and Catholic canon law recognizes, by way of exception, circumstances where Christians belonging to these communities may appropriately ask for and receive the sacraments of reconciliation, Eucharist, and anointing from a minister of the Catholic Church (CIC 844; CCEC 671).

During the closing ceremonies of Vatican II, in December of 1965, Pope Paul VI and Patriarch Athenagoras of Constantinople issued formal declarations lifting the excommunication between the churches of Rome and Constantinople, thus preparing the way for the opening of official dialogue. The framework of communion ecclesiology adopted by the Second Vatican Council enables us to recognize the many gifts that we have in common with Christians of all denominations. It establishes a firm basis for the effort of sincere dialogue "on equal footing" (UR 9) between competent experts to address together the doctrinal questions that still divide the churches. In the decades since the council the Catholic Church has taken part in more than fifteen commissions for bilateral theological dialogue with other churches at the international level. These conversations are often complemented by dialogues at regional and local levels. In addition, Catholic theologians fully participate in the multilateral Faith and Order Commission of the World Council of Churches. Through dialogue considerable progress in mutual understanding has been achieved, to the point of overcoming issues that were once considered to be church dividing, including the mutual recognition of baptism, pastoral provisions for interchurch marriage, the doctrine of justification by faith, the doctrines of Eucharist and ministry, and the exercise of authority in the church.[6] The experience of ecumenical observers at Vatican II established an important precedent as well. Today ecumenical guests and observers are invited as a matter of course to the most significant synodal gatherings, meetings of episcopal conferences, and important liturgical celebrations. We continue to learn the value of one another's perspectives and the value of common prayer.

In diocesan and parish communities the ecumenical commitment of the Catholic Church is reflected in the fact that we have come to feel more at home in one another's churches. Virtually all mainline churches in the West today follow the same Sunday Lectionary. More than 40 percent of marriages between Catholics and other Christians in North America today are interchurch marriages. This is a special calling where families are challenged to find ways to worship together in their respective churches. Christians from all denominations engage more readily in common efforts to care for the needs of the poor and works of social justice. All of these activities, if they are to help us grow together toward the fullness of unity in Christ, must be nourished by moments of common prayer and the common study of the Scriptures. The council regards this "spiritual ecumenism," which we celebrate more intensely each year during the Week of Prayer for Christian Unity, as the "soul of the whole ecumenical movement" (UR 8).

Prayer for unity and a sincere conversion of heart opens minds and hearts to recognize those aspects of the life of the church that stand in need of renewal and remain an obstacle to reconciliation with other Christians. The entire ecumenical movement is one such movement of reform calling us to greater fidelity in our living out of the Gospel. In chapter 18, we shall consider the council's humble recognition that the church stands in continual need of reform.

Notes

[1] These ideas are present from his earliest work, *Chrétiens désunis: Principes d'un "œcuménisme" catholique* (Paris: Éditions du Cerf, 1937), 288. See especially appendix VI, 381–82. (English translation: *Divided Christendom: A Catholic Study of the Problem of Reunion* [London: G. Bles, 1939].)

[2] Congregation for the Doctrine of the Faith, "Responses to Some Questions regarding Certain Aspects of the Doctrine of the Church," in *Origins* 37 (2007): 134–36.

[3] *Acta Synodalia* III/2, 335.

[4] The council clearly recognized the presence of other "churches" of the West, whose sacrament of ordination is recognized as valid, and thus, whose sacraments are also recognized as valid. These would include the Old Catholic Church (Union of Utrecht) and the Polish National Church. The term "ecclesial communities" was introduced to speak of other groups in a manner that would affirm their truly ecclesial character, and to find a term that is as inclusive as possible. A number of these groups, including Quakers and the Salvation Army, do not consider themselves to be "churches."

[5] Leo XIII, *Apostolica Curae* (1896).

[6] For a good overview of these developments, see Walter Kasper, *Harvesting the Fruits* (London: Continuum, 2009); and Edward Idris Cassidy, *Ecumenism and Interfaith Dialogue* (New York: Paulist, 2005).

Chapter Eighteen

Reform of the Church

(*Unitatis Redintegratio* 6)

> *Every renewal of the church essentially consists in an increase of fidelity to her own calling. Undoubtedly this explains the dynamism of the movement toward unity. Christ summons the church, as she goes her pilgrim way, to that continual reformation of which she always has need, insofar as she is a human institution here on earth. Consequently, if, in various times and circumstances, there have been deficiencies in moral conduct or in church discipline, or even in the way that church teaching has been formulated—to be carefully distinguished from the deposit of faith itself—these should be set right at the opportune moment and in the proper way.*

Background

The history of Christianity is in many ways a history of reformation. To be sure, early Christianity did not think about church reformation as we do today but the seeds for a theology of ecclesial reform and renewal were planted in the early centuries.[1] Those seeds were comprised of diverse theological insights into the ongoing need for men and women, even those baptized, to undergo continual spiritual renewal. One theological trajectory asserted that all humans were created in the image and likeness of God. However, that image and likeness had been defaced by human sin. Salvation consisted in the restoration of that image through the life, death, and resurrection of Christ and by the power of the Holy Spirit who transforms human hearts and draws them into saving communion with God.

As the Roman Empire began to crumble in the West, many Christians became skeptical of the possibility of pursuing an authentic life in Christ in the midst of a broken and fallen world. Some fled civilization into the desert to live as hermits. Soon many of these would create various forms of community and would envision these as contrast communities to the sinful society of the world. This development represented the birth of monasticism. The ongoing spiritual reform of the monk (almost all of whom were initially laypeople) formed the heart of the life of the monastic community. This spiritual reform was facilitated by *askesis*, the spiritual disciplines that effected detachment from a broken world and a deeper immersion into the paschal rhythms of life-death-new life. Soon this monastic path to the spiritual reform of the believer became "more structured, less severe, and increasingly communal," particularly in the form of monasticism championed by St. Benedict of Nursia in the early sixth century.[2]

Over the course of the centuries, rich spiritualities preoccupied with personal spiritual renewal would proliferate. However, beginning in the eleventh century, these would be accompanied by increasing calls for institutional church reform. The precipitating factor in this turn to institutional reform was the wedding of church structures with the feudal structure of the larger society. Now, if a nobleman decided to build a chapel on his property in order to meet the spiritual needs of his people, he presumed the right to appoint the cleric who would minister within that chapel. In like manner, if there were a cathedral within his "jurisdiction," then he presumed the right to name the bishop. The assignment of the symbols of authority (the episcopal ring and crosier) by the nobleman to the bishop was referred to as investiture, and since the nobility were mostly laypeople, this process came to be known as "lay investiture."

> Feudalism: A medieval social structure built on a set of hierarchically constructed reciprocal relationships. Peasants or serfs lived largely without benefit of personal property and survived by working the land that was the property of a local nobleman or knight. In exchange for their labor they received protection from their "lord" and judicial resolutions of various civil disputes. In turn, the local nobleman or knight owed fealty to a more powerful lord or even a king who, for his part, might owe allegiance to the emperor.

With ministerial responsibility given to the cleric, there was also attached to the appointment a guarantee of income. This came to be known as a *benefice*. Initially the granting of benefices was innocent, simply a way of providing income to a cleric. However, it was a practice easily abused; favored individuals received benefices even though many had little interest in meeting the spiritual needs of the people. It even became common to grant an individual cleric multiple benefices, making the office of priest or bishop potentially lucrative. Moreover, it was natural that the one who received the investiture from the lay nobleman would feel indebted to the nobleman, creating a potential conflict of interest for one whose primary responsibility was to be to the mission of the church and the care of God's people.

In the eleventh century a series of popes dedicated themselves to reforming the church with respect to the abuses associated with lay investiture. These reforms culminated in the reform of Pope Gregory VII, who made unprecedented claims to papal authority, including authority over bishops. The sweeping reforms he inaugurated came to be known as the Gregorian Reforms. Gregory's reformist agenda was oriented toward preserving the autonomy of the church against secular incursions, but it also dramatically redirected the course of church history. The reforms envisioned by Gregory relied on his assertions of universal papal authority. These assertions, in turn, required institutional backing. The papacy began to appropriate for itself a largely imperial style of governance. The result was the development of papal courts and legates and the establishment of canon law. As Christopher Bellitto has observed, "one of the Gregorian goals was to establish the clergy as an elite class whose authority was spiritual, not temporal."[3] The irony of these bureaucratic structures was that they were largely intended to serve the cause of papal reform. As we shall see, over time they would themselves become the objects of reform.

In the Middle Ages, much church reform was initiated "from the top." Popes used the expansion of canon law, the delegated powers of the cardinals, and a series of reforming synods and councils to fulfill papal reform initiatives. However, the bureaucratizing tendencies of these institutional structures often became an obstacle to the very reform that they were created to enact. Often lost along the way was the deep, reforming power of the Gospel itself.

Into the world of the High Middle Ages came men like St. Francis of Assisi and St. Dominic Guzman, who called for a recovery of the transformative power of simple Gospel living. In a world where success was measured by power and influence, they created new "mendicant" religious orders—the Franciscans and the Dominicans—dedicated to a lifestyle of voluntary poverty in imitation of Christ and an itinerant ministry dedicated to the priority of the Gospel. Francis and Dominic both recognized that institutional reform needed to be complemented by personal reform enabled by the liberating power of the Gospel.

Reforming impulses would continue in the church of the fourteenth and fifteenth centuries. The papacy would become less the instrument of reform than its object. In the fourteenth century the papacy capitulated to French political influence and moved to Avignon. To some this was a betrayal of the papacy's mission to serve the church and reforming voices like St. Catherine of Siena would write the pope, pleading for his return to Rome, and for a purging of ecclesiastical corruption. In the late fourteenth century, growing papal incompetence and corruption led to what is often called the Great Western Schism, in which there were two and then three different popes claiming the authority of St. Peter. As a consequence, the papacy suffered a tremendous loss of credibility. In the early fifteenth century the Council of Constance was called to resolve the crisis. Constance initiated a series of reforms intended to forestall future papal abuses and address continued problems with ecclesiastical corruption. Although successfully resolving the crisis related to the papacy itself, their other reforms were much less successful. John Wycliffe (1330–84) called for the people to have greater access to the Scriptures and denounced abuses in sacramental practices but he also ended up rejecting much of the church's sacramental system. Jan Hus (1369–1415) protested against simony and clerical immorality. Girolamo Savonarola

> **Simony: The practice of requiring payment in exchange for the administration of sacraments or provision of some other spiritual goods.**

(1452–98), a fiery Dominican preacher, denounced the immoral excesses of Florence and the corruption of the Borgian popes. Two of these three reformers would be executed with the support of church authorities.

When Christians today consider the history of church reformation, what generally comes to mind are the great Reformers of the sixteenth century like Martin Luther and John Calvin, but as we have seen, reform has been an ongoing matter of concern in the church. In substance, many of Luther's calls for reform had precedent. Luther denounced the abuse of papal and episcopal authority, clerical corruption, and the sale of indulgences. He called for a reform and simplification of the church's sacramental system. He decried the accumulation of ecclesiastical laws and customs that obscured the centrality of Scripture and called for the people to have greater access to the Bible. Calvin too repudiated the papacy and episcopate and challenged the regnant sacramental system, acknowledging only baptism and Eucharist as sacraments with biblical support. Some, like Ulrich Zwingli, were even more sweeping in their reforms. There were subsequent "reformations" like that which gave rise to the Church of England and the "radical reformation" associated with the Anabaptists.

The Council of Trent was convened from 1545 to 1563, in part as a response to the challenges of these reformers and in part out of recognition of the need for reform expressed by leading voices within the late medieval church. The council implicitly acknowledged the validity of some of the criticisms and undertook important reforms in sacramental practice, clerical education, and the ministry of priests and bishops. In the wake of the Reformation and the agenda of Trent, the papacy continued its own program of church reform. Unfortunately, this reformist program was built largely on the further expansion of papal authority and the imposition of an unprecedented uniformity in church practice, particularly regarding the liturgy. The Roman Curia was transformed from a bureaucratic entity structured on the model of an imperial court to its current structure comprised of distinct dicasteries with compartmentalized responsibilities. The reformist response to the sacramental/liturgical abuse of the period was a sweeping program of sacramental/liturgical standardization patterned on the worship of the Roman church. Trent spawned an ecclesial uniformity built on a standardized profession of faith, catechism, breviary, missal, and Vulgate Bible. Although new spiritualities would continue to emerge that would foster ongoing personal reform and renewal, the massive program for the standardization of church practice would stymie most efforts at institutional reform. Resistance to reform would be stiffened by a growing perception that the church was under siege, first by the Reformers, next by Galileo and the rise of modern science, then the Enlightenment's assertion of the autonomy of human reason, and finally assertions of the separation of church and state in the nineteenth century.

> **Dicastery:** A congregation, council, or tribunal within the Vatican that is devoted to some aspect of the church's life and mission (e.g., education, the laity, peace and justice). They might be conceived on the analogy of the various departments in the executive branch of the US government (e.g., the State Department, Defense Department).

In the nineteenth century in particular there were a number of voices calling for church reform. Johann Adam Möhler argued for a dynamic theology of tradition that was open to genuine change and development. The English theologian John Henry Newman would also embrace a positive theology of church reform, noting famously that "in a higher world it is otherwise, but here below to live is to change, and to be perfect is to have changed often."[4] However, it was only in the middle third of the twentieth century when the conviction that the church was immune to the need for reform would be challenged by the plethora of historical scholarship that revealed a church that had always been subject to reform and renewal. The Dominican theologian Yves Congar articulated a theological rationale for church reform in his work *Vraie et fausse réforme dans l'Église* (*True and False Reform in the Church*).[5] In that groundbreaking work Congar insisted that the church is always subject to authentic reform and that such reform must be candid in its criticism, focused on matters of substantial import, attentive to the impact of reform on the whole Christian faithful, and firmly grounded in the church's great tradition. Congar's prominence as a *peritus* at Vatican II helped to ensure that a theology of reform found its way into the council's documents.

Vatican II on Reform in the Church

Pope John's opening address made the reformist agenda of the council explicit. In that address he spoke of the need for an *aggiornamento* in the church, which meant to bring the church "up to date." He also articulated a distinction that would prove basic to any subsequent calls for church reform, namely, the distinction between the substance of church doctrine and its form of presentation. Even before the council had articulated a theological rationale for reform, the practice of reform was already evident in the first session of the council, particularly in the debates over the draft document on the liturgy and its call for sweeping liturgical changes.

Church Reform and the Eschatological Orientation of the Church

A key element in the council's emerging theology of church reform was found in the *De Ecclesia* draft. Early in the council Pope John had requested a draft on eschatology and the veneration of the saints. In May of 1964 Pope Paul VI asked that this text be integrated into the fast expanding *De Ecclesia* draft. That chapter was provisionally titled "The Eschatological Nature of Our Calling and Our Union with the Heavenly Church." During the third session Congar was asked to rework this text, placing a greater emphasis on the eschatological nature of the church itself. The new chapter title reflected this change: "The Eschatological Nature of the Pilgrim Church and her Union with the Heavenly Church." This change reflected a pronounced shift in the tone of the document. The church was no longer simply a church of pilgrims, each awaiting their final destiny. No, the church itself was "pilgrim" and would not achieve its perfection until the end of history (LG 48).

This text stood in sharp contrast to common attitudes toward the church. In the nineteenth century Pope Gregory XVI confidently insisted in his 1832 encyclical, *Mirari Vos*, that "it is absurd and injurious to propose a certain restoration and regeneration in [the church] as though necessary for her safety and growth, as if she could be considered subject to defect or obscuration or other misfortune."[6] By conceiving of the church not just as a collection of individual pilgrims but as itself pilgrim, the council adopted a tone of eschatological humility, a conviction that while the church was confident it was headed in the right direction as guided by the Spirit, it had not yet arrived. The council wrote, "The church, to which we are all called in Christ Jesus, and in which by the grace of God we attain holiness, will receive its perfection only in the glory of heaven, when the time for the renewal of all things will have come" (LG 48).

We are a people *on the way* who have the promise of God's presence and guidance but who still await the consummation of God's plan. In a similar way, *Dei Verbum* had, in its description of the development of tradition, presented the church not in full possession of the truth but as "always advancing toward the plenitude of divine truth until eventually the words of God are fulfilled in it" (DV 8).

By placing the church in this eschatological framework, it was now possible to acknowledge the need for ongoing reform. If the church as pilgrim has not yet arrived at its final fulfillment, then there is more work to be done. Earlier in the constitution the bishops had acknowledged this ongoing need for renewal: "It [the church] does all in its power to relieve their need and in them it endeavors to serve Christ, who, 'holy, innocent and undefiled' . . . knew nothing of sin . . . , but came only to expiate the sins of the people. . . . The church, however, clasping sinners to its bosom, at once holy and always in need of purification, follows constantly the path of penance and renewal" (LG 8). Although the council's affirmation of the eschatological character of the church played an important part in its emerging theology of ecclesial reform, we must also acknowledge the importance of the council's heightened appreciation for the work of the Holy Spirit in the life of the church.

Church Reform and the Work of the Holy Spirit in the Life of the Church

In an earlier chapter we discussed the accusation of Christomonism—a theological preoccupation with the work of Christ in the church to the exclusion of the role of the Holy Spirit—that was leveled against much preconciliar theology. The council countered this tendency by recovering the integral role of the Holy Spirit in the life of the church. Every authentic ecclesial action exercised within an authentic ecclesial relationship is effective only because it is empowered by the Spirit. The church is indeed the Body of Christ, but it is so only because it is constituted as such by the Holy Spirit who animates the church and guides it on its pilgrim journey. But how did this pneumatology contribute to a theology of ecclesial reform?

If one conceives of the church exclusively as a reality instituted by Christ two thousand years ago, substantive change will generally be viewed as a departure from the will of Christ. However, if one conceives of the church as not only instituted by Christ in the past but also perpetually *constituted* by the Holy Spirit in each present moment, then ecclesial change (and reform) might be viewed, not as a departure from the will of Christ, but as a fidelity to the guidance of the Holy Spirit. Authentic reform and renewal will always be a response to the promptings of the Spirit in ever changing historical and cultural contexts.

Church Reform in Ecumenical Context

An important new context for the council's consideration of church reform was its embrace of ecumenism. The council insisted that the work for Christian unity required Catholics to "get their own household in order." It recognized that the restoration of church unity could not happen without a commitment to authentic reform and renewal. This was most clearly articulated in the key text of this chapter. Let us consider the individual elements of the text (UR 6).

"Every renewal of the church essentially consists in an increase of fidelity to her own calling." First, the council specifies the key distinction between authentic and inauthentic reform. Authentic ecclesial reform is never about the church simply accommodating itself to the patterns and expectations of the world. Authentic reform is a matter of fidelity; it is a matter of the church looking to its deepest theological identity as the Body of Christ, the people of God, the temple of the Holy Spirit, the sacrament of salvation, the pilgrim church—and seeking concrete ways to ensure that its teachings, structures, policies, and practices are in keeping with that theological identity. Let us consider one example. Calls for church reform frequently seek more structures that would allow church leaders to consult the faithful on a variety of matters from pastoral policy to church doctrine. Now many object that such a proposal for reform mistakenly presumes that the church is a democracy. Indeed, were this call for ecclesial reform motivated by nothing more than an effort to transform the church into a liberal democracy, it could well be illegitimate. But, in fact, this reform proposal is oriented toward greater fidelity to the church's theological identity as a temple of the Holy Spirit. In pursuing such reform the church would become a community of discernment, a community in which its leaders would be dedicated to seeking out the voice of the Spirit.

"Christ summons the church, as she goes her pilgrim way, to that continual reformation of which she always has need . . ." Second, this passage teaches that ecclesial renewal and reform is not an occasional element in church life. Church reform initiatives are not like the need to occasionally adjust the hands on a grandfather clock that runs a bit slow. Insofar as the church is pilgrim, reform and renewal will not be occasional realities; they will, in fact, be constitutive of the life of the church. The church must always be about reform and renewal until Christ returns.

". . . insofar as she is a human institution here on earth." Third, this key text of the council reminds us that although the church is truly the Body of Christ, it is nonetheless a human institution. As the Body of Christ, the church relies on the presence of the Holy Spirit to preserve it in truth. But as a human institution it is also subject to failure, pettiness, closed-mindedness, and the many inadequacies that are part of the human condition. It is now and always holy *and* ever in need of reform.

"Consequently, if, in various times and circumstances, there have been deficiencies in moral conduct or in church discipline, or even in the way that church teaching has been formulated—to be carefully distinguished from the deposit of faith itself—these should be set right at the opportune moment and in the proper way." Fourth, authentic ecclesial reform will be directed at the whole of the church's life. It will be concerned with correcting abuses and shortcomings in church custom and law. It will be concerned with remedying the sinfulness of church leaders, and identifying and remedying sinful structures and policies that may be found within the church itself. The ambit of church reform will also include the formulation of church doctrine. The council here draws on a distinction made by Pope John XXIII in his opening address when he distinguished between the substance of church doctrine and its manner of presentation. This distinction is operative on several levels. The Catholic Church teaches that church dogmas are teachings that are taught infallibly as irreversible because they mediate divine revelation. Put simply, a church dogma can never be wrong. However, insofar as the specific formulation of a dogma relies on limited linguistic, philosophical, and cultural constructs, it will always be possible to find better formulations of a particular teaching. For example, the Council of Trent taught that transubstantiation was a "most apt" (*aptissime*) expression of the church's faith in the Real Presence of Christ in the Eucharist. But it is still a theological formulation, one that depends on a particular Aristotelian-Thomistic metaphysical framework. Therefore, in principle it will always be possible to find a new and more adequate philosophical/theological framework for articulating the mystery of the eucharistic Real Presence.

When it comes to church teaching that is not definitive and irreversible in character, that is, teaching that is proposed by the church's teaching office in an authoritative way but not infallibly, the change and development of such teachings may go beyond a simple change in the formulation of the teaching. In rare cases there may even be a reversal of a teaching. A classic example of this is the church's longstanding tolerance, if not acceptance, of the enslavement of other human beings. This teaching was not repudiated in any formal way until the nineteenth century.

Few teachings had greater consequence for the church in all its institutional forms than this council teaching on the need for church reform and renewal. Authentic reform and renewal must always have a place in the life of the church. Yet the council reminded us that the church seeks out this reform for but one purpose: "that the sign of Christ may shine more brightly over the face of the church" (LG 15).

Notes

[1] Much of the historical background to our topic is drawn from Christopher M. Bellitto, *Renewing Christianity: A History of Church Reform from Day One to Vatican II* (New York: Paulist, 2001).

[2] Ibid., 31.

[3] Ibid., 90.

[4] John Henry Newman, *An Essay on the Development of Christian Doctrine*, 6th ed. (Notre Dame: University of Notre Dame Press, 1989), 40.

[5] Yves Congar, *True and False Reform in the Church*, trans. Paul Philibert (Collegeville, MN: Liturgical Press, 2011; original French publication, 1950).

[6] Quoted in Bellitto, *Renewing Christianity*, 2.

Chapter Nineteen

Hierarchy of Truths

(*Unitatis Redintegratio* 11)

> *In ecumenical dialogue, Catholic theologians, standing fast by the teaching of the church yet searching together with separated brothers and sisters into the divine mysteries, should do so with love for the truth, with charity, and with humility. When comparing doctrines with one another, they should remember that in catholic doctrine there exists an order or "hierarchy" of truths, since they vary in their relation to the foundation of the christian faith.*

Background

The Lutheran New Testament scholar Oscar Cullmann, who attended the Second Vatican Council as an official observer, commented that the affirmation that a "hierarchy of truths" exists in Catholic teaching was one of the most revolutionary ideas, not only in the Decree on Ecumenism, *Unitatis Redintegratio*, but also in all the council's teachings.[1] Like many others, he felt it was an important clarification, and one that was needed in order to redress a certain maximalist tendency among Catholics to place all doctrines, forms of liturgy, and pious practice on the same plane. The notion of an ordering or of a certain prioritization of Christian truths is not entirely new, but in the period that followed the Protestant Reformation it tended to be obscured in the Catholic presentation of belief. During the Modernist crisis of the early twentieth century Catholic teaching was especially resistant to the introduction of historical-critical methods to the study of the Scriptures or Christian doctrine, especially as they gave rise to notions of growth in understanding and doctrinal develop-

> Modernism: A movement within Catholic theology that embraced modern methods inspired by the Enlightenment in the study of the Bible and Christian teaching, often in the hope of adapting the Christian faith to the times. Among those condemned for Modernist tendencies were the French philosopher Alfred Loisy and the English Jesuit George Tyrell. Pope Pius X issued a searing condemnation of Modernist errors in his 1907 encyclical letter, *Pascendi*, and subsequently required all Catholic clergy to swear an anti-Modernist oath.

ment, to distinctions between the historically and socially conditioned elements of tradition and the meaning of revealed truth, and to the idea that there is a need to differentiate among the revealed truths of Christian faith. This resistance began to soften in the 1940s when Pope Pius XII authorized the use of historical-critical methods in Catholic biblical studies, and opened up the possibility for Catholic scholars to compare various expressions of Christian doctrines in dialogue with scholars from other Christian churches.

We first discover a certain ordering of Christian values and truths in the Scriptures, where the early christological hymns place Christ at the center of creation and of God's plan for our salvation (Eph 1:3-10; Phil 2:5-11; Col 1:12-20). Paul writes of Jesus Christ as "the foundation" of God's building (1 Cor 3:11; Heb 6:1), the basis for all his teaching and ministry. Similarly, the church gives priority to some books of the Bible over others. It places the Book of the Gospels at the center of its Liturgy of the Word. Due to their apostolic origin, that is to say, their link to the first witnesses to the resurrection of Christ, the church accords a "special place" to the four gospels, and draws upon them as "our principal source for the life and teaching of the incarnate Word, our Saviour" (DV 18). We read the other books of the Bible in the light of what the gospels reveal to us concerning Christ and his teaching.

We also recognize a certain ordering among the seven sacraments of the church. It can be said that all other sacraments flow from and lead back to the sacraments of baptism, by which we enter into Christ's Body, the church, and the Eucharist, where our communion with God and one another is sealed and regularly renewed. Our baptismal initiation is deepened through confirmation as we are anointed as members of the messianic people of God. In the sacrament of reconciliation, we return to right relationship with God and are reintegrated into the eucharistic community. While the pain of illness and psychological suffering can often alienate us from God and others, the healing love of God expressed in the sacrament of the sick can restore us to our place as valued members of the Christian community who are called to share in the paschal mystery of Christ even in our very bodies. The sacraments of marriage and holy orders signify the particular way in which we are called to live out our baptismal vocation within the community.

As we saw in our discussion of the liturgy in chapter 3, participation in the communal prayer of the church takes priority over practices of personal piety. While all are bound to take part in the weekly celebration of Christ's paschal mystery in the Eucharist, none are required to practice the regular recitation of the rosary, however commendable this spiritual practice may be. Expressions of personal piety can take many forms and may be influenced by the many currents of spirituality that are found within the Catholic tradition. They complement but cannot replace the liturgical prayer of the church. All of our worship is to be clearly directed to the Father through Christ, in the power of God's Spirit. The divine Trinity, the foundation of our faith, remains the center of our prayer.

Vatican II on the Hierarchical Order of Revealed Truths

In November of 1963, during debate on the proposed text for the De-cree on Ecumenism, the archbishop of Gorizia, Andrea Pangrazio, spoke eloquently about the need to recognize in no uncertain terms that the faith Christians share in Christ and in his role in our salvation is far greater than what divides them. He offered a helpful framework for putting the com-munion we share on matters of doctrine with other Christians into proper perspective. In order to adequately evaluate both the nature of our divisions and the weight of what we have in common, he argued, it is not enough to simply list our points of disagreement and of agreement. Rather, we must carefully distinguish those doctrines or truths of the faith that have to do more directly with the goal of our salvation from those that pertain to the means of obtaining it. He rightly observed that doctrinal divisions among the churches relate more often to the means of salvation. His remarks are still worth recalling at length:

> To arrive at a fair estimate of both the unity which now exists among Christians and the diversity which still remains, it seems very important to me to pay close attention to the *hierarchical order* of revealed truths which express the mystery of Christ and those elements which make up the church.
>
> Although all the truths revealed by divine faith and all those elements which make up the Church must be kept with equal fidelity, not all of them are of equal importance.
>
> Some truths are *on the level of our final goal*, such as the mystery of the Blessed Trinity, the Incarnation and Redemption, God's love and mercy toward sinful humanity, eternal life in the perfect kingdom of God, and others.
>
> Other truths are *on the level of means toward salvation*, such as that there are seven sacraments, truths concerning the hierarchical structure of the Church, the apostolic succession, and others. These truths are the means which are given by Christ to the Church for her

pilgrim journey here on earth. When this pilgrim journey comes to an end, so also do these means.

Now doctrinal differences among Christians have less to do with these primary truths on the level of our goal, and deal mostly with truths on the level of means, which are certainly subordinate to those other primary truths.[2]

Archbishop Pangrazio asked that these distinctions be made more explicit so that Christians might better appreciate the extent to which they are united as a single family in the most important truths of the Christian faith.

The archbishop of Vienna, Cardinal Franz König, provided a helpful complement to the recognition that Christian doctrines are not all of equal importance in his written proposal to amend the text of *Unitatis Redintegratio*. He suggested that this ordering of truths ought to be understood as a kind of qualitative differentiation among them, as they do not all have the same proximity to the "center" or the "foundation" of the Christian faith. Archbishop Pangrazio had raised a similar concern when he spoke of the presentation of the elements of the church in the draft of the Decree on Ecumenism. He complained that the text read like a "quantitative" catalog, simply piling up the elements with nothing uniting or ordering them in a coherent way. "We should point to the *center*," he argued, "to which all these elements are related, and without which they cannot be explained. This bond and center is *Christ* himself, whom all Christians acknowledge as the Lord of the Church, whom the Christians of all communities unquestionably want to serve faithfully, and who graciously accomplishes wonderful things even in separated communities by his active presence through the Holy Spirit."[3]

In Relation to the Foundation of the Christian Faith

The language proposed by both Archbishop Pangrazio and Cardinal König was adopted by the Decree on Ecumenism, which explains that the order or hierarchy of the truths of faith is determined by their "relation to the foundation of the christian faith" (UR 11). At the center of our faith is Christ. As we saw in our discussion of the nature of revelation, faith is much more than an intellectual assent to a statement of truth. The assent of faith is fundamentally a personal response to God's self-disclosure in and through the person of Christ. Through this personal relationship, which entails an engagement of our whole person with Christ, we are drawn to participate in the life of the three Divine Persons in the Trinity. This mystery of personal communion is at the heart of our faith commitment.

We might understand the relationship of the various truths of faith to the center or foundation of our faith by considering the famous image of Christ the Redeemer that overlooks the city of Rio de Janeiro from Corcovado Mountain in Brazil, one of the new "seven wonders of the world." A group of Brazilian Catholics raised the funds to commission this work by French sculptor Paul Landowski in the 1920s. One hundred and thirty feet tall, and ninety-eight feet wide, it took almost ten years to build this impressive monument. From the beginning, it was designed to be lit by a complex array of floodlights illuminating every aspect of the monument and enabling people to see the image of Christ from all directions. Imagine the dismay of the artist and those who commissioned the sculpture, if upon seeing it, the people had exclaimed, "My, what gorgeous floodlights!"[4] The purpose of the floodlights is not to draw attention to themselves but rather to illuminate the figure of Christ and to draw all of our attention to him as the focal point and the source of our salvation. Without them, some aspect of Christ the Redeemer might be less apparent or remain obscured by the dark of night.

If we reconsider Archbishop Pangrazio's distinction between those truths relating to the "means" of our salvation, and those relating to the goal or end on the lines of this analogy, we might see that those truths relating to the seven sacraments and the structures of the church are like the floodlights. They are intended to direct our attention to Christ and to lead us to a personal encounter with the One who is the ultimate focus and center of our faith. In fact, all doctrines are intended to direct us toward a personal encounter with Christ, in whom we ultimately place our faith. But some pertain more directly to the mystery of Christ and the Divine Persons of the Trinity than others.

By way of example, most Orthodox, Catholic, Anglican, Lutheran, and Reformed Christians continue to confess their faith in Christ as the incarnate Son of God, and worship him together with the Father and the Spirit. The core of their faith is summed up in the creed that they profess on the day of their baptism and recite in the eucharistic liturgy. They agree that Christ is truly human and truly divine, and that he is the source of our salvation. Together they profess their faith in the triune God and look forward to the fullness of life with God in the resurrection. Most often our disagreements are centered on the means, on *how* that grace of salvation is mediated to us in and through the sacraments, ministries, and institutional structures of the church. Admittedly, those churches that do not adhere to the creeds of the ecumenical councils and their confession of faith in a triune God do not share the same degree of communion in faith with us as those that do.

Among the doctrines where ecumenical dialogues have suggested we might appropriately apply the hierarchy of truths are the dogmatic teachings relating to Mary, the Mother of the Lord. The Council of Ephesus met in 431 during a time of considerable struggle to arrive at a just understanding of the unity of the divine and human natures in Christ. The council declared that Mary is to be called "Theotokos," literally, the "God bearer" or Mother of God. The purpose of this teaching was not so much to convey the unique dignity of the Virgin but to affirm that she bore in her flesh a child that is the divine Word of God incarnate in human flesh. Similarly, the Catholic dogmas of the immaculate conception and the assumption of Mary can be seen less as attempts to clarify the facts of Mary's personal trajectory than as affirmations relating to the priority of God's offer of justifying grace and to our hope in the resurrection. Like the floodlights turned on the Redeemer of Corcovado Mountain, these teachings are intended to direct our gaze toward Christ who is truly divine and truly human, the risen One and source of saving grace. As we contemplate the mysteries of his life, death, and resurrection, we are drawn into the communion he shares with the Father and the Spirit.

> Immaculate conception: The dogmatic teaching defined by Pope Pius IX in 1854 that Mary, in view of her vocation to be the bearer of the incarnate Word, was protected from original sin from the moment of her conception by an extraordinary gift of God's justifying grace. Many church fathers reflected on the purity of Mary and presented her as the "new Eve." From the seventh century the feast of her conception was celebrated liturgically. The theological basis for this teaching can be traced to Duns Scotus in the Middle Ages.
>
> Assumption: The dogmatic teaching defined by Pope Pius XII in 1950 that Mary was taken up bodily into heaven at the end of her earthly life and now enjoys the joy of the resurrection. While the exact origins of this belief are uncertain, the liturgical feast can be traced back to the fifth century, and has long been celebrated in the West on August 15th.

The *Catechism of the Catholic Church* provides an important insight into the meaning of the "foundation of the Christian faith" in its reflection on the importance of the creed for our confession of faith: "The mystery of the Most Holy Trinity is the central mystery of Christian faith and life. It is the mystery of God in [God's self]. It is therefore the source of all the other mysteries of faith, the light that enlightens them. It is the most fundamental and essential teaching in the 'hierarchy of the truths of faith'" (CCC 234). All other dimensions of our faith and system of beliefs are secondary, in a sense, and at the service of our relationship with a loving God. This does not mean to imply that they are less true, but they do not have the same priority. The General Catechetical Directory of 1971 explains, "This hierarchy does not mean that some truths pertain to faith itself less than others, but rather that some truths are based on others as of a higher priority, and are illumined by them" (no. 43). The 1997 General Directory for Catechesis repeats that the hierarchy of truths must serve as an important principle to guide every presentation of the Catholic faith.

The Practice of Ecumenical Dialogue

Returning to our key text for this chapter (UR 11), the Decree on Ecumenism introduces the notion of the hierarchy of truths in the context of its description of the work of theologians in officially mandated dialogues that aim at overcoming the doctrinal differences at the source of the historical division of the churches. As we saw in chapter 17, the Catholic Church is engaged in formal dialogue with more than fifteen world confessional families of churches today. The Decree on Ecumenism presents the work of dialogue as a common search for the truth of the Gospel to be carried out "with love for the truth, with charity and with humility" (UR 11). Dialogue is not a process of negotiation where the convictions of one partner or another would be compromised. Rather, the partners in dialogue strive to hear, beyond the words and expressions of the other, the truth about the mystery of faith that each side has attempted to express in its listening to and receiving of the word of God through history.

They carry out this common search for the truth mindful that at times, "one tradition has come nearer to a full appreciation of some aspects of a mystery of revelation than the other, or has expressed them better" (UR 17). They are careful not to confuse content and form, unity in the meaning of faith with uniformity of expression. Indeed, the process of careful study and dialogue has led at times to the discovery that differing theological formulations ought to be "considered complementary rather than conflicting" (UR 17), or that matters once thought to be church-dividing can no longer be so considered. The Decree on Ecumenism invites us to learn from what God has done in the life of other Christian communities, recognizing that "anything wrought by the grace of the holy Spirit" among them "can contribute to our own edification" (UR 4). Some have described the process of dialogue between the churches as an ecumenical gift exchange, where each partner seeks to hear how the other has understood and received the revealed word of God in its search to remain faithful, and where each learns from the other's diverse insights into the divine mysteries. In the end, both sides are enriched. As they grow together in unity these diverse insights into the mysteries of faith help us all to better express the catholicity of our faith and "bring a more perfect realization of the very mystery of Christ and the church" (UR 4).

Officially mandated dialogue commissions often prepare reports or statements that attempt to summarize our common agreement in faith. These statements may propose "new forms of expression of the faith" or employ the language of the Bible or early Christian writings—drawing from our common heritage—in preference to the disputed language of historical controversies. These statements are not intended to avoid the controversies of the past but aim to express a common understanding of the faith in a language that can be recognized by all. An important example of where consensus has been achieved on a matter directly related to the foundation of our faith can be found in the series of agreements concluded by Popes Paul VI and John Paul II with leaders of several Oriental Orthodox churches concerning the confession of faith in Christ as true God and true man, overcoming disagreements on the christological teaching of the Council of Chalcedon, a dispute that lasted over fifteen hundred years.[5] Though consistent with the language of Chalcedon (one person, two natures), these confessions of faith give priority to the *meaning* of a dogma over the specific formulation of the teaching. In this way, the churches have shown themselves able to recognize agreement on the meaning of the fundamental dogmatic teaching of an ecumenical council beyond disputed formulae.

Ecumenical Formation for All the Faithful

In its 1993 Directory for the Application of the Principles and Norms of Ecumenism,[6] the Pontifical Council for Christian Unity helpfully suggested that the recognition of a prioritizing or ordering in both the teaching and in the life and practice of the church is something that must be clearly transmitted not only in the context of ecumenical dialogue but also in the religious instruction, catechesis, and theological education of members of the Catholic Church. The directory affirms that in its presentation of the Catholic faith, catechesis "should expound clearly, with charity and with due firmness the whole doctrine of the Catholic Church respecting in a particular way the order of the hierarchy of truths and avoiding expressions and ways of presenting doctrine which would be an obstacle to dialogue" (61). It further insists on the importance of respecting the hierarchy of truths in the theological education of all those preparing for ministry in the church: "[T]hese truths all demand due assent of faith, yet are not all equally central to the mystery revealed in Jesus Christ" (75).

By cultivating a greater awareness of the hierarchy of truths among the Catholic faithful, the Pontifical Council for Christian Unity aims to ensure that the witness and teaching of all Catholics—ordained and lay ministers, theologians, teachers and catechists, but also the daily witness of every ordinary believer—reflect the sense of just proportion conveyed by the recognition of the hierarchy of truths. This witness has profound implications for our commitment to growing together in unity with other Christians, for, as the directory suggests, a failure to respect this correct ordering of the truths of faith can become "an obstacle to dialogue." The task of restoring Christian unity "involves the whole church" and "extends to everyone, according to the talents of each, whether it be exercised in daily christian living or in theological and historical studies" (UR 5). A deeper awareness of the hierarchy of truths on the part of all is essential to ensuring that our "daily christian living" be an accurate reflection of the just ordering of doctrines in Catholic teaching.

Both the process of dialogue and the reception of its fruits into the life of the church are occasions for applying the hermeneutical principles described by the Second Vatican Council, including the hierarchy of truths. These principles enable us to recognize "whatever is truly Christian" and "genuinely belongs to the faith" (UR 4) beyond the boundaries of the Catholic Church. The principle of welcoming the work of God's Spirit wherever it is found extends to our relationship with non-Christian religions as well, a topic to which we turn in the next chapter.

Notes

[1] Oscar Cullmann, "Comments on the Decree on Ecumenism," *Ecumenical Review* 17 (1965): 93.

[2] Andrea Pangrazio, "The Mystery of the History of the Church," in *Council Speeches of Vatican II*, ed. Hans Küng, Yves Congar, Daniel O'Hanlon (Glen Rock, NJ: Paulist Press, 1964), 188–92, at 191.

[3] Ibid., 190–91.

[4] This analogy is adapted from a discussion in Richard Gaillardetz, *By What Authority? A Primer on Scripture, the Magisterium, and the Sense of the Faithful* (Collegeville, MN: Liturgical Press, 2003), 96–97.

[5] See, for example, The Common Declaration of Pope Paul VI and of the Pope of Alexandria Shenouda III (Coptic Orthodox) [1973]; Common Declaration of Pope Paul VI and His Holiness Mar Ignatius Iacob III (Syrian Orthodox) [1971]; Common Declaration of Pope John Paul II and His Holiness Mar Ignatius Zakka I Iwas (Syrian Orthodox) [1984]; Common Declaration of John Paul II and Catholicos Karekin I (Armenian Orthodox) [1996]; all at http://www.vatican.va/roman_curia/pontifical_councils/chrstuni/sub-index/index_ancient-oriental-ch.htm. See also Common Christological Declaration between The Catholic Church and The Assyrian Church Of The East [1994].

[6] Pontifical Council for Promoting Christian Unity, Directory for the Application of the Principles and Norms of Ecumenism, at http://www.vatican.va/roman_curia/pontifical_councils/chrstuni/general-docs/rc_pc_chrstuni_doc_19930325_directory_en.html.

Chapter Twenty

The Church and World Religions

(*Nostra Aetate* 2)

> *The Catholic Church rejects nothing of what is true and holy in these religions. It has a high regard for the manner of life and conduct, the precepts and doctrines which, although differing in many ways from its own teaching, nevertheless often reflect a ray of that truth which enlightens all men and women. . . . Let Christians, while witnessing to their own faith and way of life, acknowledge, preserve and encourage the spiritual and moral truths found among non-Christians, together with their social life and culture.*

Background

In the council's Declaration on the Relation of the Church to Non-Christian Religions (*Nostra Aetate*), we find the expression of the commitment of the Catholic Church to enter into dialogue with members of other religious traditions. This short text, consisting of only five articles, was hammered out over four tumultuous years of struggle. It began at the personal initiative of Pope John XXIII. The French Jewish historian Jules Isaac traveled to Rome in June of 1960 to meet personally with John XXIII. His wife and daughter had been deported to Auschwitz in 1943 and executed in the gas chambers. A historian and educator, Isaac authored works on Jesus and Israel, the origins of anti-Semitism, and the teaching of contempt. In 1947 he cofounded "Amitiés judéo-chrétiennes," a movement for Jewish-Christian friendship aimed at combating anti-Semitism and developing a deeper appreciation of Christianity's Jewish roots. During his visit with John XXIII, he confided a carefully prepared memorandum to the pope in the hope that the upcoming ecumenical council might provide an opportunity for the church to carefully reconsider its relationship with the Jews.

This visit was an important catalyst in prompting John XXIII to personally request the preparation of a draft document on the Jews for the deliberations of the council. When he founded the new Vatican Secretariat for the Promotion of Christian Unity in 1960, John XXIII entrusted this important task to Cardinal Augustine Bea and his staff, asking Bea to receive Isaac and weigh his proposals carefully. Bea also met with Nahum Goldmann, president of the World Jewish Congress and cochair of the World Conference of Jewish Organizations. These encounters secured a commitment to work toward Catholic-Jewish cooperation in the struggle against racial prejudice and religious intolerance. A small subcommittee of the Secretariat worked diligently over the next year to prepare a draft decree, On the Jews.

The "Jewish question" proved to be among the most politically charged issues treated by the council. In the early 1960s the recently established state of Israel was at war with the Arab nations. When Arab governments learned of the pope's initiative, they dispatched diplomatic envoys to the Vatican to express their displeasure. They viewed any support for the Jewish community as a political matter, not a religious one. For patriarchs of the Eastern Catholic churches living among majority Muslim populations in Middle Eastern countries, any perceived support for the embattled state of Israel raised the specter of reprisals against the Christian faithful. At one point, the proposed text was deemed so controversial that it was withdrawn from the council's agenda. As was noted in earlier chapters, it was reintroduced for debate in the second session of the council in 1963 with the full support of Pope Paul VI, appended to the Decree on Ecumenism together with the proposed text on Religious Liberty.

Thomas Stransky, a staff member of the Secretariat for Unity during the council, describes the two main tendencies that were to confront one another in the course of the conciliar debate. The first, conveyed through a long history of preaching contempt and negative treatment of the Jews, continued to be widely held by many Catholics, including a number of bishops at the council. Stransky provides a succinct summary of this position:

> God continues to punish the Jewish people for its rejection and killing of Jesus, the Son of God, Messiah and Savior of all. By this deicide Jews have forsaken all rights to God's promise in the Old Covenant, which has been completely replaced by the New, identified with the Catholic Church (supersessionism). Like sinful Cain, Jews should continue to wander the earth as vagabonds without a homeland. God sustains their dispersed existence to remind Catholics of the divine blessings of the New Covenant and Jews of their true calling to share in the same by converting.[1]

The second tendency can be characterized by an effort to reconsider the charge of deicide against the Jewish people and the theory of super-

Deicide: Literally, the killing of God; referring to the alleged guilt of the Jewish people for the crucifixion of Jesus, owing to the role of some Jews of the time in his death.

Supersessionism: A theory of salvation history that maintains the Christian church established by the new covenant in Jesus supersedes, displaces, or replaces the people of the "old" or first covenant between God and the Jewish people. According to this theory, the "old" covenant ended with the coming of the Messiah, Jesus the Christ.

sessionism on the basis of a careful reexamination of the biblical evidence. Those who shared this view were profoundly troubled by the complicity of Christians in the terrible chapter of history represented by the Shoah—the systematic genocide of six million Jews carried out under the Nazi regime of Adolf Hitler. They were led to reevaluate the relationship of the church with the Jewish people. Christian scholars, including the Reformed theologian Karl Barth, the Catholic philosopher Jacques Maritain, and the Jesuit biblical scholar Augustine Bea, mindful of how the Scriptures had been interpreted in ways that nurtured anti-Jewish sentiment, contributed toward a renewed understanding of God's covenant with the Jews. Inspired especially by the teaching of Paul's letter to the Romans, they maintained that God has not rejected the Jews but remains faithful to his unique covenant with his chosen people, since his "gifts and calling" are "irrevocable" (Rom 11:29). They argued that anti-Judaism contradicts the biblical teaching concerning the place of the Jews in God's plan for salvation history. Noting Paul's teaching that the Gentile community that gave rise to the church is "a wild olive shoot . . . grafted in their place to share the rich root of the olive tree" of Judaism (Rom 11:17), they insisted on Christianity's unique dependence upon the faith of the Jews, the people of God's enduring covenant. This more biblical perspective would prevail in the elaboration of *Nostra Aetate*.

When the text was debated by the bishops in 1964, the Eastern patriarchs continued to voice their concern that it would be "inopportune" for the Catholic Church to issue a decree that spoke positively of Catholic-Jewish relations. A small conservative minority of bishops from Italy, Spain, and Latin America expressed the view that an anti-Jewish position was an integral part of Catholic tradition supported by the Scriptures and could not be reversed. In an unanticipated turn of events, bishops from Asia and Africa protested that the church must speak not only of its relationship to the Jewish people but that it must also say a word about the other religions to which two-thirds of the world's population belong. It was therefore proposed that the material on Judaism be integrated into a larger framework of reflection on the relationship between the church and other religions. This recommendation was accepted and had the effect of providing a framework that was more clearly theological and less open to politicizing interpretations. The revised text was passed in the final session of the council with few opposing votes in November 1965.

The Council's Teaching

The final version of *Nostra Aetate* begins from a consideration of the broad scope of human relations in our day, noting that "people are drawing more closely together and the bonds of friendship between different peoples are being strengthened" (NA 1). In the 1960s, a new consciousness was taking root that Canadian philosopher Marshall McLuhan described as a sense of belonging to "a global village." In this context, the church expressed its conviction regarding the unity of the human community and the universality of God's plan of salvation in confident terms, noting the common origin and destiny of all people:

> Humanity forms but one community. This is so because all stem from the one stock which God created to people the entire earth . . . , and also because all share a common destiny, namely God. His providence, evident goodness, and saving designs extend to all humankind . . . against the day when the elect are gathered together in the holy city which is illumined by the glory of God, and in whose splendor all peoples will walk. (NA 1)

In placing its consideration of other religions within the framework of salvation history and against the eschatalogical horizon of God's destiny for humankind, *Nostra Aetate* echoes the perspectives found in the council's teaching in chapter 2 of the Dogmatic Constitution on the Church. Building on a biblically based theology of God's will that all humanity be saved, *Lumen Gentium* does not hesitate to affirm that all people of faith belong or are related to the people of God in different ways: the members of the Catholic Church (LG 14), other baptized Christians (LG 15), and "finally all of humankind, called by God's grace to salvation" (LG 13, 16).

Lumen Gentium notably grants first consideration to the Jews when treating the relationship of the other religions to the people of God. The text indicates the esteem of the church for the Jewish people and repeats Paul's teaching that God remains faithful to his covenant with them: "There is, first, that people to whom the covenants and promises were made, and from whom Christ was born in the flesh (see Rom 9:4-5), a people in virtue of their election beloved for the sake of the fathers, for God never regret[s] his gifts or his call (see Rom 11:28-29)" (LG 16). Next, it considers the adherents of Islam, a faith tradition that is related to both Christianity and Judaism: "[T]hey profess to hold the faith of Abraham, and together with us they adore the one, merciful God, who will judge humanity on the last day" (ibid.). These three monotheistic or Abrahamic religions are presented together in recognition of their common foundation of faith in one Creator God.

Religion and the Human Search for Meaning

Lumen Gentium does not refer directly to any other religion by name but alludes to them broadly as "those who in shadows and images seek the unknown God" referred to in the Acts of the Apostles (17:25-28). The account in Acts refers to an episode where Paul proclaimed the Gospel to the Athenians in the Areopagus. While traveling through Athens, Paul came across many monuments erected to the pagan gods of the Greeks, among them an altar bearing the inscription "To an unknown god." He appealed to the Athenians by suggesting that the "unknown god" they were seeking was none other than the God of Jesus Christ. The Gospel that he preached was not a message concerning a reality foreign to them but was already implicit in their own search for a transcendent being at the source of creation. Paul sees Christ as the answer to their quest for meaning and fulfillment. Similarly, *Lumen Gentium* affirms that all those who "seek God with a sincere heart" or "strive to lead a good life" do so with the help of God's grace, and considers "[w]hatever of good or truth" found among them as "a preparation for the Gospel" (LG 16).

Adopting a similar approach, *Nostra Aetate* proceeds from the horizon of the human search for meaning in its treatment of other religions. Just as all human persons are created in the image and likeness of God, they are created for communion with God. This thirst for communion and fulfillment is at the heart of our deepest questioning. Religion provides a framework of meaning, "an answer to the unsolved riddles of human existence" (NA 1). The human longing for God is expressed whenever we ask, "What is humanity? What is the meaning and purpose of life? What is upright behavior, and what is sinful? Where does suffering originate, and what end does it serve? How can genuine happiness be found? What happens at death?" (NA 1). These are among the most basic questions belonging to our experience as human persons. They point to our search for the "ultimate mystery," that something bigger than ourselves and beyond our capacity to explain, the source of life and its ultimate fulfillment.

This basic human experience is shared by all humanity. As Christians, we are convinced that Christ, the Alpha and Omega, is the answer to all our searching, "the goal of human history, the focal point of the desires of history and civilization, the center of humanity, the joy of all hearts, and the fulfillment of all aspirations" (GS 45). He is at work in the lives of all those who respond in sincerity to these God-given aspirations. *Gaudium et Spes* affirms, "grace is active invisibly" in the hearts of all people of goodwill (GS 22; see also LG 16). For this reason, the council seeks to affirm "all that is good and holy" in other religions. It aims to instill a spirit of respect for their rich traditions and to promote genuine dialogue with them in the hope that we might work together for the betterment of the human community (NA 2). Without renouncing their own convictions and way of life, nor condemning those who believe differently, Christians are urged to "acknowledge, preserve and encourage the spiritual and moral truths found among non-Christians" (NA 2).

Nostra Aetate, mindful of the expressed desire of many Asian bishops, explicitly mentions Hinduism, where people explore and express the divine mystery within "the limitless riches of myth and the accurately defined insights of philosophy," and Buddhism, which acknowledges "the essential inadequacy of this changing world" (NA 2). The church's encounter with these religions in both historic missionary efforts and in the contemporary context has instilled a deep respect for their rich traditions.

An entire article is devoted to the faith of Islam, which the Catholic Church holds in "high regard" (NA 3). The declaration notes that Muslims "venerate Jesus as a prophet" and honor "his virgin Mother" in accordance with the Quran, the book of Scripture they regard as the word of God dictated to the prophet Mohammed. Their religious practice is expressed through the observance of prayer, almsgiving, and fasting. Recognizing that the long history of Christian-Muslim relations has been marked at times by "many quarrels and dissensions," the council issues a plea to set aside the ways of the past and "urges that a sincere effort be made to achieve mutual understanding" and work together to "preserve and promote peace, liberty, social justice and moral values" (ibid.).

Spiritual Ties with God's Chosen People

The fourth and most extensive article of *Nostra Aetate* is devoted to the relationship between the church and the Jewish people. It begins with the affirmation that the church is spiritually joined to the Jews. As people of the new covenant, members of the church are "daughters and sons of Abraham (see Gal 3:7)" and heirs of God's covenant with the chosen people through the patriarch Abraham. Because the church sees itself "mystically prefigured in the exodus of God's chosen people from the land of bondage"—that is to say, it sees in the liberation of Israel from slavery a foreshadowing of the paschal mystery of Christ—it continues to regard the Old Testament texts as an expression of God's revelation in history (NA 4). Further, it recalls that Jesus himself, his family, and the early community of disciples were all members of the Jewish community. The Pauline teaching adopted by *Lumen Gentium* is reiterated. While Jews do not recognize in Christ the promised Messiah, God has not withdrawn from God's covenant with them (Rom 11:28-29; LG 16).

A dense and carefully worded paragraph takes up the questions of deicide and supersessionism. While the council does not employ the term "deicide" directly, its teaching precludes any interpretation of Scripture that would inculpate the entire Jewish community for the death of Jesus. "Even though the Jewish authorities and those who followed their lead pressed for the death of Christ . . . , neither all Jews indiscriminately at that time, nor Jews today, can be charged with the crimes committed during his passion" (NA 4). Similarly, it would be incorrect to reason that God's covenant with the Jews is no longer valid, or has been replaced by the new covenant in Christ: "It is true that the church is the new people of God, yet the Jews should not be spoken of as rejected or accursed as if this followed from holy scripture" (ibid.). All members of the church, especially those with the responsibility of preaching the word of God and handing on the faith of the church as religious educators or catechists, are exhorted not to teach what is contrary to the Gospel. All forms of persecution and anti-Semitism are reproved in light of this renewed understanding of the "common heritage" of the church and the Jewish people. The council urges dialogue and a renewed study of theology and the Scriptures so that we might continue to grow in mutual understanding and in appreciation for the bonds that unite Jewish and Christian communities.

Since the Second Vatican Council, a number of official interreligious dialogues have been established at both the international and regional levels.[2] The relationship of the church to the Jews is recognized as distinct from the church's dialogue with other religions, given the unique common patrimony that we share. A special Commission for Religious Relations with the Jews is charged with overseeing this relationship. It remains under the care of the Pontifical Council for Promoting Christian Unity (the successor to the Secretariat established by John XXIII), and is distinguished from the work of the Vatican's Pontifical Council for Interreligious Dialogue.

In its desire to affirm all that is good and true in other religions and to recognize their source in the one, loving God of all, Vatican II marks the commitment of the Catholic Church to live in a religiously pluralist world with an attitude of humility, respect, and mutual esteem. By affirming the many values that are shared by the church and non-Christian religions, the council gives expression to the church's solidarity with all humanity and its deep desire to be an agent of peace and reconciliation in the world. The fundamental stance of the church as one of dialogue and willingness to collaborate with all people of God will hasten the coming of God's reign in the world.

Notes

[1] For a more detailed account, see Thomas Stransky, "The Genesis of Nostra Aetate," *America* (October 24, 2005).

[2] For an overview, see Edward Idris Cassidy, *Ecumenism and Interreligious Dialogue* (New York: Paulist, 2005).

Conclusion

We began our exploration of the Second Vatican Council by indicating some of the ways that its teaching differs from that of previous ecumenical councils. The sheer volume of material represented by the sixteen documents has made it a challenge to choose just twenty texts that might serve as interpretive "keys" that can "unlock" the richness of the council's most central teachings. There is, of course, an inherent danger in any process of selection, namely, that one might neglect some important element or another. We have attempted to make use of these key texts as a springboard for reflection on the broad orientations of Vatican II. It is our hope that this rather organic approach to the council documents will provide insight into the substance of the council's teaching and the far-reaching consequences of the reform undertaken at Vatican II. As we saw in chapter 18, the process of reform in the life of the church is an ongoing one. The orientations provided for the life of the Catholic Church by the Second Vatican Council continue to provide an impetus for the ongoing renewal of the Catholic community in our time. The interpretation of the council's teaching is, by necessity, dynamic since the global Catholic community and the broader human community today face many challenges that differ from those which confronted the church in the 1960s.

Fifty years have now passed since the opening of the Second Vatican Council. Fifty years is but a heartbeat in the long view of church history. From a historical perspective, we know that the momentous occasion in the life of the church represented by an ecumenical council is most often followed by a long period of "reception." It is in this long and complex process of reception that the council's teachings are integrated into the practical living of the Christian faith in the celebration of the liturgy, in the structuring of church ministries, administration, policies, and ecclesiastical laws. The revision of the Lectionary and all the liturgical rites of the Latin church was a task that took over ten years of concerted effort. It took twenty-five years following the council to carry out the revision of the Code of Canon Law, which sought to set out in practical terms many of the norms for the implementation of the council's teaching on the rights and responsibilities of the baptized faithful, and the functioning of the structures of the Latin church.[1] It took another seven years for the completion of a new Code of Canon Law for the Eastern Catholic churches in 1990.[2]

It should not be surprising, therefore, to discover that some of the council's teachings have not been easily appropriated or received into the life and culture of the Catholic Church. The recognition of the collegial nature of the episcopal office, in the view of many, has thus far been given a rather hesitant embodiment in a purely consultative international synod of bishops, or again in the carefully circumscribed role of the conferences of bishops. And as the widening scandal of clerical sexual abuse continues to come to light in many countries, it is becoming apparent that while Vatican II recognized the rights and obligations of all the faithful, the provision of appropriate procedures and tribunals to ensure that the causes of those who are wronged may receive a just hearing, and that any of those who abuse their pastoral authority will be held fully to account, remain inadequate.

Since the close of the council in 1965, the decline in candidates for ordained ministry, a decline that began prior to the council, has continued. At the same time, we have witnessed an unprecedented explosion of new lay ecclesial ministries: laypeople around the world now study theology in great numbers and serve as professors, religious educators, catechists, pastoral care givers, canon lawyers, and parish and diocesan administrators. New experiments have been undertaken to restore the permanent ministry of the diaconate (LG 29). These developments invite renewed reflection in our own context on forms of ecclesial ministry and their structured collaboration within the life of the church.

As the Catholic Church has continued to expand in the southern hemisphere, the need for greater inculturation and adaptation—a question that was very much on the minds of the bishops at the council— continues to make itself felt ever more urgently. The population of the global Catholic community has more than doubled in the past fifty years, and its center of gravity has shifted to the south. Today the largest Catholic populations are to be found in Brazil, the Philippines, and Mexico. By the year 2050, it is expected that 75 percent of Catholics will live south of the equator, completely reversing the situation of a century ago. According to the Vatican's annual yearbook, the Catholic population of Africa alone increased by 33 percent in the decade from 2000 to 2010. The bishops at Vatican II could not have anticipated the nature or pace of these and other social and cultural changes that are giving rise to a whole host of new questions today.

That being said, Vatican II remains a fundamental turning point in the history of the Catholic Church, and indeed of world Christianity. Its commitment to renewal and reform has been embraced by many other

Christian families who sent observers to the council. As we have tried to show, its teaching represents an important shift in the stance of the Catholic Church from one of isolation, fear, and condemnation to one of humble openness and willingness to learn through dialogue with other Christians, with other religions, and with the wider world.

This stance of confident engagement is the fruit of a century of renewed biblical, patristic, liturgical, and theological scholarship that helped the Catholic Church to rediscover the centrality of the encounter with the risen Christ for the whole of Christian life. A deeper awareness of the role of the paschal mystery in the life and prayer of the church is grounded in the revealed word of God contained in the Scriptures that are now placed more decisively at the heart of the church's prayer, theology, teaching, and witness. The study of church history and tradition led to the recovery of the basic equality and shared dignity of all the baptized faithful, reversing almost a millennium of teaching and practice based on the notion of two "classes" of people in the church—laypersons and the ordained.

The principal teachings of Vatican II constitute a sustained reflection on the vocation of the church. One of the most important structuring principles that helped to organize the council's teaching was introduced by Cardinal Suenens at the close of the second session in 1964. In his influential speech he proposed that the council's documents be structured according to a reflection on the life of the church *ad intra*, that is, its inner life and structuring, and on the calling of the church *ad extra*, its mission to the world and its relationships with other Christians and other religions.

Three of the four constitutions produced by the council pertain to the inner life of the church. The Constitution on the Sacred Liturgy, the Dogmatic Constitution on Divine Revelation, and the Dogmatic Constitution on the Church relate primarily but not exclusively to the internal life of the church: its source in the revelation of the divine Word in the person of Christ, which is communicated in Sacred Scripture and made actual in the sacraments. Christ and the communion of Divine Persons in the Trinity are the source and the model of the communion that we are called to live within the church (UR 2). The Decree on the Pastoral Office of Bishops, the Decree on the Ministry and Life of Priests, the Decree on the Up-to-Date Renewal of Religious Life, and the Decree on the Apostolate of Lay People can all be seen as further reflections on the particular vocations of the baptized faithful against the horizon of the collective calling of the whole church. Together they are all called to a life of holiness and of witnessing to Christ through the outpouring of their lives in love for others. The Decree on the Catholic Eastern Churches provides an orientation to guide the communion existing between the twenty-two Eastern Catholic churches and the Roman Catholic Church, a relationship that enriches the catholicity of the whole church of Christ. In the Declaration on Christian Education (*Gravissimum Educationis*) the Catholic Church commits itself to ensuring that the right to education is realized for every person. It calls for making use of the most advanced learning and methods of pedagogy in order to contribute to the formation of men and women as well-informed and responsible citizens.

The church does not exist as an end in itself but is called to be of service to the whole human community, helping all of humankind to live in accord with its God-given purpose. For that reason, the Pastoral Constitution on the Church in the Modern World, a text for which there was no preparatory draft and that is entirely a child of the council, reflects perhaps more than any other the conscious turning of the church outward to the world and its deep-felt solidarity with all of humanity. These perspectives are widened and the church's engagement in dialogue is given a firm foundation in the Declaration on Religious Liberty, the Decree on the Church's Missionary Activity, the Decree on Ecumenism, and the Declaration on the Relation of the Church to Non-Christian Religions. These new and renewed relationships are taking on even greater significance today, as the global context reveals the necessity for collaborative efforts to overcome violence and meet the basic needs of humanity. In a world where religious diversity is now commonplace, we are perhaps more deeply aware than a half century ago of the necessity of witnessing to the world that people of faith can be a positive force for nonviolent and constructive social transformation. Finally, the Decree on the Mass Media, one of the least mature documents of the council and perhaps the most outdated today—given the veritable revolution in communications technology that has ensued over the past two generations—still stands as a witness of the church's desire to make use of every means possible to effectively communicate its message to all of humanity.

Debate has ensued in recent years among scholars and church leaders regarding the best way to interpret the Second Vatican Council. Some have inaccurately characterized the work of historians as an effort to portray the council as a moment when the Catholic Church made a definitive break or rupture with the past. They argue that instead of seeing Vatican II as a moment of historic change, it must be understood as standing in serene continuity with all that went before it.[3] No serious scholar of the council would advocate either of these positions as an adequate interpretation of the conciliar event or of the council's teaching. Pope Benedict XVI has characterized the council as a moment of "reform in continuity."[4] There is no denying that the Second Vatican Council initiated a number of far-reaching changes and reforms. Yet it did so out of fidelity to the Gospel and the tradition of the church.

Our approach to the council drew inspiration from the orientation provided in the decisive speech of Pope John XXIII at the opening of the council on October 11, 1962. Throughout our presentation of key teachings of Vatican II we have attempted to show how the renewal and reform of the church sought by the council was based on a concerted effort of *ressourcement*, of returning to the sources of the great Christian tradition in the Scriptures, in ancient Christian writings, and in the earliest sources of the Christian liturgy. In many cases, the reforms proposed by the council—including those relating to the liturgy, the role of the laity, the renewal of religious life, and the collegial governance of the church—must be seen as efforts to reappropriate a number of forgotten elements uncovered by a scholarly return to the sources. The council's commitment to *ressourcement* was complemented by its equal commitment to renewing the life of the church—to an *aggiornamento* or updating necessary to make the church's teaching and witness accessible to contemporary men and women. *Aggiornamento* drew on that same tradition to develop new insights for recognizing the fruits of the Spirit in the experience of other Christian communities and religions, and in the aspirations and developments of contemporary human society and culture.

The teachings of the council contain both *nova et vetera*, new things and old, all drawn from the treasure of God's household (Matt 13:52). The dynamic of continual renewal belongs to the very nature of our faith, as it is continually enlivened and rejuvenated by the Holy Spirit. Saint Irenaeus, the second-century bishop of Lyon, describes the living reality of faith to which he himself gives witness: "Our faith which, having been received from the Church, we do preserve, and which always, by the Spirit of God, renewing its youth, as if it were some precious treasure in an excellent vessel, causes the vessel itself containing it to renew its youth also. For this gift has been entrusted to the Church, as breath was to the first created man, for this purpose, that all the members receiving it may be vivified."[5] The vessel of the church, carrying within it the treasure of the Gospel, is continually renewed and made young by that to which it testifies.

In our day, no less than in 1962, we are called to give a more faithful and effective witness to the Gospel. The key orientations of the Second Vatican Council, if they do not provide detailed answers to every question, can nonetheless continue to guide our discernment as we seek to respond to the challenges of our time. The Benedictine abbot, and later bishop, Christopher Butler, who served as a member of Vatican II's Theological Commission, has written that the council's teaching "offers us a key to the Christian and human future."[6] As a faithful expression of the heart of our faith, Vatican II continues to unlock for us the meaning of our call to follow Christ even as it evokes hope for the destiny of humankind.

Notes

[1] *Code of Canon Law*, Latin-English Edition, New English Translation (Washington, DC: Canon Law Society of America, 1999 [original edition in 1983]).

[2] *Code of Canons of the Eastern Churches*, Latin-English Edition, New English Translation (Washington, DC: Canon Law Society of America, 2001 [original edition in 1990]).

[3] For a good overview of this discussion, see John O'Malley, "Vatican II: Did Anything Happen?," in *Vatican II: Did Anything Happen?*, ed. David G. Schultenover (New York / London: Continuum, 2007), 52–91.

[4] See Benedict XVI, Address to the Roman Curia (December 22, 2005), http://www.vatican.va/holy_father/benedict_xvi/speeches/2005/december/documents/hf_ben_xvi_spe_20051222_roman-curia_en.html.

[5] Irenaeus, *Against Heresies*, III, 24, 1.

[6] Christopher Butler, *In the Light of the Council* (London: Darton, Longman and Todd, 1968), 7.

Further Readings

General

Alberigo, Giuseppe. *A Brief History of Vatican II*. Maryknoll, NY: Orbis, 2006.

Alberigo, Giuseppe, and Joseph A. Komonchak. *History of Vatican II*. 5 vols. Maryknoll, NY / Leuven: Orbis / Peeters, 1995–2006.

Doyle, Dennis M. *The Church Emerging from Vatican II: A Popular Approach to Contemporary Catholicism*. Rev. ed. Mystic, CT: Twenty-Third Publications, 2002.

Hahnenberg, Edward P. *A Concise Guide to the Documents of Vatican II*. Cincinnati: St. Anthony Messenger Press, 2007.

Lamb, Matthew L., and Matthew Levering, eds. *Vatican II: Renewal within Tradition*. New York: Oxford University Press, 2008.

Latourelle, Rene, ed. *Vatican II: Assessment and Perspectives*. 3 vols. New York / Mahwah: Paulist, 1988–89.

Marchetto, Agostino. *The Second Vatican Council: A Counterpoint for the History of the Council*. Chicago: University of Scranton Press, 2010.

O'Collins, Gerald. *Living Vatican II: The 21st Council for the 21st Century*. New York: Paulist, 2006.

O'Malley, John W. *What Happened at Vatican II*. Cambridge: Harvard University Press, 2008.

Orsy, Ladislas. *Receiving the Council: Theological and Canonical Insights and Debates*. Collegeville, MN: Liturgical Press, 2009.

Pesch, Otto Hermann. *The Ecumenical Potential of the Second Vatican Council*. Milwaukee: Marquette University Press, 2006.

Ratzinger, Joseph. *Theological Highlights of Vatican II*. New York: Paulist, 1966.

Rush, Ormond. *Still Interpreting Vatican II*. New York / Mahwah: Paulist, 2004.

Schultenover, David G., ed. *Vatican II: Did Anything Happen?* New York / London: Continuum, 2007.

Stacpoole, Alberic. *Vatican II Revisited by Those Who Were There*. Minneapolis: Winston Press, 1986.

Sullivan, Maureen. *The Road to Vatican II: Key Changes in Theology*. New York: Paulist, 2007.

Wilde, Melissa J. *Vatican II: A Sociological Analysis of Religious Change*. Princeton: Princeton University Press, 2007.

Reports and Memoirs from the Council

Congar, Yves. *My Journal of the Council.* Collegeville, MN: Liturgical Press, 2012.

Hurley, Denis, OMI. *Vatican II: Keeping the Dream Alive.* Pietermaritzburg, South Africa: Cluster Publications, 2005.

Kaiser, Robert. *Inside the Council.* London: Burns & Oates, 1963.

MacAfee Brown, Robert. *Observer in Rome: A Protestant Report on the Vatican Council.* Garden City: Doubleday, 1964.

Outler, Albert C. *A Methodist Observer at Vatican II.* Westminster, MD: Newman Press, 1967.

Rynne, Xavier. *Vatican Council II.* New ed. Maryknoll, NY: Orbis, 1999.

Suenens, Leon-Joseph. *Memories and Hopes.* Dublin: Veritas, 1992.

Wiltgen, R. M. *The Rhine Flows into the Tiber: The Unknown Council.* New York: Hawthorn Books, 1967.

Wycislo, Aloysius. *Letters from Rome During Vatican II: The Personal Letters of a Vatican II Bishop to his Parishioners.* De Pere, WI: Paisa Publishing, 2005.

———. *Vatican II Revisited: Reflections By One Who Was There.* New York: Alba House, 1987.

On the Documents

Cassidy, Edward Idris. *Ecumenism and Interreligious Dialogue : Unitatis Redintegratio, Nostra Aetate.* Rediscovering Vatican II Series. New York / Mahwah: Paulist, 2005.

Confoy, Maryanne. *Religious Life and Priesthood: Perfectae Caritatis, Optatam Totius, Presbyterorum Ordinis.* Rediscovering Vatican II Series. New York / Mahwah: Paulist, 2008.

Ferrone, Rita. *Liturgy: Sacrosanctum Concilium.* Rediscovering Vatican II Series. New York / Mahwah: Paulist, 2007.

Gaillardetz, Richard R. *The Church in the Making: Lumen Gentium, Christus Dominus, Orientalium Ecclesiarum.* Rediscovering Vatican II Series. New York / Mahwah: Paulist, 2006.

Gros, Jeffrey, and Stephen B. Bevans. *Evangelization and Religious Freedom: Ad Gentes, Dignitatis Humanae.* Rediscovering Vatican II Series. New York / Mahwah: Paulist, 2009.

Leckey, Dolores R. *The Laity and Christian Education: Apostolicam Actuositatem, Gravissimum Educationis.* Rediscovering Vatican II Series. New York / Mahwah: Paulist, 2006.

Tanner, Norman P. *The Church and the World: Gaudium et Spes.* Rediscovering Vatican II Series. New York / Mahwah: Paulist, 2005.

Vorgrimler, Herbert, ed. *Commentary on the Documents of Vatican II.* Vols. 1–5. Freiburg: Herder and Herder, 1967–69.

Witherup, Ronald D. *Scripture: Dei Verbum.* Rediscovering Vatican II Series. New York / Mahwah: Paulist, 2006.

Index to Conciliar Document References